*Indexing Books*

# Indexing Books

**SECOND EDITION**

Nancy C. Mulvany

THE UNIVERSITY OF CHICAGO PRESS · CHICAGO AND LONDON

Nancy C. Mulvany is a professional indexer and past president of the American Society of Indexers. She has written articles on indexing for a variety of publications and taught book indexing courses for fifteen years.

The University of Chicago Press, Chicago 60637
The University of Chicago Press, Ltd., London
©1994, 2005 by Nancy Claire Mulvany
All rights reserved. Published 2005
Printed in the United States of America
14 13 12 11 10 09 08 07 06 05    1 2 3 4 5
ISBN: 0-226-55276-4 (cloth)

Library of Congress Cataloging-in-Publication Data
    Mulvany, Nancy C.
    Indexing books / Nancy C. Mulvany.— 2nd ed.
        p. cm.
    Includes bibliographical references and index.
    ISBN 0-226-55276-4 (alk. paper)
    1. Indexing. I. Title.
    Z695.9.M8 2005
    025.3—dc22

                            2005004214

♾ The paper used in this publication meets the minimum requirements of the American National Standard for Information Sciences—
Permanence of Paper for Printed Library Materials, ANSI Z39.48-
1992.

# Contents

# Preface

Many times during the writing of this book I asked myself why I had taken on the task. My first motivation was quite pedestrian: I needed a text for my classes. After teaching book indexing for several years, I grew tired of piecing together course materials. I exposed my students to a bit from here and a bit from there, often contradictory material that had to be put into perspective through lectures or with my own additional written material. While G. Norman Knight's book *Indexing, the Art of* (1979), or Martha Wheeler's treatise "Indexing: Principles, Rules, and Examples" (1968), would have been a fine primary text, both are out of print. Also, I recognized that not every aspiring indexer could take my class or one of the few others offered in this country that are devoted to book indexing. Those who wish to know about book-indexing methods have few places to turn for reference.

Like my classes, this book attempts to address the real-world aspects of book indexing. But I must include here the caveats I present to my students during our first class session.

Book indexing is something you will either enjoy or detest; there is little middle ground. You will have a knack for it or you won't. I do not believe that indexing can be taught. Rules, and the reasons for following or not following them, can be presented. Various index formats can be discussed. However, the ability to analyze text objectively and accurately and to produce a conceptual map that directs readers to specific portions of the text involves a way of thinking that can only be guided and encouraged, not taught. I compare my book-indexing class to a studio painting class. I can tell you various methods for preparing a canvas and for mixing pigments. We can discuss types of paints and brushes. We can look at the work of other painters to see how they handled color or perspective. But I cannot turn you into a painter.

So, too, in indexing. Although many rules can indeed be taught and learned, a very important aspect of this work comes down to the individual indexer's judgment and communicative abilities. Indexing cannot be reduced to a set of steps that can be followed. It is not a mechanical process. Indexing books is a form of writing. Like other types of writing, it is a mixture of art and craft, judgment and selection. With practice and experience, indexers develop their own styles—as do other writers. The best we can do as teachers of indexing is to present the rules and offer guidance.

So much for my first and most immediate reason for writing this book. While satisfying my desire to present the many diverse practices in indexing, the book attempts to come to terms with the seemingly elusive aspects of our craft. After grading hundreds of indexes of the same material, I have learned from my students that good indexes come in a variety of forms. Just when I think I have seen all the possible permutations of the one standard index assigned in all of my classes, someone comes up with a new and quite brilliant way of handling the material. Perhaps I shouldn't be surprised at this. After all, an index by its very nature is interpretive. Therein lies the challenge and creativity in indexing. In this book I have attempted to explain what it is we indexers *really* do. But I feel my efforts are preliminary in this regard. My discussions with other indexers clearly reveal that in the midst of following rules and creating entries in an accurate and complete fashion, a synergy is at work that is difficult to describe.

This is not a "how-to" book in the sense that its rules, if followed, will result in a perfect index. I do hope, however, that readers seeking information about how to handle a particular aspect of an index will find direction here. Nor is this book intended to be an encyclopedic or historical treatment of indexing like Hans Wellisch's fascinating book *Indexing from A to Z*. My book primarily addresses authored indexes such as those found in books. Unlike F. W. Lancaster's *Indexing and Abstracting in Theory and Practice*, my book does not provide detailed treatment of indexing methods used for online information retrieval. Readers interested in the intricacies of Web-site indexing will find valuable information in Glenda

Browne and Jonathan Jermey's Website Indexing: Enhancing Access to Information within Websites.

This book pulls together various approaches to book indexing. It is about practice, not theory. It is my hope that novice indexers will find within these pages the guidance they seek and that my colleagues, experienced book indexers, will find that I have described our methods and our profession well.

When I first considered writing about book indexing, I wondered who might publish such a book. I decided quite early that I wanted the University of Chicago Press to publish my book. In my mind, it would be a perfect match. I am honored and extremely pleased that this book is published by Chicago. However, I caution readers to keep in mind that much of the material presented in these pages does not reflect the recommendations of the University of Chicago Press. Because of the widespread acceptance by the North American publishing community of the indexing guidelines in *The Chicago Manual of Style (CMS)*, Chicago's preferences for index presentation are of course discussed. But the opinions expressed in this book are mine and are not necessarily endorsed in CMS. If you are preparing an index for the University of Chicago Press, do review the guidelines presented in the fifteenth edition of *CMS* before proceeding.

# Acknowledgments

This book is the result of both the knowing and the unknowing collaboration of many people in the indexing and publishing community. I am indebted to those who so willingly shared their thoughts with me and gave of their time.

During my fifteen years of teaching I came to know many students. I want to thank all of them for contributing greatly to my abilities as a teacher. There is one three-letter word that all good students have on the tip of their tongue—"why." I thank all the students who wouldn't let me get away with answers like "It's the rule" or "That's the way we've always done it."

I appreciate the many comments that were made by readers of the first edition of this book. In late 2002 five readers were commissioned by the University of Chicago Press to review the first edition and offer suggestions for the revision. Thanks are due to Victoria Agee, Sylvia Coates, Jean Mann, Thérèse Shere, and Do Mi Stauber. Additionally, three of them agreed to review the first draft of the second edition: Victoria Agee, Jean Mann, and Do Mi Stauber.

Several colleagues offered comments on various sections of this revision or answered my spur-of-the-moment questions without hesitation: Victoria Baker, Hazel K. Bell, Jessica Milstead, Janet Shuter, and Jan Wright. A special thanks goes to Victoria Baker, who bravely agreed to index this book.

I truly appreciate the support of the University of Chicago Press for publishing a new edition of my book. Linda J. Halvorson and Mary Laur guided the book through the revision process. Christopher Rhodes helped out with countless details. I am delighted with my editor, Carol Saller. Carol has helped me clarify important issues, and this is a better book because of her efforts.

Excerpts from Facing the Text: Content and Structure in Book Indexing are reprinted with permission from Do Mi Stauber. Figure 3.1 is reprinted from *The Chicago Manual of Style*, 15th edition, © 2003 by The University of Chicago. The quotations from Jan C. Wright in chapter 10 are printed with her permission.

# Chapter One

## INTRODUCTION TO BOOK INDEXING

I just googled Google. I typed "google" into Google's search field and in 0.10 seconds over 152 million results were returned. Yes, this is an extreme example of being flooded with information. However, in early 1998, Google did not even exist. No one would have understood my first sentence at that time. Very quickly, Google would become the most popular search engine on the Internet. The explosive growth of the Internet combined with increasingly sophisticated search tools has made us all more aware of the need to access relevant information efficiently.

## Information Overload

In 2003 the School of Information Management and Systems at the University of California, Berkeley, released a report, *How Much Information? 2003* (Lyman and Varian 2003). The study attempted to estimate how much new information is created each year. The report surveys a broad spectrum of information sources: "Newly created information is stored in four physical media—print, film, magnetic and optical—and seen or heard in four information flows through electronic channels—telephone, radio and TV, and the Internet."

These researchers found that in 2002 the print, film, magnetic, and optical storage media produced five exabytes of new information. "How big is five exabytes? If digitized, the nineteen million books and other print collections in the Library of Congress would contain about ten terabytes of information; five exabytes of information is equivalent in size to the information contained in half a million new libraries the size of the Library of Congress print collections." Furthermore, the report estimates that the amount of stored information in these four physical media grew by 30 percent per year between 1999 and 2002.

The sheer volume of information has led to the coining of the phrase "information overload." Donald O. Case (2002) devotes a portion of a chapter to "Information Overload and Anxiety" and offers this amusing thought:

Given the proliferation of media in our time, with the World Wide Web
now competing with television in the degree to which it juxtaposes
strange images on a screen, it is inevitable that overload will become an
ever more present distraction in making sense of the world. A January
1999 feature in *Inc.* magazine claimed that there had been over 3,000
newspaper and magazine articles on "information overload" published
in the previous two years, and that there were over 15,000 Web sites that
mentioned that concept. What irony: even our awareness of overload
is overloaded! (101)

A Google search on "information overload" produced 620,000 results
in early 2005. I am sure that all would agree that a massive amount of
information is of little value if there is no access to relevant content of
that information. What is not so well understood is that an index is a device for providing access to relevant information—and that is what this
book is about.

We see the word *index* in many contexts—index of leading economic
indicators, mutual fund index, consumer price index, indexed database
files, the Roman Catholic Church's *Index Librorum Prohibitorum,* index of
refraction, index finger. Even within the indexing and information science
communities, indexing processes cover a wide spectrum of applications.
There are indexes to books, periodicals, databases, newspapers, e-books,
Web sites, and in help files for software.

## Open-system vs. Closed-system Indexing

A useful framework for discussion of indexing is provided by Susan Klement in "Open-system Versus Closed-system Indexing: A Vital Distinction"
(2002). Klement distinguishes the two systems in this way: "Closed-system indexing assists people in finding a unit or units of relevant information *within a document,* while open-system indexing is designed to
facilitate the retrieval of one or more *documents* that contain relevant
information" (23–24). Internet search engines are examples of open-system indexing. The back-of-the-book index is an example of closed-system
indexing. Open-system indexing often deals with collections that grow,
while the focus of closed-system indexing is on a text that is static and
fixated in a particular form. For information about open-system indexing
processes, see F. W. Lancaster's *Indexing and Abstracting in Theory and
Practice* (2003). We are concerned here with the preparation of a closed-
system index. The focus of this discussion is the indexing of books. Most
books are closed systems that contain a beginning, middle, and end.

Books have two delivery formats: printed on paper and displayed as pixels on a screen.

## The Future of the Book

It may seem quaint in the twenty-first century to discuss the printed book—after all, the demise of the printed book has been predicted for years. In the concluding volume of his trilogy about the world of books, Nicholas A. Basbanes (2003, 311–312) reminds us:

> When people gather today to talk seriously about "books of the future," the discussion inevitably is driven by what some see as the ubiquitous triumph of modern technology and the certain obsolescence of print. The book as we know it, in other words, if not dead, is certainly moribund. Curiously enough, this kind of debate is not especially new, and has been argued in one form or another for decades, often with great passion and conviction on both sides of the issue.

In November 2003 the Italian novelist and scholar Umberto Eco spoke at the newly opened Bibliotheca Alexandria. He has no doubts about the future of books:

> Good news: books will remain indispensable, not only for literature but for any circumstances in which one needs to read carefully, not only in order to receive information but also to speculate and to reflect about it.
>
> I think that computers are diffusing a new form of literacy, but they are incapable of satisfying all the intellectual needs they are stimulating.
>
> Up to now, books still represent the most economical, flexible, wash-and-wear way to transport information at a very low cost. Computer communication travels ahead of you; books travel with you and at your speed.

The future of book indexing is intricately tied to the future of the book. Keeping the notion of a closed system in mind, I have no doubts about the continued existence of the book. It matters not what delivery format the book takes on, print or electronic. While the e-book industry strives to standardize itself, the printed book will continue as the most efficient and pleasurable reading device ever invented.

Although the discussion in this book will focus on closed-system indexing, the methods presented have far-reaching applications. It is worth recalling what Jessica Milstead wrote: "Whenever a collection of information, by reason of its size, its location, or the medium on which it is stored, cannot conveniently be scanned in its entirety by any would-be user, the quality of the index determines its value perhaps more than any other factor" (Milstead 1984, 192).

## The Index as Paratext

Another way to think of book indexes is as paratext. This term was introduced in the 1980s by Gérard Genette. In the foreword to *Paratexts: Thresholds of Interpretation* (Genette 1997) Richard Macksey includes this description of paratextuality: "liminal devices and conventions, both within the book (*peritext*) and outside it (*epitext*), that mediate the book to the reader: titles and subtitles, pseudonyms, forewords, dedications, epigraphs, prefaces, intertitles, notes, epilogues, and afterwords" (xviii). Nicholas Basbanes (2003, 229) provides an enhanced list of paratexts: "titles, illustrations, dust jackets, indexes, appendices, paper, type design, and bindings." The paratexts all contribute to how a book is received. For example, a poorly chosen typeface or an unappealing dust jacket will not encourage sales of a book. The paratexts, when done well, add value to a book.

Genette points out that the "most essential of the paratext's properties . . . is functionality. Whatever aesthetic intention may come into play as well, the main issue for the paratext is not to 'look nice' around the text but rather to ensure for the text a destiny consistent with the author's purpose" (1997, 407). He concludes, "The paratext is only an assistant, only an accessory of the text" (410).

As paratext, the book index bridges a gap between author and reader. It reconciles the vocabulary of the reader with that of the author. The functionality of an index, and other paratexts, was described well in the preface of *The Columbia Guide to Digital Publishing* (Kasdorf 2003) in this way:

> The third major avenue into the Guide is the Index. This is a particularly notable feature of the Guide. Indexes are taken for granted in print and, unfortunately, rarely provided online. Whereas the Glossary provides a shallow, topical view of the content, and the Table of Contents provides a logical, structured view, a good index provides an intellectual view of the content unavailable by any other means. It is the result of an intelligent reading by an indexer trained in recognizing and documenting the interrelationships of the intellectual content; the indexer not only notes topics and subtopics, but also makes judgments about them, selecting the most important and relevant sections to direct readers to. (lvi)

## The Long History of Indexes

Information that cannot be located might as well not exist. The index is one of the oldest information retrieval devices. When the earliest scribe produced a document that could not be easily browsed, the need for an index emerged. Hans Wellisch (1992, 70) writes,

> Indexing of books did not begin, as is commonly thought, after the invention of printing. It started with the rise of the universities in the 13th century. Although no two manuscripts of the same work were exactly alike and folio or page numbers were seldom used, indexes to theological treatises, lives of the saints, medical and legal compendia and, most of all, to collections of sermons were compiled, using chapter and section numbers instead of pagination.

Bella Hass Weinberg (1997) has dated a Hebrew manuscript citation index back to the twelfth century. Although the exact date of the first index is a matter of debate, we can safely say that indexes have been around for several hundred years. Nonetheless, the answer to the question What is an index? is not self-evident.

## What Is an Index?

In the United States, the National Information Standards Organization defines an index as "a systematic guide designed to indicate topics or features of documents in order to facilitate retrieval of documents or parts of documents" (Anderson and NISO 1997, 39).

The International Organization for Standardization's *ISO 999* (1996) defines an index as an "alphabetically or otherwise ordered arrangement of entries, different from the order of the document or collection indexed, designed to enable users to locate information in a document or specific documents in a collection" (3.5).

The *Oxford English Dictionary* (*OED*) takes us back to the Latin root *index* (n), the forefinger; *index* (v), to point out. The *OED* devotes many column inches to the various meanings of the word *index*, both as a noun and as a verb. For more on the history and meaning of *index*, see the fascinating discussion "Index: The Word, Its History and Meanings," provided by Hans Wellisch in his *Indexing from A to Z* (1995, 199–210).

*Merriam-Webster Unabridged* online dictionary produces no fewer than 107 entries that include the word *index*. These entries run the gamut from *alveolar index* to *wholesale price index*. The type of index of interest to us is defined as "a usually alphabetical list that includes all or nearly all items (as topics, names of people and places) considered of special pertinence and fully or partially covered or merely mentioned in a printed or written work (as a book, catalog, or dissertation), that gives with each item the place (as by page number) where it may be found in the work, and that is usually put at or near the end of the work."

In his classic *Indexing, The Art of* (1979), G. Norman Knight turns to the *British Standard* of 1976, the standard current at the time he wrote his book, for a full, cogent definition: that work states that an index is "a systematic guide to the location of words, concepts or other items in books, periodicals or other publications. An index consists of a series of entries appearing, not in the order in which they appear in the publication, but in some other order (e.g. alphabetical) chosen to enable the user to find them quickly, together with references to show where each item is located."

I myself find the following definition useful: An index is a structured sequence—resulting from a thorough and complete analysis of text—of synthesized access points to all the information contained in the text. The structured arrangement of the index enables users to locate information efficiently.

### What an Index Is Not

An index is *not* a concordance, a list of all the words that appear in a document. A concordance lacks analysis and synthesis. It is simply a list of words. (See chapter 10 for an example of a concordance.) A concordance, even in alphabetic order, does not provide an "intellectual view of the content unavailable by any other means" (Kasdorf 2003, lvi).

An index is *not* a mere appendage to a book. It is a separate and distinct written document. Indexes are written, not generated. As creative, authored works, indexes are granted copyright registration. Like other types of writing, indexes are communicative by nature. The writing of an index differs from other types of writing in that an index employs only the most basic writing tools needed for ultimate clarity. Index writers strive for directness, succinctness, and clarity without the use of prefatory remarks or complete sentence structures. Communication goals are achieved with a minimum number of communication tools.

An index is *not* a more elaborate version of the table of contents. Neither is the index simply an outline of the book. The term *index*, as it will be used in this book, is not an umbrella under which any alphabetic list can huddle. An index serves only one purpose: it enables readers to locate information efficiently.

## The Index as Hypertext

Hypertext is a method used to link related information within a document or between documents. Readers can choose to review linked topics in a nonlinear way. For example, an electronic encyclopedia that discusses Abraham Lincoln may refer to the Gettysburg Address. The phrase "Gettysburg Address" may be highlighted in some way to convey to readers that it is a linked topic. If they wish, readers can select the Gettysburg Address link and be shown its complete text.

While Ted Nelson is credited by some with popularizing the notion of hypertext, the theoretical prototype of hypertext can be traced back to the early twentieth century. W. Boyd Rayward (1994, 237) writes, "In 1934, some ten years before Vannevar Bush published his ideas about a memex, some 35 or 40 years before Ted Nelson began to develop his ideas of a fabled information Xanadu, Paul Otlet published a magisterial work of synthesis, the *Traité de Documentation*. . . . The *Traité is* perhaps the first systematic, modern discussion of general problems of organizing information." In 1918 Otlet described his Monographic Principle based on note cards. "What fired his imagination was the realization of the bibliographical uses to which standard three-by-five-inch cards and later loose sheets or leaves of standard sizes could be put. Here was a simple technology to be exploited by those who had the imagination to see the potential implicit in it. Cards permitted the 'analytical' recording of single, separate pieces of information, be they bibliographical or substantive, and so effectively the creation of what in hypertext are nodes or chunks of text" (Rayward 1994, 238).

Another seminal contribution was an information retrieval and annotation system described by Vannevar Bush in his 1945 article in *the Atlantic Monthly*, "As We May Think."

Bush describes a device called a memex that will be used by individuals to store "books, records, and communications." How will people locate information in the memex? "There is, of course, provision for consultation of the record by the usual scheme of indexing." For example, if someone is looking at a book on their memex, "a special button transfers him immediately to the first page of the index. Any given book of his library can thus be called up and consulted with far greater facility than if it were taken from a shelf." Bush describes the memex machinery in fascinating detail. However, it is not the mechanics of the memex that is fundamental, it is something else:

> All this is conventional, except for the projection forward of present-day mechanisms and gadgetry. It affords an immediate step, however, to associative indexing, the basic idea of which is a provision whereby any item may be caused at will to select immediately and automatically another. This is the essential feature of the memex. The process of tying two items together is the important thing.

Hypertext linking allows us to read in a nonlinear manner and follow trails. The book index likewise allows readers to jump into a text in a nonlinear fashion. Readers looking for specific information do not need to begin at page 1; a good index can send them right to the specific place in the book where the information is located. In this regard, the index is historically one of the first hypertext tools made available to readers.

### The Index as a Knowledge Structure

The value of an index lies in how it is organized. While a poor index may contain references to all the important information in the text, if it is not systematically organized for easy access, such an index has limited value to the user.

A proper index is an intricate network of interrelationships. The very nature of the hierarchical arrangement implies a graded series of relationships and results in an obvious structure for access to the information. Ideally, this structure is transparent to readers. A reader turns to an index with a specific purpose, to locate information about a topic. When that topic is easily located, the reader's needs are satisfied; he can leave the index and return quickly to the text. However, when readers are unable to locate their topics, they must stop and more closely examine the structure of the index. At this point the index has failed to provide quick and easy access to information. In order to better understand the components of the index network we must go beyond definitions and examine the purpose of an index.

### The Purpose of an Index

One of the most cogent discussions of the purpose of an index can be found in the *British Standard* (BS 3700: 1988, sec. 3; numbering added):

FUNCTION OF AN INDEX

1. Identify and locate relevant information within the material being indexed.
2. Discriminate between information on a subject and passing mention of a subject.
3. Exclude passing mention of subjects that offers nothing significant to the potential user.
4. Analyse concepts treated in the document so as to produce a series of headings based on its terminology.
5. Indicate relationships between concepts.
6. Group together information on subjects that is scattered by the arrangement of the document.
7. Synthesize headings and subheadings into entries.
8. Direct the user seeking information under terms not chosen for the index headings to the headings that have been chosen, by means of cross-references.
9. Arrange entries into a systematic and helpful order.

The first three items above require that the indexer judge the difference between relevant and irrelevant information. That indexers should actually pass judgment on the relevancy of information in a text makes some observers uncomfortable. Often indexers are instructed to index every name in the text regardless of relevancy. We have all looked up entries in an index only to find nothing of value in the text at the point referenced. It is indeed the job of indexers to distinguish between substantive information and passing mention of a topic. If we do not make these distinctions, we waste the readers' time.

Item 4 addresses two important functions of an index. First, concepts are to be identified and analyzed. Concepts in a book are not always stated verbatim. For example, in a book about raising dogs, several paragraphs may be devoted to various types of dog food. Never is the word *nutrition* mentioned; however, the concept *nutrition* should be in the index. The indexer reads between the lines, analyzes text, and identifies relevant concepts whether they are mentioned or not.

Second, item 4 directs us to use the terminology of the document. The author's language should always take precedence over alternative terms. Later in this book I will discuss various ways to handle synonyms. In regard to indexes in general, the language of the text dictates to a great degree the language that should be used in the index. An indexer should not impose an external taxonomy that is not reflected in the document itself. If the author uses the term *autos* in the text, then the information about autos should be posted at *autos,* not at *cars.* Strict adherence to this guideline does become difficult when working with multiauthored works, which will be discussed in more detail in chapter 6.

Items 5 and 6 relate to building the network of interrelationships in the index. The basic hierarchy of an index entry—that is, main heading with subheadings—indicates a relationship between concepts. The *See also* cross-reference is another tool used in the index to indicate relationships. However, item 6, "Group together information on subjects that is scattered by the arrangement of the document," refers to a much more subtle aspect of the index network. When readers look up a particular term in an index, they should find references for all relevant information about that term. Using the earlier example about dog food and nutrition, we might find an index entry like the following:

> nutrition
>   and bone development in puppies, 67–70
>   food and, 30–35
>   skin problems and diet, 120–25
>   vitamin supplements, 89

As we can see from the page references in the example above, information about nutrition was presented in various parts of the book. The indexer has assembled for the reader the relevant information about nutrition. Identifying related information and gathering it together in an appropriate place is one of the more difficult aspects of indexing. All too often inexperienced indexers focus on the minutiae of the text and neglect the big picture.

When readers discover that information in an index is scattered, their confidence in the index suffers, and rightly so. Users of an index should be able to look up a term and feel confident that all the relevant information has been gathered there. They should not have to second-guess the indexer and try to figure out if more information might be found at some other place, or, worse, at many other places in the index.

Item 7 instructs the indexer to "synthesize headings and subheadings into entries." The indexer's ability to put together distinct topical and conceptual elements so as to form a whole, synthesized entry contributes greatly to the integrity of the index network. At times this effort is as simple as resolving differences between synonymous terms. At other times the synthesis process is more complex, as when, say, objective realism is discussed in a passage in which the phrase is not stated verbatim.

While item 7 refers to the design of individual index entries, item 9 discusses the arrangement of index entries. The most common arrangement order for index entries is alphabetic. However, as we shall see in chapter 5, there is more than one way to alphabetize.

Item 8 addresses the crucial element of cross-references in an index— in particular, the *See* cross-reference. Cross-references are an integral part of the index network. *See* cross-references control the scattering of information in an index. They anticipate the language of index users and reconcile the language of the document with the users' language.

In the *autos* example used earlier, although the information about automobiles should be listed at this term, there should also be a cross-reference ("cars. *See* autos") in the index. Judicious use of cross-references can greatly enhance the usability of an index. Without cross-references, readers have no guidance; they must spend time discovering the various ways a topic has been cited. When appropriate cross-references are lacking, the cadence of their search for information is disrupted; the usability of the index has been compromised.

In order to provide appropriate cross-references the indexer must be intimately familiar with the language of the book and the readers' language. Again, the primary purpose of an index is to enable readers to locate information efficiently. Indexers must always ask themselves, Who are these readers?

## The Audience: Who Uses Indexes?

We can begin by dividing the audience into two general categories: those who have read the book and those who have not. There are books that are read from cover to cover. Readers of these books inevitably become familiar with the author's language. They are the readers who are likely to look up terms that were used by the author. This is one reason it is so important for the indexer to retain the author's terminology. An index that is thorough and complete will meet the needs of this portion of the audience.

Meeting the needs of those who have *not* read the book is far more difficult. People who have not read the book are not familiar with the author's language. The burden is on the indexer to anticipate the language of readers that may differ from that of the author, and to anticipate the expectations of different readers.

We can assume that most index users will not have read a book in its entirety. This is particularly true of reference books. By their very nature reference books are designed to be referred to, not to be read straight through.

Reference books deserve further comment. Included in this category are a wide range of books: computer software manuals, cookbooks, employee benefits handbooks, style manuals, corporate policy and procedures manuals, and many gardening books. However, the audiences for reference books can be quite different. We need to ask, Will the readers have specialized subject knowledge? How will they use the index?

### Specialized Subject Knowledge

Some books clearly require of their readers specialized subject knowledge. A general trade book about growing roses will have an audience very different from a book about chemical pest management in citrus groves. In the book on growing roses an entry for *aphids* may be sufficient, whereas in the pest management book we may need an entry for *Aphidoidea* as well as for the various genera and species using their Latin names.

Generally speaking, the more specialized knowledge that is required of readers, the easier it is to identify their language needs. For example, in a book that assumes a background in information science an entry named *search techniques* will be adequate; the index does not need to provide access for those readers who might look up *find* or *locate*.

In a mass-market book that assumes little or no specialized knowledge the indexer must anticipate that some items may be looked up by readers in a variety of ways. A reference manual for a word-processing program may have an entry *searching for text*. This time the indexer cannot assume that most readers will know that information about finding or locating text will be posted at *searching for text*. The indexer anticipates that readers may look up *finding text* or *locating text* and provides cross-references to direct readers to the *searching for text* entry.

There are books whose audience is composed of readers with and without specialized subject knowledge. Cookbooks are a good example. One cook may look up *sauces*, while another cook may be more focused and look up *Madeira sauce*. A thorough cookbook index will anticipate the needs of both types of readers.

### How Are Indexes Used?

Depending on the type of book, we can make some general assumptions about the way indexes are used. Although there are exceptions—some people actually do read indexes—for the most part, readers turn to the index because they want information about a specific topic. Let's look at the way two users approach an index.

We will begin with Sally Serendipity, an index user who has time and patience. Suppose Sally wants to use leftover chicken for dinner. She turns to her cookbook index and looks up *kung pao chicken* in the *K*s. Not finding it there, she then looks under *chicken* and, if unsuccessful there, she looks under *poultry*. Although Sally might experience some irritation on the third try, she would continue her search. She might even browse the index casually and discover a more appropriate recipe, *chicken with almonds in ginger sauce*.

At the other end of the spectrum is Peter Perplexed, who has no time or patience. The users of computer manuals and online help files often fall into this category. Peter has a problem that needs to be solved immediately. He is trying to print a report that he must deliver in twenty minutes to his boss. The paper has jammed in the laser printer. He doesn't know how to open the printer to dislodge the paper. Peter grabs his printer manual. It turns out that paper jams are discussed in the "Troubleshooting" section along with a myriad of other problems. He is lucky that the indexer thoroughly indexed this three-page section. He finds an entry for *jammed paper*. The topic was also indexed as *paper, jamming of* and *troubleshooting*.

Imagine a more serious situation. A mother frantically turns to a home medical guide to find out how to stop her child's arm from bleeding. This index user has no time to examine the internal structure of the index or to think about whether she should look up general terms or specific terms. If she is fortunate, the indexer will have provided several access points for the information she needs.

The indexes for the printer manual and the home medical guide should address the needs of both types of index users. For users like Peter Perplexed, the index should be action-oriented. These index users should be able to locate terms like *jammed paper* and *stopping bleeding* in the indexes.

To provide reasonable access points for information, indexers must have a thorough understanding of a book's audience. As a communicative network, the index does not exist independently of its audience. As a rich paratext, the index mediates the book to the reader. Users of an index that anticipates their needs find its internal structure transparent. They need not think about the index structure or spend a lot of time searching.

They turn to the index, find the information they seek, and immediately return to the text.

## The Ideal Index

As we shall see in the chapters that follow, many factors contribute to the writing of an excellent index. A stellar index that meets the needs of a majority of users does not emerge without careful thought and design choices by the indexer. There are times to follow rules; there are times to break rules. Our mission is always to provide efficient access to information.

It can certainly be argued that there is no such thing as a perfect index. Every index can be examined and found wanting in some respects. However, the indexer's goal is to write the best index possible given the circumstances. There are indeed circumstances that by their very nature compromise the quality of the index. Some of these will be discussed in chapter 2.

The American Society of Indexers (ASI) has formulated criteria for judging an annual book-indexing competition. Two sections of the criteria—"Content of the Index" and "Structure and Accuracy of the Index Entries"—clearly list many of the components of a high-quality index (American Society of Indexers 2004).

### CONTENT OF THE INDEX

The index must bring together references to similar concepts that are scattered in the text, or that are expressed in varying terminology. This can be done by establishing a single heading with subheadings, by using cross-references, double-postings, or with other appropriate devices.

All significant items in the text must appear in the index. However, if there is a category of material that is not indexed, this should be stated in the introductory note.

Items and concepts in the text must be represented in the index by appropriate, precise, accurate, and unambiguous headings. The index headings should be consistent in form and in usage. Inclusion of synonymous headings and spelling variations, if used, should be intentional to facilitate access.

The index should represent the text and not be a vehicle for expressing the indexer's own views and interests.

### STRUCTURE AND ACCURACY OF THE INDEX ENTRIES

The index entries should be arranged in a recognizable or stated searchable order, such as alphabetical, classified, chronological, or numerical order.

The locators given in the index should tally with the text.

Strings of undifferentiated locators should generally be avoided by use of appropriate subheadings or other appropriate devices. If the number of locators in a given entry is so large that the aspects of the heading are not adequately differentiated, additional headings, sub-headings, or modifiers should be introduced. Headings should be as specific as the nature of the collection permits and the purposes of the users require.

There must be a sufficient number of cross-references in the index so that related items are connected, and obsolete or idiosyncratic terms in the text are related to terms in current use.

Abbreviations, acronyms, symbols, or other abridgments of word or phrases should be explained in an appropriate manner.

Careful readers will notice many similarities between the ASI judging criteria and the *British Standard's* "Function of an Index." If we ever lose sight of what the purpose of an index is, rereading of these excerpts should refresh our minds. Lastly, Christopher Alexander (2002, 15) uses a phrase to describe the nature of order that I think applies to the well-designed index. There is a "harmonious coherence" in an orderly and functional index that users recognize immediately.

## Terminology

> Would that the indexing profession could agree on terms so that
> the members of the profession could understand each other.
> —Dorothy Thomas (1989, 18)

In May of 1988, Dorothy Thomas, an indexer and a past president of the American Society of Indexers, spoke at the annual ASI conference about a variety of topics, including the lack of standard terminology within the indexing profession. Since 1988 the profession has done a better job standardizing our terminology.

There are five terms that will be used throughout this book that require identification: *main heading, subheading, reference locator, cross-reference,* and *entry.* Figure 1.1 includes these five items.

## Main Heading

This is the top line in the index entry hierarchy. As Thomas points out, it has been referred to by at least six terms: *access point, entry, index entry,*

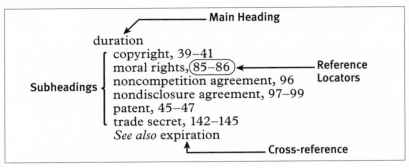

Figure 1.1. The index entry

heading, *main heading*, and *subject heading*. Wellisch (2000, 44) defines the main heading as the "first heading in a multilevel heading."

### Subheadings

The lines of indented text that immediately follow the main heading (and are not cross-references) will be referred to here as *subheadings*. Or, "a modifying heading subordinated to a main heading in a multilevel heading" (Wellisch 2000, 65). Other writers refer to them as "subentries."

### Reference Locator

Usually in a book index the reference locators are page numbers. However, in some books the reference locator is not a page number. For example, many legal books are indexed to section numbers. In this book both terms, *reference locator* and *page number,* will be used. Wellisch uses the term *locator* and defines it as "the part of an entry in an index that indicates the location of the documentary unit to which the entry refers. Locators may range from brief notations, such as page or paragraph numbers, to full bibliographic descriptions" (2000, 42).

### Cross-reference

*Cross-reference* will refer to internal index navigation guides. These guides generally take the form of *See* or *See also*. The *See* cross-reference performs a vocabulary control function. It directs readers from a term not used in the index to the term that is used: "cars. *See* autos" is an example. The *See also* cross-reference directs readers to closely related index entries; "digital photography, 3, 15. *See also* image-processing software" is an example.

## Entry

A main heading along with the entire block of information that follows it will be referred to as an *entry*. In figure 1.1, *duration*, its reference locators, subentries, and the cross-reference together constitute the entry. The term will be used in a general sense, such as "index entries are alphabetized." The term, when qualified, such as in "the *duration* entry," will refer to the main heading and everything that follows it. Bella Hass Weinberg (2004, 42) prefers the phrase *entry array* as coined by James Anderson: "A sequence of entries sharing the same heading in a displayed index" (1997, 38).

## References

Several texts will be referred to frequently throughout this book. While only portions of these references will be discussed here, all are deserving of a complete reading and all would make a valuable addition to an indexer's library.

### Standards

The United States does not have a standard for preparation of indexes. In the early 1990s the National Information Standards Organization (NISO) set up a committee to revise the then-current American standard, ANSI Z39.4–1984. The work of this NISO committee did not garner enough votes to become a standard. NISO has released the revision as a technical report, *Guidelines for Indexes and Related Information Retrieval Devices* (Anderson 1997). This report will be referred to as *NISO TR02*.

*British Standard Recommendation for Preparing Indexes to Books, Periodicals, and Other Documents* (BS 3700: 1988). The *British Standard* has been used in this book primarily because of its lucid discussion of germane topics. Much of BS 3700 has been incorporated into international standard *ISO 999*.

The International Organization for Standardization (ISO) is a federation of national standards bodies from around the world. The ISO headquarters is in Geneva. In 1996 the organization released *ISO 999: Information and Documentation; Guidelines for the Content, Organization, and Presentation of Indexes*. This standard will be referred to as *ISO 999*.

### Style Guides

Three style guides that include substantive discussion about indexes and indexing will be referenced.

*The Chicago Manual of Style*, fifteenth edition, frequently referred to as "Chicago," is the de facto standard for indexes in the United States, published by the University of Chicago Press (2003).

*The Oxford Guide to Style*, released in 2002, is a revised and enlarged edition of *Hart's Rules*, published by Oxford University Press (Ritter et al. 2002).

*Read Me First! A Style Guide for the Computer Industry*, second edition, published by Sun Technical Publications (2003), provides some guidance about special concerns that arise in the indexing of technical documentation.

# Chapter Two

## THE AUTHOR AND THE INDEX

Whether authors decide to prepare indexes for their own books or instead engage a professional indexer, a few preliminary matters should be addressed. A little planning early in the writing process will reap rewards later during the indexing.

## The Book Contract and the Index

A standard clause in most American nonfiction book contracts states that the author will provide an index. Should the author fail to provide an index or fail to provide a satisfactory index, the contract often states that the publisher may supply an index and charge the cost of the index against the author's royalty account. Either way, the author pays for the index in time or money.

The clause in the contract regarding the index is often given little scrutiny by authors. In the whirlwind of activities that surround the signing of a book contract, neither party, publisher or author, is likely to be thinking of the index. Yet the index for some books can have a direct impact on sales. It is in the interest of both parties that the best possible index be written for the book.

Later in this chapter the pros and cons of author-prepared indexes will be discussed. Here I shall focus solely on the contractual provisions regarding the index. Even those authors who are committed to writing their own index should consider revising the index clause in their book contract. The contract should state that the cost of the index shall be shared jointly between the publisher and author, and that the author's portion shall be charged against future royalties. This type of provision provides the author with more financial flexibility should a professional indexer be required. In 1988 the British journal the *Indexer* reported in the article "Contracted Indexes" that the Society of Authors and the Writers' Guild of Great Britain had reached agreements with several British publishers regarding a fifty-fifty division of the cost of indexing as a standard clause in a book contract.

When the author is completely responsible for provision of an index, an unfortunate chain of events is often set into motion. Although many authors realize that by the time the book pages are paginated they will be quite tired of dealing with the book, they often think that the indexing will not take much time. It is certainly something they can whip out in a couple of days or a week, they think. Their editor has sent them a copy of the press's indexing style guide or has referred them to *The Chicago Manual of Style*. But they have rarely read any of this material prior to receiving the first set of page proofs; they've been too busy writing the book.

Perhaps the author has tagged index terms in the word-processor files. Or perhaps the author has highlighted some index terms in the proofs while proofreading the book. Some authors do both, thinking that, without too much trouble, they can repaginate their word-processor files to match the typeset pages so that the final page numbers can be assigned to index entries. In fact this is a time-consuming, tedious, and error-prone process. But, even today, some publishers actually encourage their authors to prepare an index in this manner. For example, Columbia University Press's *Guide for Authors* begins discussion of author-prepared indexes in this way:

> The following discussion assumes that you will be compiling your index with the aid of your computer's word-processing program. However, you may wish to use index cards in the traditional way. Whether you choose to compile your index on cards or onscreen, we strongly urge you to put the final version on a computer disk, even if the original manuscript itself was not so prepared.
>
> If you prepared your manuscript on a disk, we suggest that you begin compiling the index from another copy of the disk you submitted to CUP. Major word-processing programs all have index features, and the latest versions of these are quite powerful, although they remain a poor substitute for the human brain. State-of-the-art programs will, however, be able to insert the page numbers of the original printout of the manuscript, which you can use as temporary numbers until page proofs arrive.
>
> If you take the time to compile the index while you are awaiting page proofs, all that you will need to do when they arrive will be to replace these temporary numbers with the actual page numbers. Simplicity itself! (2002, 29)

Finally, the author gets around to reading the index style specifications. Let's say the index is to be provided in run-in (or run-on) format with letter-by-letter alphabetizing. Leading prepositions, articles, and conjunctions in subheadings are not to be alphabetized. Page ranges are to be elided in a specific way. The *See* cross-references are to run off from the main entry while the *See also* cross-references are to be placed as the last subheading. And all of this has to be done within two weeks of receiving the page proofs, which arrived yesterday.

The clock is ticking, the author is exhausted, and the editor is waiting for the index. The author calls the editor and asks about finding someone to do the index. Since editors know that most experienced indexers are booked weeks if not months in advance, locating an indexer who will be able to provide an index quickly enough to maintain the printing schedule will not be an easy task. Sometimes the editor is lucky—an indexer is free because the schedule for another book has slipped. More often than not, the editor is not lucky. Phone calls produce only referrals to other indexers. The search goes on across the country for any indexer who happens to be free.

Authors who are new to publishing often do not know that contractual indexing services can be expensive. Presuming a good indexer can be located at all, the cost of indexing often shocks the author who must pay for it. A typical three-hundred-page book can easily cost a thousand dollars or more to index, especially if it is a rush job. How many books will have to be sold to pay for that out of royalties? Some editors, appearing as advocates for the author, quite blatantly ask indexers to lower their fee "because the author has to pay for this." Of course, the author has to pay for it because the publisher wrote that clause into the contract and the author did not object.

The scenario above is not far-fetched. It happens far too frequently. The moral of the story is simple: arrangements for the index should be planned; the author should have the financial flexibility to contract for indexing.

## The Writing Process and the Index

Indexers know that a well-written, well-edited, structured book is far easier to index than a poorly written book. While writing, the author can maintain some simple lists that will help to resolve mundane indexing problems later.

### Names of People

If a book refers to people, these names are often included in the index. Superficially, indexing names of people may seem quite easy. However, the task is often complicated because of the variations in references to names (see chapter 7). When citing an individual in the index, the indexer must cite the most complete name used in the text. The individual's complete name is usually provided when the person is first mentioned in the text. Later an abbreviated name or even a nickname may be used. It would be helpful if the author maintained a list of important names in full, with entries such as "Butler, James Francis—AKA—Frank Butler." A simple list of personal names can save indexing time. For example, James Francis Butler may be introduced on page 78 and not appear again until page 310, when he is referred to as Frank Butler. If a list of names is available, the indexer can quickly locate the formal name and check the text to be sure these two names in fact refer to the same individual.

### Names of Organizations

Like names of people, names of organizations should be cited in full in the index. It is hoped that, when an organization is first mentioned in the text, the complete name will have been provided along with any acronyms or abbreviations associated with it. A simple list of organization names, acronyms, and abbreviations can help the indexer maintain consistency in the index. Such a list can also help proofreaders spot name errors, which easily creep into the text. For example, on page 35 we find a reference to the "Society of Indexers" while on page 210 we find the "Society for Indexers." Which is correct? An author's list of organization names would quickly resolve such discrepancies, avoiding last-minute queries from the indexer to the editor.

### Names of Places

Some geographic names pose the same problems as names of people and organizations. Let's take a book called *A Climber's Guide to Mountains of the Western States and Alaska*. While many geographic names are straightforward, such as the Rocky Mountains or Half Dome in Yosemite, others are troublesome. Many readers of this book may not know that in 1980 Mount McKinley National Park was renamed Denali National Park and Preserve, so the index will need an entry for "McKinley National Park. *See* Denali National Park and Preserve." If the author maintains a list of such idiosyncrasies, checking the index for term consistency will be much easier.

## Vocabulary List

As a book is being written, terms that have synonyms will be introduced. The author should decide upon a term of choice and use it consistently throughout the book. The index will cross-reference from synonymous terms to the term of choice. In a book called *Getting the Most Out of Your Computer in Ten Easy Steps* we find the following statement: "Throughout this book we will not distinguish between the various types of video monitors such as CRTs and LCDs. Instead, we will refer only to video monitors."

These two sentences cleanly resolve a potential vocabulary problem. The indexer will provide two cross-references:

> **CRTs.** *See* **video monitors**
> **LCDs.** *See* **video monitors**

Authors should be encouraged to offer synonymous terms in the text. In some cases it might help to keep a list of such terms. The list can be used by both the editor and the indexer to ensure term consistency throughout the book and the index.

## Deciding Ahead of Time What Gets Indexed

Several years ago I indexed a book that contained a lot of footnotes. Before I turned the index over to the editor, I sent a copy to the author for review. She called me and was quite pleased with the index except for one thing: she had expected to see several more names in the index. I was alarmed to learn that I had missed so many names! When we went through her list, name by name, I discovered that each was mentioned only in a footnote citation. Often the mention took the form of

> 19. For a useful discussion of this concept, see Joseph Tussman, *Government and the Mind* (Oxford: Oxford University Press, 1977), 149.

In the example above, *Joseph Tussman* would not ordinarily be indexed. The general rule is not to index the footnote (or endnote) if it merely serves as a bibliographic reference. Footnotes are indexed when they add substantive information not otherwise included in the text. Authors should put indexable names in the body of the text rather than burying these names in notes if they want them to appear in the index. Or the author can request that a separate index of "Authors and Works Cited" be prepared. If such an index is desired, the request should be made early so that additional index pages can be allowed for in the production phase.

Another portion of a book that is often not indexed is the appendixes. Some editors routinely tell indexers not to index the appendixes. In many books a wealth of information is contained in the appendixes that should be indexed. If authors want the appendixes indexed, they may need to express this desire to the book editor.

## Who Should Prepare the Index?

Much debate has been devoted over the years to the virtues of author-prepared indexes compared with indexes written by professional indexers. It is interesting to note the opinion of *The Chicago Manual of Style* as presented in the last four editions.

The twelfth edition (1969):

> The ideal indexer sees the book as a whole—both in scope and in arbitrary limitations—understands the emphasis of the various parts and their relationships to the whole, and—perhaps most important of all—clearly pictures the potential reader and anticipates his special needs. . . . The author most nearly approaches the ideal as indexer. . . . The professional has the advantages of objectivity and experience in many fields of interest and scholarship. His acquaintance is seldom as deep as that of an author in any particular field, and so he may miss some subtleties. . . . (18.13–15)

The thirteenth edition (1982):

> [In this edition the language is almost the same as the twelfth edition, except that it is not gender specific (18.19–21).]

The fourteenth edition (1993):

> The ideal indexer sees the book as a whole, both in scope and in arbitrary limits; understands the emphasis of the various parts and their relation to the whole; and, perhaps most important of all, clearly pictures potential readers and anticipates their special needs. . . . Clearly, authors know better than anyone else both the scope and the limits of their work and the nature of the audience to whom the work is addressed. It might be supposed, therefore, that authors are their own ideal indexers, and sometimes this is indeed the case. . . . Professional indexers have the advantages of objectivity and experience in many fields of interest and scholarship. The most valued have mastered the craft of indexing, are familiar with the publisher's style and with

standard publishing practices, and are accustomed to timely delivery of their product. (17.20–22)

The fifteenth edition (2003):

The ideal indexer sees the work as a whole, understands the emphasis of the various parts and their relation to the whole, and knows—or guesses—what readers of the particular work are likely to look for and what headings they will think of. . . . Although authors know better than anyone else their subject matter and the audience to whom the work is addressed, not all can look at their work through the eyes of the potential reader. Nor do many authors have the technical skills, let alone the time, necessary to produce a good index that meets the publisher's deadline. Some authors produce excellent indexes. Others would do better to enlist the aid of the professional indexer. (18.2)

According to John A. Vickers (1987), an author and a winner of the esteemed Wheatley Medal (for indexing), "It may well be true in general that the author should be the last person to index his own book, being too close to the text" (165). Hans Wellisch echoes Vickers's thoughts when he writes (1995, 32–33),

Unfortunately, authors are often not only admonished but actually forced by the terms of their contracts either to index their work themselves or to find an indexer and to pay the costs of indexing out of their own pockets, whereupon many an author starts compiling an index that turns out to be woefully inadequate or that has to be abandoned after some feeble and often misguided attempts. The reasons for such failures are easy to understand. The author may be exhausted from the arduous work of writing and finishing the book (often against a tight deadline) as well as proofreading it, and has neither the inclination nor the experience to undertake the time-consuming and tedious task of indexing. Authors are also in most cases too close to their own work and may fail to index important facts, events, relationships, or even names, assuming either that "everybody knows that" or "nobody will ever look for this."

In 2002 David Henige commented on the problem of unindexed and poorly indexed academic books in the *Journal of Scholarly Publishing*:

Not long ago, I happened to consult four books in a single day that did not have indexes. Had the books been published in France, I would have been primed to expect this, but three had been published in the United States, the fourth in the United Kingdom. One was a university press book. Perhaps because of this, I felt cheated and aggrieved.

Either I would have to forgo consulting these as I had intended, or I would need to put in far more time than I had allocated. Either way it was my loss. (232)

    The indexing process begins—and should end—with the author, who must, if he needs, insist that his work contain all necessary means of access. He should remember how often his own research had been facilitated by good indexes, and take it for granted that his responsibility is to pass the favour along to his own readers. (234)

Unfortunately Henige urges authors to reject contracting with a professional indexer. His cavalier treatment of indexers generated many letters to the editor in the next two issues of the *Journal of Scholarly Publishing*.

    While this debate will certainly not be resolved here, we can say that it is difficult to generalize about author-prepared indexes. Some authors take to the task of indexing well and prepare useful indexes for their books. Others will flounder and develop an intense dislike for the entire process. A common pitfall is deciding to index one's book without knowing what is actually involved. Aside from a familiarity with the mechanics of indexing, which will fill the remaining chapters of this book, there are some practical issues that should be considered before anyone decides to index a book.

### Authors as Indexers: Strengths and Weaknesses

The primary strength authors bring to the indexing process is familiarity with the text and general subject matter. Authors, better than anyone else, know what is covered in their books and are in a good position to anticipate the needs of the audiences for which they have written the books. Many authors, particularly textbook authors, realizing that the index will play a crucial role in many buying decisions, have a vested interest in the publication of a good index. A good index will help the sales of the book. With this synergy of crucial elements in place, what could possibly go wrong?

    Two factors that can greatly hinder authors who prepare their own indexes are (1) a lack of knowledge of the indexing process and (2) general fatigue and too much self-involvement with the book when it is ready for indexing. The extent to which these factors apply to an author's situation should help authors decide whether or not to index their own books.

    Virtually all who encourage authors to prepare their own indexes insist that authors learn the mechanics of indexing. Some publishers send authors attractive pamphlets that outline the indexing process in quite simple terms. Other publishers refer their authors without additional comment to the discussion of indexing in *The Chicago Manual of Style*. If indexing were such a straightforward and simple task, there would be no need for a book such as this; we could issue a training leaflet instead.

It is not my intention to inflate the index-writing process. On the contrary, I wish to provide information about the substance and nuances of the process to improve the performance of those who undertake the writing of an index. However, after teaching book-indexing techniques to over two thousand students, I've discovered that the art and craft of indexing is mastered by few (Mulvany 2002). Even after thirty hours of classroom instruction, matched by at least thirty hours of outside preparation time, some students learn the rules but still cannot write a proper index. Other students do an excellent conceptual job with term selection but muddle up the rules so badly that their indexes suffer. Hans Wellisch (1995, xxiii) sums up the situation as follows:

> Indexing does not come naturally, like breathing. It is rather more like playing the fiddle: some learn to do it reasonably well, a few will become virtuosi, but most people will never know how to do it at all. This simple truth seems to be lost on publishers and editors, who almost always assume that someone who can write a book will also be able to index it. But this assumption, enshrined in most authors' contracts, is tantamount to the belief that an author can also design and cut the type from which the book will be printed.

To suggest that writing an index can be done by anyone with a minimum amount of preparation is a disservice to author-indexers. At the same time, to suggest that indexing is best tackled by a professional indexer is not fair either. Some authors naturally want to index their own books; the index is a crucial component of the book. Authors who wish to index their own books should be encouraged to do so, provided they are made aware of the demands of the task. Index writing is indeed a form of writing, but one very different from expository writing. Book writers will have to switch creative gears when they become index writers. There will be rules to follow, deadlines to meet. Indexing one's own book is certainly not an impossible task, but it is a demanding task when done well.

In addition to learning how to index, author-indexers must also face the problem of exhaustion and overinvolvement with the book by the time it is ready for indexing. As I contemplate the indexing of this book, I am quite concerned about my own ability to index it well. I will have written and rewritten, edited and rewritten the book many times. I will have proofread pages at least once, if not twice. I suspect that by the time this book is ready for indexing I will be quite tired of it!

The element of fatigue should not be overlooked. Many authors turn the indexing task over to someone else simply because they are too tired of the book to write the index themselves. This is as good a reason as any to hire a professional indexer.

We can generally gauge the amount of fatigue we are feeling; it can be more difficult, however, to ascertain the degree of self-involvement we have with our books. Author-indexers must be true not only to themselves but also to the readers of the index. In order to anticipate the needs of their readers, they must become somewhat detached from the book. While authors know their own language quite well, this language may not be helpful to people who use the index. Even though the author has deliberately chosen particular terms for use in the book, the author-indexer must methodically consider various ways to provide the reader access to those terms and concepts. Intense involvement with one's book can make it difficult to anticipate the index user's needs accurately.

Those authors who will be writing indexes for their own books can rest assured that they will not need to know every tidbit of information that follows in the remaining chapters. They may wish to jump ahead to the next chapter, "Getting Started," paying particular attention to the section on deciphering indexing style guides.

### Professional Indexers: Strengths and Weaknesses

The primary strength a professional indexer brings to the task can be summed up in one word: experience. Professionals know how to index. They know how to budget their time so that the publisher receives the index on schedule in the desired format. Also of extreme importance, professionals can be objective about the book. The professional can read the book with fresh eyes. Even those indexers who specialize in a particular field realize that each book is unique; each index is a special blending of the language of the text with the language of the audience.

Indexers have also mastered the nuances of their dedicated indexing software (discussed in more detail in chapter 10). This software is expensive and definitely has a learning curve. Indexers who know how to use their software properly can work very quickly to meet the publisher's deadlines.

Professional indexers are familiar with publishing practices. They frequently work with authors, manuscript editors, production editors, and compositors/typesetters. Instructions full of publishing jargon that may sound like gibberish to the uninitiated make complete sense to the professional.

Many indexers specialize in subject areas. Some may have advanced degrees, while others may have years of hands-on experience. Often indexers who specialize join appropriate professional organizations and keep current with the language of the field by regularly reading the professional literature.

Indexers must be able to empathize with both the author and the readers. Indexers must possess an array of inductive and deductive thinking skills. Additionally, the professional must work in a detailed, careful, and accurate manner. Indexers must also possess the rare commodity of common sense. When the rules do not apply and there is nowhere to turn for guidance, common sense and sound judgment will provide an answer.

The most obvious handicap that a professional indexer may have is lack of familiarity with the subject matter. With many mass-market books, this is not an issue. Any book written for a literate, general audience can be indexed by a well-read, intelligent indexer. Books that contain specialized and complex subject matter will often require the indexing skills of an individual with a substantial background knowledge of the subject. For example, any good indexer could index a mass-market book about reducing cholesterol with a vegetarian diet. The indexer would not need an advanced degree in nutritional science. However, a medical school text about renal disease can be an indexing challenge. While the indexer of such a book need not have a medical degree, knowledge of medical terminology will be important. Ideally, the indexer of the book about renal disease will be an experienced medical indexer familiar with the nuances of medical indexing and the standard vocabulary of the discipline.

Without a doubt some books contain such specialized subject matter that locating a professional indexer with the appropriate background may be difficult. Some argue that a good indexer can index anything; I believe that indexers often need subject-area expertise to index well.

At the other end of the spectrum are authors and editors who assume that the material is so complex that the indexer will need help with term selection. Often this "help" takes the form of lists of terms to be included in the index, or manuscripts in which the author has highlighted indexable terms. These lists of terms or author highlights are usually not helpful or necessary. I have often found that the material to be indexed is not complex but quite straightforward to anyone with a rudimentary background in the field. It is important to maintain a clear picture of the nature of the material to be indexed and to locate an indexer with an appropriate background.

## Relationship between Author and Indexer

When authors decide not to index their own books, they must locate someone who will do the indexing. By now it should be clear that indexing is not a task to carelessly hand over to a graduate student or somehow persuade a brother-in-law to do. The index will reflect upon both the author and the publisher. A poorly written index will be a source of embarrassment to both parties. Authors are advised to spend time and locate an appropriate indexer.

### Locating an Indexer

An indexer should be selected well in advance of the date that final, paginated pages are expected. Given the typical turnaround time for an index, the indexer will need to plan for a book. Usually six weeks to a month is enough notice for an indexer to block out the time needed.

Indexers are often located by referral. Most editors have a list of indexers with whom they have worked. Your colleagues can be another source of information. If you liked the index in a particular book, try to locate the indexer who wrote it.

Another source of information are the directories published by the various indexing societies. Please see appendix B for society addresses and Web sites. Indexers are also listed in the *Literary Market Place (LMP)*, the sourcebook for the American publishing industry.

When time allows, it is often a good idea to interview and accept bids from several indexers. You need to find an indexer with whom you can work. The author and the indexer must be able to communicate clearly. Ask if the indexer has worked on books similar to yours. The indexer will surely ask you to describe your book and its audience. If you do not feel comfortable with the conversation, then most likely you are not talking to the person who should index your book.

If the interview goes well, you will undoubtedly be asked questions you may not be able to answer. You might be asked if the index is to be in indented or run-in style, or what format will be used for the electronic index file. Authors should feel free to refer all questions regarding index specifications to their editors (see the section below, "What the Indexer Needs").

Many authors turn the entire matter of indexing over to their editors. However, a complete lack of author involvement in the indexing process is far from ideal. In response to a negative review of an index that placed blame on the indexer and the publisher, British author Bernard Levin (1987) addressed the matter of the author's responsibility:

> This authorial willingness to be left out of the picture is widespread; I cannot count the number of fellow-authors who have complained in my hearing about, say, a rotten jacket for their books. When I ask why they did not demand to see the jacket in all its stages, from the first sketch, it almost invariably transpires that it never occurred to them to ask, whereupon I have a struggle to refrain from telling them that they have no one to blame but themselves. When I wrote my first book, some seventeen years ago, I announced that I was going to interfere in every stage of the publication, right down to the typeface it was set in, and I have done so ever since. And surely if a book includes an index, a self-respecting author should be as jealous of its quality as of his own. (238)

Authors are advised to make clear to their editors early in the book production schedule the degree of involvement they wish to have with the index. If an author wants to review an index before it goes to press, time will need to be allocated for that review. When an author demands to see actual page proofs of the index, planning for this time is even more crucial. Time for thorough author review of the index needs to be budgeted from the very beginning of the production cycle.

### Contractual Matters

When an index is paid for either by the author alone out of royalties or jointly by the publisher and author—again, the author's portion out of royalties—typically the publisher formally contracts with the indexer. Authors who will pay the indexer directly will need their own contract with the indexer.

Most problems between indexers and their clients arise from a lack of communication about aesthetic and practical expectations. Many indexers have their own contracts. Publishers have their own contracts. Often publishers' indexing contracts are woefully lacking in clarity and professionalism.

At the very least, an indexing contract should cover the following items:

- the work to be indexed; expected length of the work
- time schedule for delivery of final proofs to indexer and delivery of the index to the client
- provisions regarding late delivery of material to the indexer; provisions regarding late delivery of the index to the author/publisher
- provisions for additional indexing caused by pagination changes in the text
- complete specifications regarding index format and submission format for the index
- rate of pay for the index; the payment schedule
- assignment of rights for the index

▮ *Written contracts.* Like any other contract, the indexing contract must be signed by both parties. A surprising number of publishers and indexers work without written contracts; they rely solely on oral agreements. This arrangement appears to work well until there is a problem. When a problem does arise, the lack of a written contract does not reflect well on the professionalism of either the indexer or the publisher.

▮ *Assignment of rights.* Many people within the publishing community mistakenly assume that an index is automatically considered a "work made for hire." The U.S. Copyright Act of 1976 (§101) clearly states that a work is a work made for hire only "if the parties expressly agree in a written instrument signed by them that the work shall be considered a work made for hire" before works begins. Without a written agreement signed by both parties an index cannot be considered a work made for hire. If both parties sign an agreement stating that the index will be a work made for hire, then the commissioning agent, usually the publisher, will be the copyright owner (see §201).

Many indexers prefer to use an "assignment of rights" clause rather than a "work for hire" clause. Frequently the indexer will assign all rights to the client upon full payment for the indexing work. More disturbing than misconceptions about work-for-hire agreements is the widespread lack of any written agreement specifying the assignment of rights for the index. It appears that some people do not realize that indexes are creative, authored works entitled to copyright registration. For the record, I have filed for and was granted copyright registration for three indexes (Copyright Registration Numbers: TXu-399–379, TXu-401–792, TXu-448–434). At a 1989 meeting with Harriet Oler, chief of the Examining

Department of the U.S. Copyright Office, it was confirmed that an authored index that is not a work for hire is deemed a compilation entitled to copyright registration.

Of course, copyright registration does not necessarily mean that the indexes are copyrightable. Miller and Davis (1990, 307) write about this issue regarding the copyrightability of computer programs: "Mere registration did not make them copyrightable, of course, but did reflect the view of many respected persons both within and without the Copyright Office that programs have sufficient originality and authorship to be copyrightable." For more information about copyright and indexes, see the article "Copyright for Indexes, Revisited" (Mulvany 1991).

■ *How much will it cost?* Generalizing about the cost of an index is difficult. Indexing rates vary greatly depending upon the type of material to be indexed.

One of four basic formats is used by an indexer when preparing a bid. Some indexers charge by the hour; many charge by the page or by the entry. Other indexers will present a flat-fee bid.

When an indexer charges by the hour, the indexer must stipulate, in writing, an expected range, with the maximum number of hours clearly understood by both parties. An experienced indexer is able to judge accurately how much time an assignment will take. Hourly rates generally range from forty to fifty dollars.

Most indexers bid jobs on a per-page rate. This way both parties know exactly how much an index will cost. When calculating a per-page rate, the indexer will be taking into account the density of text per page. Clearly, if a book is three columns of 8-point type, the per-page rate will be higher than for a book of less densely printed material. Another item considered in this type of bid format is the amount of illustrative material. Are there tables or photographs or line drawings? Is the illustrative material to be indexed? If not, does it take up space on the pages, reducing the amount of indexable material? Are footnotes or endnotes to be indexed? Another important consideration is the nature of the material. For example, a multiauthored graduate-level text about economics will very likely cost more to index than an introductory, single-authored text about economics. Per-page rates generally start at four dollars, depending on the type of book; many medical texts, for instance, are indexed at a rate of six dollars or more per page.

Some indexers submit per-entry bids. This format requires a clear understanding of what constitutes an entry. For example, is "dogs, 34–37,

55, 103–4" one entry? Is it three entries? Or is it seven entries? In my opinion, it is three entries—the indexer had to type or tag the entry three times because "dogs" appeared in three separate locations in the text. Others would consider the example as one entry. In this case, the per-entry rate is really a per-line rate. Another concern with this type of bidding is the possibility that an index will become padded with entries. Given the disparity in the interpretations of what constitutes an entry, it is difficult to arrive at a general rate for this type of bidding. Usually, the rate is less than a dollar per entry or per line.

Indexers who provide a flat-fee bid have undoubtedly taken into account the various bidding formats used. In any type of contract work, all parties like to know what it will cost. This is not always possible, but it is always desirable.

One last remark about fees. Occasionally an editor will call and say, "We need a really short index, only about 900 lines," implying that it takes less time to design a short index than to design a longer index for the same material and that therefore the price should be less. This reasoning is flawed. First, regardless of the size of an index, the indexer must still read the same number of words. Second, it is not only difficult but also time-consuming to produce a 900-line index instead of the 1,500 lines that may really be called for. Many indexers index a book the way it should be indexed, then edit it to meet space requirements. It is difficult to distill five entries to one entry and remain fair to the material. Short indexes do not necessarily imply reduced fees.

Another way to look at the cost of the index is to calculate how much the index costs in relation to the number of copies of the book that are published. This calculation will show us how much the index adds to the unit cost of a book. Let's use the example of a 300-page book whose index costs $1,200.00. Table 2.1 shows how the unit cost of the index decreases as print runs increase.

Table 2.1. The unit cost of a $1,200 index

| Copies printed | Unit cost ($) |
| --- | --- |
| 5,000 | 0.24 |
| 10,000 | 0.12 |
| 15,000 | 0.08 |
| 50,000 | 0.024 |
| 100,000 | 0.012 |

## What the Indexer Needs

The following items are indispensable to the indexer:

- page proofs that are clear and readable
- index specifications
- author's list of names (if available)
- editor's style sheet (if available)

The indexer will need a complete set of page proofs for the book. It is usually the publisher's responsibility to provide a set of these pages to the indexer. Often the typesetter is asked to send final pages by overnight delivery to the indexer at the same time that the pages are sent to the publisher. If the book is in camera-ready PDF format, indexers may be sent the book as an e-mail file attachment. Most indexers would then print out the PDF and charge for this service.

The indexer's copy of the final pages must be clear and readable. Poor photocopies will slow down the indexing, cause the indexer grief, and possibly lead to errors in the index.

A few comments about *final* pages are warranted. Publishers who generate final pages in-house often succumb to the temptation to make last-minute adjustments that change the pagination of a book. Since the indexer is assigning page numbers to index entries, any changes in pagination will affect the index. It can be very time-consuming, and therefore costly, for the indexer to readjust reference locators in the index. Once pages have been sent out for indexing, every effort should be made to ensure that the pagination of the book does not change. If the pagination does change, the indexer should be notified immediately.

The indexer must be given specifications for the index or a comprehensive style guide. Index specs should cover such things as rules of alphabetization, format of the index (run-in or indented), format and placement of cross-references, and electronic formatting requirements. The likely source for this information is the editor at the publishing house. More on index specifications will be presented in chapter 3.

If the author has maintained lists of personal names, geographic names, or names of organizations, these lists should be given to the indexer. A copy of the editor's style sheet can also be helpful to the indexer. Any general editorial guidelines regarding such matters as transliteration or density of indexing should be discussed prior to the beginning of indexing work.

## Collaboration between Author and Indexer

A cooperative working relationship between the author and the indexer can be extremely beneficial. An author who is available for consultation during the indexing process can be a valuable technical resource for the indexer.

In some books the indexer may have questions about the organization of certain terms. "Would it be better to list this as *xyz,* or would people tend to look it up first as *abc?*" Authors should respond to such questions with directness; there is no time to give the indexer a graduate-level education in the topic at hand. If the author and the indexer have established a good rapport, the indexer will feel free to call upon the author as need arises; a much better index will result. This is one reason authors should be involved in the selection of the indexer.

Alternatively, authors (and editors) can become overinvolved in the indexing process, much to the dismay of the indexer. Calls to the indexer to say, "I just want to make sure you indexed *xyz* on page 52" are not helpful. A more difficult situation arises when the indexer is provided with a long list of terms that the author wants to see in the index. Such lists are distracting to the indexer. The cadence of indexing is disrupted when the indexer must double-check selected index terms against the author's list. Another problem with these lists is the assumption that the indexer needs help. It would be more productive for the author to hold on to such a list and use it later when the index is being reviewed. If there are terms on the author's list that do not appear in the index, the author can discuss these terms with the indexer and the two of them together can figure out how to integrate the missing terms into the index.

■ *Author highlights.* Equally unhelpful, in my experience, are "author highlights." An author highlight is a set of page proofs on which the author has highlighted the terms that should be indexed. The quality of highlights varies greatly. I have seen pages with practically nothing marked. Others have been so heavily marked up with various DayGlo colors representing different levels of entries that the pages resembled a psychedelic smorgasbord. One editor went so far as to tell me that the only terms that should be in the index were those terms that were highlighted. The editor should have hired a data entry clerk, not an indexer, for this task.

There are several problems with author highlights. First, it is the indexer's job to know what should be indexed. If the editor's or author's confidence in the indexer is so low that they feel the indexer needs to be told what to index, then perhaps they have not found the right indexer for the job.

Second, working from pages that have been marked up by someone else is, again, distracting. The rhythm of indexing is interrupted as the indexer second-guesses every decision. It is difficult for the indexer to see the book on its own terms; the highlights interfere with the indexer's perception of the book. Given the short amount of time available for indexing, anything that slows the process should be eliminated.

Third, some author highlights are not only distracting but impossible to work with. I have seen pages with thirty or more terms marked per page. An indexer needs clear, legible copy. When an editor insists on providing an author highlight, I insist on a second set of unmarked pages. Usually I put the author highlight in a corner and never look at it. It takes a great deal of the author's time to highlight pages. This time could be better spent putting together lists of names or synonyms for the indexer.

∎ *Interim review of the index.* Sometimes an author or editor asks to see the index while it is in progress. The value of an interim review of the index is that the author or editor can check to see that certain types of material are being handled as desired. The disadvantage of an interim review is that it places the indexer in an awkward position. Writing an index is not a linear process. As an index evolves, changes are made to various parts of it. The structure of entries on Wednesday may bear little resemblance to the structure of entries on Friday.

Again, given the typical time allotted for indexing, there is little chance that an interim review of an index can be scheduled at a productive point. When an indexer works on the usual deadline, stopping midway to wait for interim review comments is not possible. By the time review comments come back to the indexer, the index at hand will very likely be different from the index that was reviewed. It is also important to keep in mind that some of the editing of the index does not occur until the end of the indexing process.

There are some situations when an interim review might be desirable to all parties. An interim review can be helpful in a very large indexing project, particularly if multiple indexers are involved. Such review periods need to be specifically scheduled, with time allowed to incorporate the reviewer's comments.

∎ *Final review of the index.* Ideally, the indexing schedule will allow time for author review of the index. Author review is separate from the editor's review. While the publishing house editor will be concerned primarily with index format and length, the author will be concerned with the content of the index.

Authors must be prepared to review the index quickly, usually within a day or two of its receipt. Authors are intimately familiar with the content of the book. When reviewing the index, authors must evaluate the index's ability to provide access to the content of the book. One way to do this is to randomly choose a page of text to look at. Imagine how readers might look up information appearing on that page. Check to see if those terms are in the index.

The index should also be reviewed as a whole. Authors should read through the index. Check for cross-referencing of synonymous terms. Do not forget to truly read the entries. Do not scan them. Do the entries make sense? If an entry does not make sense, look it up. Perhaps you, as the author, can provide a better term.

Make notes and keep a list of questions. The next step is to talk with the indexer. The author and indexer should have prearranged a time to talk. At this point time is crucial. The editor is waiting for the index. Quite likely, the indexer will send the index to the publisher within twenty-four hours of conferring with the author.

Most indexers are pleased to work with authors who have carefully reviewed the index. Often authors' insights result in a better index. It is also important for authors to listen to the indexer, who may have sound reasons for designing the conceptual structure of an index in one way and not another. At the same time, indexers must remember that authors know their books best. This is not the time to be overly defensive about one's work. It is the time to listen to the author and attempt to integrate the author's suggestions into the index.

Some authors have no desire to become involved in the indexing process. The editors of books by such authors will find themselves responsible for the entire review and editing cycle. Chapter 9, "Editing the Index," will present a detailed discussion of the index editing process.

# *Chapter Three*

## GETTING STARTED

This chapter will provide a general overview of the indexing process, beginning with a brief description of the book production process. I will discuss what is and is not indexable and offer suggestions about how to index the indexable material. Lastly, I will look at various index style specifications and a handy way to estimate the size of an index.

## The Book Production Process

A general understanding of how a book is physically produced can be very helpful to the indexer. For example, decisions regarding the actual page size of a book and the typography and layout will affect the cost of indexing. Decisions regarding the printing and binding of a book directly affect the number of pages that will be allotted to the index. A thorough overview of typography, layout, design, production, and printing methods can be found in *The Chicago Manual of Style (2003)*, appendix A: Design and Production.

### Typography and Layout

There are many reasons why indexers should have a familiarity with the principles of typography and book layout. First, indexers often work with production editors rather than manuscript editors. Indexers need to be able to interpret the language used by production editors. Second, when space is at a premium, indexers can sometimes have some influence over the typography and layout of the index. Effective communication between indexers and production editors can mean the difference between cutting an index down to size and printing the index in its entirety. Third, indexers familiar with typography will understand the difference in text density per page when the type is "10 on 12" compared to type that is "9 on 10." Lastly, indexers are only one of several types of professionals who work in the publishing industry. A general knowledge of publishing is appropriately expected of indexers.

Books are printed using particular *typefaces* in specific sizes. Typefaces have names such as Times Roman or Helvetica. The size of a typeface is expressed in points. The larger the point size, the larger the characters. Many books are printed in 9- or 10-point type. The spacing between the lines of type is referred to as *leading*, which is also measured in points. The expression above, "10 on 12," refers to a book that is printed with 10-point type on a 12-point base that allows 2-point leading.

The layout of book pages affects the density of type on the page. The pages for many software manuals have a lot of "white space"—wide margins with the body text in one column. On the other hand, the pages for a graduate-level college textbook may be quite dense, with two columns of text and footnotes at the bottom of the page. The density of text on a page impacts not only the *density of indexing*, that is, the average number of index entries per page, but also the time it takes the indexer to read and extract index entries from a page of text. Thus, the cost of indexing is related to the layout of the book pages.

### Printing and Binding of a Book

Production editors and indexers may find themselves at odds regarding the space allocated for the index. Often the indexer feels that the index needs more pages than are available whereas the production editor insists that the index fit into the specified number of pages. Unfortunately, such disputes arise at a time in the production cycle when little can be done to accommodate an index that is too long.

When a book is printed, the pages are not printed one at a time. Instead, the printer uses large sheets of paper, often called *press sheets*. Such a sheet might be 49 inches by 37 inches, with 64 pages to a sheet, 32 pages on each side. A sheet of this sort will be cut and folded into groups of 16 pages. These groups are called *signatures*. When a book is laid out, the production editor will arrange the book so that it will come out in even signatures. A 320-page book that is printed on a sheet that produces 32 pages on each side, 64 pages total, will require five 64-page press sheets for one copy of the book (320 pages divided by 64). If 10,000 copies of the book are printed, 50,000 press sheets will be required.

When a book is prepared for binding, the press sheets are folded and gathered into signatures in numerical order. The signatures are then sewn together, individually and to each other. Various methods are used to physically bind the signatures into one unit.

Long before a book goes to press, paper is ordered for the book. The cost of the paper is of real concern to a publisher; it directly affects the unit cost of a book. When an editor tells an indexer that only a specific number of pages are available for the index, that number is not arrived at capriciously. Most likely, front matter pages have been counted and re-counted. Perhaps a half-title page and the blank page behind it have been removed so that two more pages can be set aside for the index.

It is highly unlikely that an additional signature will be added to a book to accommodate an index. Remember, in the 320-page book example above, the press sheets hold 64 pages. The printing press is set up for this particular paper size. Adding another signature will involve order-ing more 64-page press sheets. This can be not only costly but difficult to do at the last minute. The paper manufacturer may not have the paper in stock. Or the paper manufacturer may not be able to ship the paper to the printer in time for the printer to get the pages to the binder. Also, the bindery is expecting to bind a book of a particular size. Adding another signature may affect the binding.

With careful planning, the production editor will give thought to the number of pages required for the index. Later in this chapter, estimating index size will be discussed.

## The Nature of Indexing Work

Before diving into the intricacies of indexing, I shall describe the way many indexers work. Most professional book indexers do not begin work until page proofs of the book are available. *Page proofs* are typeset and pag-inated book pages that reflect the placement of text, display material, and other design elements. Some publishers produce page proofs in multiple stages. Indexers must have the most stable proofs in hand in order to be able to assign correct page numbers to index entries.

## Production Schedule and Indexing

Indexers should understand where indexing falls in the book produc-tion cycle. The general sequence of events in the book production cycle is as follows:

Copyediting

Author review of copyediting

Cleanup copyediting

Page proof production

Author review of proofs

Revised page proof production

Proofreading/Indexing (one or the other may come first; both may go on simultaneously)

Even in this age of electronic manuscript preparation, there is still a gap between the first run of typeset copy and the final page proofs. Despite the use of sophisticated book design software, inevitably changes will be made to various pages of the book. Some page breaks will not be quite right. Sometimes an illustration that falls at the bottom of a page will need to be moved to the top of the next page. Any adjustments to book pages that affect the pagination should be completed before indexing begins.

Since so many books are now written on personal computers, it would at first glance seem to make sense to index the book using the indexing module in the word-processing program. A lot of time could be saved this way, one would think. If the index entries were already embedded in the text files, one would not need to wait for page proofs before beginning the index. The many problems with this approach to indexing will be discussed in chapter 10, "Tools for Indexing."

The page proofs are delivered to the indexer either as hard copy or electronic files. Hard copy is produced by the typesetter and delivered directly to the indexer. Some publishers send the indexer the book by e-mail, often as a PDF file. The indexer will then print the file. Since most printers used by indexers print on letter-sized paper, this method will not work well for books with large pages. The pages will shrink to fit the indexer's printer but will likely be difficult to read, much less to index from.

Once the indexer receives final book pages, time is of the essence. The publisher has a firm date set with the printer and binder of the book. That date is rapidly approaching. Presumably the production editor or production controller has scheduled a reasonable amount of time for indexing, editing the index, typesetting the index, proofreading the index, and laying out and producing the final proofs of the index.

An informal survey of production editors revealed that once copy for an index is received by a publisher, usually a week or less remains before the index must be delivered to the printer. There is no time for slipped schedules at this point. Missing a date with the printer can have dire consequences. Publishers with a high printing volume may have some leeway insofar as rescheduling the printing date is concerned. However, a slipped print schedule can be very expensive when the book must be printed as a rush job in order to meet a binding and shipping date. Or a book could miss its shipping date altogether. It will be late going to distributors. Orders from bookstores will be placed on back order. The book cannot be presented at an important conference or will not be ready for the beginning of fall classes.

When the indexing work begins, often production schedules have already slipped—the copyeditor was late, the author was late getting corrections back, or the typesetter was delayed and the page proofs are late. There is often no cushion in the schedule by the time the indexer gets the pages. Indexers must be able to work within the bounds of rather tight schedules. Indexing is not a leisurely activity.

## How Indexers Work

The way indexers work will vary from individual to individual and from project to project. Some indexers will receive the entire set of book pages at one time. Others will receive pages in batches, such as chapters 1 through 3, then 4 through 6, and so on. When pages are sent in batches, the indexer often has more time to devote to the index. Ideally, the batches are sent in order so that the indexer can work through the text in a linear manner.

Believe it or not, one question frequently asked of indexers is, "Do you really have to read the whole book?" Yes, we read the whole book, every word. Once in possession of book pages, some indexers skim through the book. Others thoroughly read the book, marking appropriate entries as they go. Still others sit down with the pages and jump right in on page 1 and create index entries.

Chapter 10, "Tools for Indexing," discusses the various methods used by indexers to collect the entries and turn them into a formatted index. Here I wish only to discuss the general nature of indexing work.

Reading a book as an indexer is very different from reading the book as an interested reader. The indexer must be able to read quickly and at the same time accurately synthesize the material being read. In well-written and well-edited books, the overall structure of the index emerges in tandem with the discussion in the text. Highly structured books are often the easiest books to index. For example, a programmer's reference guide for a Java programming product will be much easier to index than Martin Heidegger's *Being and Time*. Reference books for programming languages are often highly structured documents that discuss discrete elements one at a time. *Being and Time* is also highly structured, but the discussion deals with complex conceptual issues that build upon one another.

The indexer becomes immersed in the flow of the writing. It is inevitable that the indexer will internalize the voice and tone of the author. At the same time, though, the indexer must consider the reader's perspective, adding cross-references where needed and picking up on nuances that are not clearly stated. The indexing process is intense. Chances are that no other reader will read the book in such a focused manner in such a short amount of time as does the indexer.

Many indexers hold the structure of the index in their minds as they work. It always amazes me that while indexing page 324 I can remember that the same topic was discussed earlier, although that earlier discussion may have been as far back as page 98. For the length of time an indexer works on a book, the indexer lives and breathes the language of the book. This is why some experienced indexers turn down work they are quite capable of doing; they do not want their consciousness flooded with the theme of the book!

Indexers must be able to recognize details. More important, the indexer must be able to see relationships between details and organize them into meaningful order. While indexers must be detail-oriented, they must also be able to synthesize information and communicate the synthesis to the readers. This ability requires sharp communication skills and the ability to empathize with the audience.

The indexer is constantly balancing the words of the author with the needs of the reader. The index is ultimately an interface between the author and the reader. It is the most heavily used portion of some books. The indexer's ability to meet the demands of the text and the reader's needs will determine the overall usability of the index, and of the book as well.

Indexing by its very nature is intense. The intensity is compounded by the pressure of the book's production schedule. A two-week period to index a three-hundred-page book is not uncommon. A three-week schedule is considered generous.

As G. Norman Knight (1979) so clearly pointed out in the title to his book, indexing is an art. We can isolate the methodological components of indexing, but there is another dimension to indexing that does not lend itself to such rigorous examination. Indexing skills can be nurtured and rules can be learned. But the indexer's ability to thoroughly digest the intentions of the author and anticipate the needs of the readers, thereby producing a knowledge structure that is sensible and usable, involves the application of abilities and skills that are inherent in some individuals and not in others.

After the indexer has edited the index, the work is prepared for submission. Frequently the indexer delivers the index electronically as an e-mail attachment. (Chapter 8, "Format and Layout of the Index," provides information about final submission formats.) For many indexers, delivery signals the end of their involvement with the index. But indexers should always be available to answer any questions the editor may have.

## What Not to Index

Before we look at what parts of a book are indexed, let's discuss what portions are not. There are some gray areas within a book that are indexed in some situations but not in others. Most books can be divided into three major sections: front matter, text, and back matter.

### Front Matter

Generally the front matter of a book is not indexed. Included as nonindexable front matter are the following: title page or pages, copyright and printing history page, dedication or epigraph, table of contents, lists of illustrations or tables, and acknowledgments.

Many books also include a foreword, a preface, and an introduction. The foreword and preface that describe how a book came to be written should not be indexed unless the actual substance of the book is discussed therein. Certainly an introduction to the subject matter of the book is indexable.

Lowercase roman numerals are generally used to paginate front matter pages. These reference locators precede the arabic page numbers regardless of their numeric value. Note the order of the reference locators in the following entry:

>  atoms, discovery of, xv, 5–8

Although the front matter appears first in a book, it is often the last set of pages the indexer will receive. Some of the front matter sections, such as the table of contents, cannot be composed until the entire book is in pages. As noted above, it is often necessary to juggle the pagination of the front matter so that the book will fit within the desired number of signatures. A book that is running one page too long, perhaps because of the index, can sometimes be shortened by removing a blank page in the front matter. But removing pages from the front matter is easier said than done. Often the front matter pages are typeset and paginated by the time the index is submitted.

If there will be indexable material in the front matter, providing the copy to the indexer early on can be very helpful. The material need not be in final pages at this point; even manuscript will do. For example, if a true introduction to the book appears as front matter, the indexer could benefit from reading the introduction before beginning work. The indexer would then have a general perspective on the entire work. The foreword or preface can also inform the indexer of the book's intended audience.

Many editors do not routinely provide front matter material for indexing. It is up to the indexer to inquire about the substance of the foreword, preface, or introduction and to ask for a table of contents even if the final version is not yet available.

### Text

For the purposes of this discussion, the *text* of a book shall be defined as the main body of the book, often divided into chapters or sections. Most of the text of a book is routinely considered indexable.

In some books each chapter or section begins with a detailed table of contents. These "minicontents," like the contents page at the beginning of the book, are not indexed. Similarly, some books are divided into parts, which begin with display pages that list the title of the part. Such display pages are not indexed.

Chapters in textbooks often end with a series of questions for students. These pages are not usually indexed. But like many guidelines in indexing, *not usually* does not mean *never*. A fine example of an exception to this guideline is Schaum's 3000 Solved Problems Series (McGraw-Hill), books that are composed entirely of questions and answers for students.

Footnotes or endnotes that serve only a bibliographic purpose are usually not indexed. In other words, if the function of the note is solely to provide a reference to discussion in the text, it is not usually indexed. The matter of indexing footnotes or endnotes is discussed in more detail later in this chapter.

### Back Matter

The back matter of a book often comprises appendixes, notes, glossary, bibliography, and, of course, the index. As a general rule, the contents of the bibliography and glossary are not indexed. However, if the back matter is lengthy, it may be helpful to readers to cite in the index the presence of the glossary or bibliography:

> **glossary of terms, 535–66**

Although many technical publications contain glossaries, indexers are not always provided with them. Some editors assume that the glossary will not be indexed, so they do not provide the indexer with a copy. Or it may be that the glossary is not yet set in pages when indexing begins. Whenever possible, the indexer should receive the glossary: it can be used as a quick reference during indexing and as a handy checklist during the editing of the index. While not every term that appears in the glossary necessarily appears in the index, a great majority of glossary terms do.

Although the content of appendixes may or may not be indexed, the presence of the material should be cited. Let's suppose that a book about civil liberties has an appendix containing the text of the Declaration of Independence. While the substance of the Declaration of Independence is not indexed, the presence of the document is cited. Readers who want to locate the actual text of the Declaration of Independence should be provided with access to that text. The civil liberties book may contain the following entry:

> Declaration of Independence
> authors of, 38–39
> French Revolution and, 45–48
> text of, 430–35
> writing of, 39–44

In the above, the subheading "text of" clearly references the presence of the document in the appendix. This subheading provides direct access to the reproduced document in the appendix.

In technical documentation, particularly that of the computer industry, a great deal of important information is often included in the appendixes. This information is not always indexed as thoroughly as it might be. Contract indexers are often not even given the appendix pages. Because the appendixes are frequently the last portion of the book to be written, there may be little time for thorough indexing. Unfortunately, appendixes in computer documentation may contain crucial information, such as troubleshooting tips, configuration tables, and hardware switch settings. Access to information like this is important to the users of the product. Although the general feeling among editors and indexers is that appendixes that reproduce material cited in the text should not be indexed, it is definitely a mistake to assume this without consideration.

It is important when deciding whether to index appendixes to distinguish between indexing the appendixes in detail or indexing them in a general manner, simply citing the presence of certain material. Given the cost and effort that goes into publishing a book, it is difficult to imagine material in appendixes being of such minor importance that their indexing is not required. The indexer's duty is to index the entire book. If a decision has been made to restrict the indexing, a statement to this effect should appear in an introductory note to the index.

## What Is Indexable?
### The Text
All information presented in the body of the text that is directly relevant to the subject matter, scope, and audience of the book is indexable. An indexer with a clear idea of the scope of the book and a general understanding of the subject matter and the audience will be in a position to distinguish between relevant and peripheral information.

Distinguishing between relevant and peripheral information involves judgment. Careful exercise of such judgment is what sets a true index apart from a computer-generated list of words. A computer could easily scan the text of a book and produce a listing of every occurrence of the words "Yellowstone Park." An indexer, however, has the ability to distinguish between passing mention of Yellowstone and information of substance relating to it. Users of indexes seek access to specific, relevant information. They do not expect to be guided to peripheral material.

Relevant information in a book can be both explicit and implicit. *Explicit information* is that which is stated verbatim in the text. Simple examples of explicit information are the names of people or organizations discussed in the text. *Implicit information* is that which is implied but not stated word for word in the text. Quite often, general concepts are implicit information that must be identified by the indexer.

To expand on the example of implicit information mentioned above, consider the discussion of the mineral and vitamin content of dog food in a book about raising dogs. Although many types of minerals and vitamins are discussed in relation to wheat-based and corn-based dog food, never is the word *nutrition* used. In a case like this, *nutrition* is an implicit concept that will be identified by the indexer and added to the index.

It is the reasonable and experienced application of judgment and interpretation by the indexer that greatly contributes to the overall quality and usefulness of an index. Just because a term is mentioned does not necessarily mean that it is indexable. The indexer is responsible for each element in the index as well as for its general character. Later in this book we shall see that computers are capable of automatically manipulating the text of a book in a variety of ways. Yet the computer is incapable of exercising the type of judgment and interpretation applied by experienced indexers.

Unlike the computer, the indexer is constantly filtering information: separating the trivial from the substantive, making the implicit concepts explicit in the index. The complex network of decisions that lie behind the successful index are often transparent to the index users. For a more detailed discussion, see "Inside an Indexer's Brain" (in Stauber 2004, 327–343).

## Footnotes, Endnotes

The general rule regarding footnotes and endnotes is to index their contents only when they present material not found in the text. Notes that provide only a bibliographic reference for material in the text are not generally indexed. Scholarly books that contain notes often have a bibliography that lists all the references cited in the text. If a bibliography is not present, however, a strong argument can be made for the indexing of references in footnotes as this will be the only access to these references provided for readers. Also, because the bibliography does not include page references for the discussion in the text, it is often difficult, if not impossible, for readers to work backward from an entry in the bibliography to its context in the text.

There are certainly times when readers' needs will be better served if the reference material in notes is indexed. For example, most of the text in *Labor Management Laws in California Agriculture* was written in "plain English" rather than in legalese. Very few case law citations found their way into the body of the text. Instead, the book made heavy use of footnotes to list the many pertinent case law citations. In the interest of attorneys who might use the book, all footnotes containing case law citations were indexed.

As with any general rule in indexing, it is always important to apply the rule judiciously within the context at hand. In some books, the reference material found in footnotes is of great importance. We have all wanted to locate a reference that appeared in a footnote only to discover that this material was not indexed. Keep in mind that properly indexing all reference material in footnotes can greatly add to the length of the index. In a heavily referenced book, the decision to index all reference material should be evaluated carefully in light of the space available. Additionally, the cost of indexing will increase when all references are included in the index. (See chapter 4 for a discussion of the reference locator format for footnote and endnote entries.)

### Illustrations, Tables, Charts, and Other Display Material

Before indexing begins, a decision should be made regarding the indexing of display material in the text. In the context of this discussion, *display material* refers to line drawings, photographs, tables, maps, charts, screen displays, block diagrams, flowcharts—any special element that is not text.

If the display material appears on the same page as textual discussion of the material, it is usually not necessary to index the display individually. If a photograph of a kung pao chicken dish appears on the same page of a cookbook as the recipe, one entry is sufficient. But if the photograph is ten pages away, two entries will be needed: one for the recipe, another for the photograph.

A distinction should be made between indexing the presence of a display and indexing the contents of a display. Let's take the example of a DVD player user's guide. Frequently a user's guide will begin with illustrations of the DVD player labeling its various parts. In one illustration there may be an arrow indicating where the S-video output plug is located. The discussion of how to connect the S-video cable may be separated from this illustration by twenty or thirty pages. It may help the reader to cite the illustration in the index. In a case like this, indexing the contents of display material contributes to the usability of the text.

When display material is indexed, the reference locator format often differs from that used to indicate textual entries. In chapter 4 various ways of citing display material will be discussed.

## How to Index the Indexable Material

While most of the remainder of this book is about "how to index," some general comments are warranted here.

### Depth of Indexing

Depth of indexing is defined in the International Standard ISO 5127/3a-1981 as "The degree to which a topic is represented in detail in an index" (International Organization for Standardization 1981) and in NISO Z39.4 as "The result of the combined effects of exhaustivity and specificity in an index." It is thus not, as stated in some textbooks, merely the equivalent of exhaustivity (the number of terms representing a document in an index). It is a function of both the indexer's assessment of the amount of detail needed and degree of specificity of the indexing language employed to index a document. (Wellisch 1995, 137)

As Wellisch notes above, *depth of indexing* is often discussed in relation to *exhaustivity* and *specificity*. Gerard Salton, in his book *Automatic Text Processing*, makes the following point:

> The effectiveness of any content analysis or indexing system is controlled by two main parameters, indexing exhaustivity and term specificity. Indexing exhaustivity reflects the degree to which all aspects of the subject matter of a text item are actually recognized in the indexing product. When indexing is exhaustive, a large number of terms are often assigned, and even minor aspects of the subject area are reflected by corresponding term assignments. The reverse obtains for nonexhaustive indexing, in which only main aspects of subject content are recognized. (1988, 277)

Book indexes tend to be exhaustive and specific. When a book is cataloged for inclusion in a library, the cataloger is often restricted to the assignment of three to five terms that describe the content of the book. In contrast, the index in the book itself may well have over two thousand terms that reflect the subject matter of the book. The exhaustivity of a book index is greatly influenced by the indexer's analysis and synthesis of the text. Wellisch writes that "exhaustivity refers to the extent to which concepts and topics are made retrievable by means of index terms" (1995, 175). The book index that provides complete access to all the information in a document is exhaustive and satisfies the goal outlined in BS 3700 (sec. 3) to "identify and locate relevant information within the material being indexed."

Salton defines term *specificity* as "the degree of breadth or narrowness of terms" (Salton 1988, 277). As Wellisch points out in his discussion of specificity (1995, 439–442), the terminology used in the text will influence the specificity of the index. I would add that the anticipated language and needs of the readers will also help the indexer determine the degree of breadth or narrowness of terms in the index. The index in a highly specialized text that will be read by readers fluent in the technical language of the text will very likely be composed of a large percentage of specific and precise terms, whereas a book written for a larger group of readers some of whom are not specialists will have a greater mixture of broad and specific terms in the index.

I am not convinced that exhaustivity and specificity provide a useful framework for the discussion of depth of indexing in regard to book indexes. The book indexer must work with restrictions imposed by the time available for indexing and the space allotted for the index. The amount of detail to index will be influenced by the nature of the text itself and any restrictions placed upon the indexer.

In the early portion of the indexing process, it is better to overindex than to underindex. Include every topic you think may be important. It is irritating to discover, midway through a book, detailed treatment of a topic that was discussed earlier but not indexed. Returning to the earlier chapters and searching for the initial discussion of the term can be quite tedious. It is much easier to codify or eliminate superfluous material than it is to locate information that was not indexed and later proves to be significant.

### Term Selection

What terms go in the index? What is indexable? How do I know what readers will look for? What rules are there for selecting terms? There are no rules, and this is perhaps one of the most frustrating issues for students. *Term selection* is composed of two parts: identifying indexable topics and deciding how to present the topic in the index.

Sylvia Coates (2002) points out that "students do not approach the term selection curriculum on an equal footing: some will have tremendous cognitive advantage over others" (15). Coates describes certain cognitive skills that are necessary for good term selection: reading comprehension, classification ability, and conceptualization skills particularly regarding thematic relations. "It is evident, from the findings of the Lin and Murphy study, that using thematic relations is an uncommon trait in adults. Students with the ability to conceptualize using thematic relations have a distinct advantage in applying term selection, creating main heading/subentries groupings, and designing the index structure" (16).

As a former teacher of book-indexing courses, I found that most students were not proficient in term selection abilities. These abilities are essential, but they are rare. Of course, as a teacher it is frustrating when so few students demonstrate the ability to index well. In "Teaching Book Indexing: A Curriculum" I wrote:

> At times I am disturbed that only 10% of the students seem to have "learned" the material covered in the course. Recently I found some solace in Steve Lohr's book, *Go To*. This is a book about a group of gifted programmers. In the introduction Lohr quotes Donald Knuth, "There are a certain percentage of undergraduates—perhaps two percent or so—who have the mental quirks that make them good at computer

programming. They are good at it, and it just flows out of them. . . . The two percent are the only ones who are really going to make these machines do amazing things. I wish it weren't so, but that is the way it has always been" (Lohr, 9). Mental quirks cannot be taught; as adults you either have them or you don't have them. This is the element that I believe accounts for the lack of stellar students in book indexing courses. Anyone can learn the "rules" of indexing or least know where to find them. Anyone can type index entries into an indexing program and set up the format properly. But this is not enough to produce a quality index, much less an amazingly good quality index. (Mulvany 2002, 14)

Do Mi Stauber, on page 1 of her book, *Facing the Text (2004)*, offers these thoughts:

So here you are, with a new indexing job sitting in front of you. The stack of pages looks a little intimidating. You have set up your software, counted your pages, laid out your purple pen. You have opened your statistics document or your note page. You have made your cup of tea.

And, even if you have plenty of indexing experience, you may have a breathless moment, a hesitance, a pause—there is a gap between you and those pages that for a moment seems very wide. This book is called *Facing the Text* because indexing comes down to this: you and an actual text. A different text each time. An imperfect text, created by an author with her own idiosyncratic agenda, as yet unknown to you. Your task as an indexer is to bridge the gap between you and that text. You must reach out to the text, embrace it, absorb it, and then you must give it a different form, one that makes its riches accessible to the reader.

Yes, our job is to make the text accessible to readers. Our success as indexers is closely related to our term selection abilities. When selecting terms for the index, always attempt to structure the terms in a way that will enable readers to locate them. Consider how the term will appear in the index. In an alphabetic index it is crucial that the first word be a word that readers are likely to look up. It is important to bring the significant term forward within main headings and subheadings.

Term selection plays a significant role in determining the overall structure of the index. The wording of main headings in particular is of crucial importance, since main headings are the primary access points in the index. Readers conduct their search for information at the main heading level. However, the ultimate structure of an index is often not fully intact until the indexer has gone through the entire document. For this reason much of the manipulation of terms is performed as an editing task. See the discussion "Substantive Editing Tasks" in chapter 9 for more detailed treatment of this topic.

### Succinct and Clear Entries

Entries should be as succinct as possible while remaining clear. Avoid long, verbose entries whenever possible. When indexes are printed, they are often printed in multiple columns in a type size smaller than that of the text. Succinct entries help to reduce the density of the printed index pages. Dense index pages compromise the ability of readers to quickly scan the index and locate information. When the index entries are kept to the minimum number of words needed for clarity, the usability of the index is enhanced.

### Terms from the Title; Subject Matter of the Book

Be wary of creating entries for the whole topic of a book or from terms in the title. Generally, such entries will be far too broad to serve a useful purpose in the index. A book called *A Guide to Michigan* will most likely not need an entry in the index for Michigan. The entire book is about Michigan, so the entire index would be in the *M*'s! It will be assumed that the entries are related to Michigan and that they will be found in different sections of the index.

Stauber (2004, 9) applied the term *metatopic* to this concept, defining it as "the structural center of the index: every single heading you create will be implicitly related to it." She adds: "Sometimes identifying the metatopic involves simply reading the title of the book. Sometimes it is a gradual process of revelation that is only finished in the final stages of editing. In either case, you must have it firmly in mind before your index structure can be completed."

Some indexers add an introductory note that explains the way particular terms have been handled in the index. In F. W. Lancaster's 2003 book *Indexing and Abstracting in Theory and Practice,* we find the following introductory note for the index: "Because the entire volume is about indexing and abstracting, the use of these terms as entry points has been minimized in this index."

### Marking the Page Proofs

In chapter 10, "Tools for Indexing," the details of the mechanics of indexing, ranging from index cards to software for indexing, will be presented.

Here the focus will be on the steps taken before entries are entered into the computer.

The first step for many indexers is to mark up page proofs. For some, a great deal of the actual indexing process is done right on the page proofs. Others find that heavily marking up page proofs is a step that takes additional time without providing comparable benefits.

Inexperienced indexers are urged to mark up the page proofs to some degree. One advantage of marked pages is that they make it easy to locate the context of an entry later during the editing process. Also, if entries are in page number order, marked pages can be used to help check that the correct page number has been assigned to index entries.

One primary goal of marking pages for indexing is to indicate the possible index entries on each page of text. Indexers use their own shorthand notations for page markup.

In figure 3.1 main headings are underlined. Subheadings are preceded by a colon. At this stage include all the subheadings that appear reasonable. During the editing process unnecessary subheadings can be removed.

An unedited extraction of the marked entries would yield the following list, written in order of appearance on the page, including marginal entries, in reading order, from left to right, moving down the page.

> work: as play, 54–56
> play: as work, 54–56
> Perry, Bliss, 54
> amateurs, 54
> professionals, 54
> work: loving one's, 54
> love: of one's work, 54
> Churchill, Winston, 54
> politicians: work celebrated by, 54
> Huizinga, Johan, 54
> *Homo Ludens*, 54
> Shattuck, Roger, 54n
> *Forbidden Knowledge*, 54n
> art-for-art's-sake movement, 54n
> Pater, Walter, 54n

After the indexer has marked up the pages, the next step is to extract the entries from the pages. The indexer will end up with citations like those above with reference locators attached to the ends of the entries.

Some indexers are not concerned with comprehensive term selection when marking pages. Instead they highlight particular types of terms that will be indexed. For example, if a book contains a great many personal

Within the figure (sample page proof):

54 ❧ CHAPTER THREE

those who find the hurting of others fun, no arguments against it can fully succeed, and the history of efforts to explain why "human nature" includes such impulses and what we might do to combat them could fill a library: books on the history of Satan and the Fall, on the cosmogonies of other cultures, on our genetic inheritance, including recently the structure of our brains, on sadism and why it is terrible or defensible. And so on. I'll just hope that here we can all agree that to hurt or harm for the fun of it is self-evidently not a loving choice.[1]

One embarrassing qualification: we amateurish amateurs do often inflict pain on others. We just don't do it on purpose.

*Work and Play, Work as Play:*          *as play –56          work as –56*

To celebrate playing for the love of it risks downgrading the work we do that we love. In fact we amateurs are often tempted to talk snobbishly about those who cannot claim that what they do they do for the love of it. As Bliss Perry put the danger: "[T]he prejudice which the amateur feels toward the professional, the more or less veiled hostility between the man who does something for love which another man does for money, is one of those instinctive reactions—like the vague alarm of some wild creature in the woods—which give a hint of danger."

*: loving one's*

The words "professional" and "work" are almost as ambiguous as the word "love." Some work is fun, some gruesome. Churchill loved his work—but needed to escape it regularly. I hated most of the farm work I did as an adolescent, and escaped it as soon as possible. I hated having to dig ditches eight hours a day for twenty-five cents an hour. Yet working as teacher and a scholar, I have loved most of my duties—even the drudgery parts. A member of the Chicago Symphony Orchestra told me that he hates his work—his playing—and is eager for retirement. Politicians celebrate work as what will save welfare recipients from degradation; for them, to require people to work, even if they're underpaid and even if the job is awful, is a virtuous act.

*Winston*

*: of one's work*

*: work celebrated by*

Such a mishmash of implied definitions makes it impossible to place work in any simple opposition to play or pleasure. In *Homo Ludens* Huizinga occasionally writes as if the whole point of life were to have fun by *escaping*

*Johan*

1. A fine discussion of the dangers threatened by "doing things for the love of the doing" is given by Roger Shattuck in *Forbidden Knowledge*. Shattuck argues that the art-for-art's-sake movement, with its many echoes of Pater's celebration of "burning" with a "hard, gemlike flame" and living for the "highest quality" of a given moment, risks moving us toward "worship of pure experience without restraint of any kind." The temptations of sadistic ecstasies lurk in the wings. As I shall insist again and again, to make sense out of a title like *For the Love of It* requires careful distinction among diverse "loves," many of them potentially harmful.

*Walter*

Figure 3.1. A sample page proof marked for indexing. From *The Chicago Manual of Style*, 15th ed. (Chicago: University of Chicago Press, 2003), 792.

names, it may be helpful to use a highlighting pen to mark the names. This way there is less chance that a name will be missed. Skimming through the book in this way gives the indexer an opportunity to get an overview of the material. When the writing of the index begins, the indexer has a good perspective on the overall structure of the book.

## Interpreting the Publisher's Instructions

Before any indexing begins, the indexer must understand what the publisher expects. Aside from the desire for the most brilliant and thorough index possible, the expectations of most publishers can be reduced to three: the index should conform to the house style, the index should be of the desired length, and the index should be delivered on time.

### Deciphering Indexing Style Guides

Some publishers provide the indexer, be it the author or a professional indexer, with a booklet outlining the house index style. Other publishers provide a less polished, often much-photocopied list that describes the style required. A surprising number of publishers simply tell the indexer to "follow Chicago." What this means is that the indexer is to follow the guidelines outlined in *The Chicago Manual of Style (2003)*, published by the University of Chicago Press. Because the indexing section of *CMS* has been published separately and is widely used within the publishing community, I will devote some discussion to the basic style requirements of the University of Chicago Press. It is interesting to note that a survey of 104 publishers by Liddy, Bishop, and Settel (1991, 68) revealed that the majority of the respondents (84 percent) viewed *CMS* as the preferred style guide for indexing.

Most publishers specialize in particular types of books. Their index style guides have emerged from years of experience with a particular type of book. At the very least, the style guide is an attempt to distill general indexing guidelines as they apply to a particular type of book. Many publishers know that not every book will fit into this general mold. So it is important to know that not every facet of a publisher's style guide is cast in stone. When there is good reason to change a specification, many editors will accommodate the indexer. But such changes should not be made lightly. The indexer will have to present a strong and persuasive argument regarding any changes to the house style. Unfortunately, the indexer will very likely be dealing with an editor who knows little about indexing and nothing about the raison d'être of the house index style.

It is crucial that the indexer correctly interpret house style and understand the implications of specifications on the usability of the index before suggesting any change in the specifications. Five elements will be covered in any indexing style guide. Here these five elements are discussed in a general way. Later in this book I will discuss these elements in far more detail. In appendix A you will find a worksheet which will provide an easy way to outline the index specifications of your publisher.

The five basic elements of index style are presented below. Keep in mind that there are many other elements that are commonly dealt with in an indexing style guide.

> Alphabetizing of main entries
> Arrangement of subheadings
> Format of entries
> Format of reference locators
> Format and placement of cross-references

■ *Alphabetizing of main entries.* Most publishers want main headings in an index alphabetized in one of two orders: either letter-by-letter order or word-by-word order. (For further discussion of this topic, see chapter 5.)

■ *Arrangement of subheadings.* The prevalent choice for the order of subheadings is alphabetic. The particular type of alphabetic order is the same as that used for sorting the main headings. However, some publishers want subheadings sorted not in alphabetic order but chronologically. Frequently the chronological order is obtained by sorting the subheadings in ascending page number (or reference locator) order. (For further discussion of this topic, see chapter 5.)

■ *Format of entries.* The *format of entries* refers to the way the entries will appear in print. The format is usually either indented style or run-in style. Within these two styles are many variations. (For further discussion of this topic, see chapter 8.)

■ *Format of reference locators.* The variations in specifications for reference locators often focus on different ways to cite inclusive discussion of a topic. In the case of page numbers, an indexing style guide will cover the way that page ranges are expressed. Often page ranges are not expressed in full but, rather, are compressed (or elided) by dropping some of the repeated digits. For example, a page range such as "232–239" has two repeated digits, the "2" and the "3." There are different rules for handling the compression of such numbers. If the inclusive page numbers are not to be expressed in full, the indexing style guide will outline the publisher's rules for compression. (For further discussion of this topic, see chapter 4.)

■ *Format and placement of cross-references.* There are many variations in the format and placement of cross-references, particularly the *See also* cross-references. Some publishers will want the *S* in the *See* capitalized; others will want it lowercased. Many will want the *See* and *See also* in italics. Sometimes the *See also* cross-reference will be placed at the beginning of an entry right after the main heading and its page numbers. Other times the *See also* will be placed at the end of the entry after the subheadings. (For further discussion of this topic, see chapter 4.)

### Sample Index Styles

Four common index styles are illustrated below. All use the same set of entries, including some strange entries to demonstrate differences. The first two examples illustrate the style presented in *The Chicago Manual of Style*. The other two styles are not attributable to any particular publisher, but they are used by many publishers.

▌ *Sample 1*

Alphabetizing of entries: letter-by-letter

Arrangement of subheadings: letter-by-letter

Format of entries: run-in

Format of reference locators: compressed

Format and placement of cross-references: *See* is run off from the main entry, and *See also* is the last subheading; a period and space precede both

> dog food, 125–29
> dogs, 10–18; beagles, 75–83; collies, 1122–29; coonhounds, 243–49; English setters, 35–42; Gordon setters, 282–89; Great Danes, 1541–49; Irish setters, 700–712; poodles, 342–56. *See also* American Kennel Club
> Dog Tooth Mountain, 56
> hounds. *See* dogs

▌ *Sample 2*

Alphabetizing of entries: letter-by-letter

Arrangement of subheadings: letter-by-letter

Format of entries: indented

Format of reference locators: compressed

Format and placement of cross-references: *See* is run off from the main entry preceded by a period and a space, and *See also* is the last subheading

> dog food, 125–29
> dogs, 10–18
>   beagles, 75–83
>   collies, 1122–29
>   coonhounds, 243–49
>   English setters, 35–42
>   Gordon setters, 282–89

    Great Danes, 1541–49
    Irish setters, 700–712
    poodles, 342–56
    *See also* American Kennel Club
Dog Tooth Mountain, 56
hounds. *See* dogs

∎ *Sample 3*

Alphabetizing of entries: word-by-word

Arrangement of subheadings: word-by-word

Format of entries: indented

Format of reference locators: in full

Format and placement of cross-references: *See* and *See also* are run off from the main heading; a period and space precede both

    dog food, 125–129
    Dog Tooth Mountain, 56
    dogs, 10–18. *See also* American Kennel Club
      beagles, 75–83
      collies, 1122–1129
      coonhounds, 243–249
      English setters, 35–42
      Gordon setters, 282–289
      Great Danes, 1541–1549
      Irish setters, 700–712
      poodles, 342–356
    hounds. *See* dogs

∎ *Sample 4*

Alphabetizing of entries: letter-by-letter

Arrangement of subheadings: page-number order

Format of entries: run-in

Format of reference locators: compressed

Format and placement of cross-references: *see* is run off from the main heading, and *see also* is the last subheading; both are enclosed in parentheses

    dog food, 125–9
    dogs, 10–8
      English setters, 35–42; beagles, 75–83; coonhounds,
      243–9; Gordon setters, 282–9; poodles, 342–56;
      Irish setters, 700–12; collies, 1122–9; Great Danes,
      1541–9 (*see also* American Kennel Club)
    Dog Tooth Mountain, 56
    hounds. (*See* dogs)

Most index style guides will include far more instructions than those outlined above. Some will indicate whether main headings should always be capitalized, whether there is a preferred citation format for notes and illustrations, or whether run-in subheadings should start on the line below the main heading or run off from the main heading line. Later in the book these format topics as well as many others will be discussed.

■ *Sample style preferences.* Table 3.1 lists some of the style preferences of the University of Chicago Press, Oxford University Press, *ISO 999*, *NISO TR02*, and Sun Microsystems. The table demonstrates both conformity and variety regarding index style. It is important to keep in mind that most publishers are willing to adapt style guidelines as necessary in order to present an index in the best possible manner. Table 3.1 lists only the *preferred* style, not necessarily every style allowed by the publishers.

Indexing style information for British publishers has been compiled by Jean Simpkins in the article "How the Publishers Want It to Look" (Simpkins 1990). The publishers represented in this article are Blackwell, Butterworths, David and Charles, HMSO, Hutchinson, Oxford University Press, Routledge, Sage Publications, and Unwin Hyman. American indexers working for British publishers will find this article quite valuable. One of Simpkins's observations regarding British publishers is also generally applicable to the American publishing industry: "On many points remarkable unanimity is apparent on the part of publishers—as though they had all been studying the same handbook before compiling their lists of requirements" (41).

### Usability and Index Style

The use and usability of book indexes has been studied from various perspectives. Corinne Jörgensen and Elizabeth Liddy (1996, 67) found that "index features which theoretically should facilitate searching may have complex effects and index features may interact together in unexpected ways." An earlier study (Liddy and Jörgensen 1993, 134) concluded,

> In terms of format, there are serious questions about what is successful. Users seem more keyed in to what they have learned from Madison Avenue advertising than to the traditional accepted format of an index. Rather than relying on intellectual mechanisms such as syndetic structure for intellectual access, indexers need to rethink the use of layout and typestyles to communicate such information. For instance, these could be used effectively to indicate levels or amounts of information (users already interpret text in bold print as being more significant).

In her paper, "Let's Get Usable! Usability Studies for Indexes," Susan Olason found that indented indexes are preferred over run-in style, that

Table 3.1. Comparison of basic index specifications

| | Chicago | Oxford | ISO 999 | NISO TR02 | Sun |
|---|---|---|---|---|---|
| Alphabetizing order | Letter-by-letter | Word-by-word | Word-by-word | Word-by-word | Word-by-word |
| Index format | Indented/run-in | Indented/run-in | Indented | Indented | Indented |
| Locator format | Compressed | Compressed | In full | — | In full |
| Cross-references from main headings: Format | *See*<br>*See also* | *, see*<br>*see also* | *see*<br>*see also* | *see:*<br>*see also* | *, See*<br>*See also* |
| Cross-references from main headings: Placement | *See* run off from main heading<br>*See also* last subheading | *see* run off from main heading<br>*see also* last subheading | *see* run off from main heading<br>*see also* first subheading | *see:* first subheading<br>*see also* first subheading, clearly distinguished from other subheadings by deeper indention or within boxes | *, See* run off from main heading<br>*See also* first subheading |
| Cross-references from subheadings: Format | (*see* . . .)<br>(*see also* . . .) | — | *see* . . .<br>*see also* . . . | — | — |
| Cross-references from subheadings: Placement | (*see*) run off from subheading<br>(*see also*) run off from subheading | — | *see* run off from subheading<br>*see also* first subheading | — | — |
| *See under/See also under* allowed? | Yes | — | — | Yes | — |

subheadings should not begin with function words, and that users expect "table-of-contents-like" main headings. In regard to run-in style, some user comments "included frustration about being forced to read rather than scan, confusion about which page references went with which subentry" (Olason 2000, 93). Barnum et al. (2004, 199) found that users will use the table of contents in addition to an index, and that users "like synonyms, lots of them, in the index" (202).

While these usability studies are interesting, it is difficult to establish hard-and-fast rules for index presentation. For example, it appears obvious that an indented index is easier to use when compared to a run-in index. However, there are exceptions. The index in the fifteenth edition of *The Chicago Manual of Style* is a combination of both styles; subheadings are indented, sub-subheadings are run-in. This index is lengthy. The hybrid format allows for detailed indexing and the ability to easily scan the index pages. The index design works well for this particular book.

## Estimating the Size of an Index

Before indexing begins, the indexer must know if there is a size limitation on the index. By the time a book is in final pages, ready for indexing, the production editor will have a fairly good notion of the number of pages available for the index.

Frequently, an editor will tell an indexer that there are $x$ number of pages available for the index. This is not enough information for the indexer to work with. The indexer needs to know how the index will be laid out. For example, will the index pages contain two columns or three columns of text? Type size and leading also influence the number of index lines per page. Chapter 8, "Format and Layout of the Index," presents the details of page design and typography as they relate to the index.

Earlier in this chapter the point was made that a publisher will not be likely to add an additional signature of pages just to accommodate an index. If an index is too long, it is better that the indexer, rather than the in-house editor, reduce its size. Because the indexer knows the index intimately, she or he is in a far better position to edit the index to size than someone unfamiliar with the index. Chapter 9 will present techniques for reducing the size of an index. For the discussion at hand, suffice it to say that it is best to deliver an index that fits. When the indexer knows that space for the index is severely limited, he or she will make certain editorial decisions that will affect the density of indexing before indexing begins.

When an index must be short, the indexer, after consulting with the editor, may decide to restrict certain types of entries. For example, the indexer may post (enter) all book titles only as main headings rather than double-post the title both as a subheading under the author's name and as a main heading. Similarly, the indexer may decide against using subsubheadings; or perhaps material in the notes will be excluded.

The guidelines that follow are general in nature. The great number of variables that affect the length of an index make it extremely difficult to offer a set of rules that will apply to all circumstances. The entries in some indexes will be very short, and in others, quite long. An entry that is long most likely will not fit across the width of one column. The line will "turn over" (or "run over") and continue onto the line below. Naturally, entries with runover lines take up more space. An index formatted in run-in style will frequently take up less space than an index in indented style. An index page with three columns will often hold more entries than a page with two columns.

### Guidelines for Editors

Estimating the number of pages to reserve for the index should begin early in the design process. Once the estimate of the length of a book manuscript based on a castoff is made, it is possible to add on a specific number of pages for the index. *The Chicago Manual of Style* has a very good discussion of determining a castoff (2003, 807–810).

Using simple arithmetic, the editor can arrive at a percentage figure. Assume that a book has 200 indexable text pages. If a 5 percent index is desired, then 10 pages should be reserved: $200 \times 0.05 = 10$.

Deciding on the percentage to use is tricky. Table 3.2 provides some general guidelines for estimating the percentage of index pages for various types of books.

The ratio of indexable text pages to index pages varies for different types of books. The index for a stylebook such as *CMS* can be expected to be somewhat dense and lengthy. Following are index page percentages for three style books:

*The Chicago Manual of Style*: 9 percent
*The Oxford Guide to Style*: 5 percent
*Read Me First! A Style Guide for the Computer Industry*: 6 percent

An extreme example of a dense index can be found in *The Oxford Dictionary of Quotations*. The index included in this book is a 54 percent index! At the other end of the spectrum, in general trade books, we often find 2 or

3 percent indexes. Theodore Roszak's book *The Cult of Information* has a 2 percent index, and John Muir's *Travels in Alaska* has a 2.3 percent index. A quantitative study of back-of-the-book indexes by Bishop, Liddy, and Settel (1991) found that the average ratio of index pages to book pages of all books reviewed (433 books) was 3.3 percent. Diodato and Gandt (1991), although working with a smaller sample of books (73 books), also found the average ratio to be 3 percent.

### Guidelines for Indexers

Index length estimates affect indexers in two important ways. First, the percentage of book pages available for the index can be roughly correlated with the density of indexing expected by the editor. Second, and perhaps most important, the indexer must deliver an index that fits the length estimate (see "Copyfitting an Index" in chapter 9).

Knowing the number of pages that have been reserved for the index can be very helpful for the indexer. Some indexers work with clients who do not impose strict length requirements. Others constantly work with clients who do not set aside enough space for a thorough index.

I remember an indexing project in which the client told me that space was not a problem; my index could be as long as necessary. The day before the index was due, an embarrassed editor phoned to tell me that there were only ten pages available for the index. I needed to reduce my index by 46 percent! Had I known before indexing began how many pages were available I would have written a very different index. Certain types of topics would not have been indexed. Actually, I probably would have declined the job, because the number of pages available was so inadequate it was impossible to write a good index under those circumstances.

When the indexer knows how many pages are available for the index, it is easy to determine the proportion of the number of index pages to the number of indexable text pages of the book. As in the example above, we assume that a book with 200 indexable pages has 10 extra pages reserved for the index. If we divide 10 by 200, we end up with 5 percent: $10 \div 200 = 0.05$, or 5 percent.

We can refer to this as a 5 percent index. As a general rule of thumb, a 5 percent index is not exceptionally dense. Remember that the type of books in table 3.2 that have 5 percent indexes are described as "light text, not heavy on details." To an indexer, this means that a moderate amount of indexing is expected, perhaps averaging five entries per indexable page. Problems arise when the indexer is confronted with a request for a 5 per-

Table 3.2. Estimates of percentage of index pages and entries per page, by type of book

| Type of book | Percentage of index pages | Entries per page |
|---|---|---|
| Mass-market trade books<br>Light text, not heavy on details | 2–5 | 3–5 |
| General reference books<br>College textbooks<br>Cookbooks<br>Medical texts<br>Scholarly texts | 7–8 | 6–8 |
| Technical documentation I<br>General end-user manuals<br>Policy & procedures manuals<br>Training manuals | 10 | 8–10 |
| Technical documentation II<br>Codes & regulations<br>Corporate bylaws<br>Service & repair manuals<br>Systems manuals | 15+ | 10+ |

cent index when a 10 percent index is needed. The indexer must pay close attention to the density of indexing. Decisions will be made not to include a certain level of detail. Instead of providing eight to ten entries per page, which would be typical for a 10 percent index, the indexer will work with three to five entries per page.

As the value of the percentage figure increases, the density of indexing increases. When an indexer is told that 6 percent (or more) of the indexable text pages have been reserved for the index, it is reasonable to assume that a fairly detailed index is desired. When the percentage drops below 5 percent, it is reasonable to assume that light indexing is desired. Table 3.2 provides density of indexing rates typically associated with various types of books.

In the case of technical manuals, a 10 percent index is not uncommon. Some complex manuals have 20–25 percent indexes. For example, the WordStar 6.0 reference manual (1989, rev. a) included a 17 percent index. This manual averaged about 15 entries per indexable page. The significance of the variation in density becomes apparent when we realize that in a 200-page book the difference between an index with 5 entries per page and one with 15 entries per page is 2,000 entries.

The general nature of the figures in both tables is revealed when we examine two indexes. The index of the January 1967 edition of *The Joy of Cooking* occupied 60 pages of the book; the indexable text took up 787 pages. This is an 8 percent index. All who have used this index know that it is dense. Terms are often double- and triple-posted. Cross-references abound.

On the other hand, *Greenhouses: Planning, Installing, and Using Greenhouses,* published by Ortho Books in 1991, includes a 3 percent index. On the face of it, one might assume that the book is not thoroughly indexed or that the indexable text is not as dense as in *The Joy of Cooking.* On the contrary, this book is very densely indexed. The indexer reports that there is an average of 8.6 entries per page. The figures for entries per page in table 3.2 demonstrate that this index would fall into the Technical Documentation I category, which often has 10 percent indexes.

The critical difference between these two indexes is a matter of typography and layout. *The Joy of Cooking* index is set in 8-point type with 9-point leading at two columns per page, on a six and one-half inch by eight and three-quarters inch page. The *Greenhouses* index is set in 7-point type with 9-point leading at four columns per page, on an eight and one-half inch by eleven inch page. It is important to keep in mind that even when an adequate number of pages are not available for the index, it is still possible to provide a thorough index. The wizards in the production department have a variety of options available to fit a large number of index entries on a page.

The problem with setting up a table like table 3.2 is that some editors and indexers will consider the numbers immutable. Every book must be evaluated on its own terms—and according to its readers' needs. Some medical textbooks will need a 10 percent index, not a 7 percent index. If a 10 percent index is called for, then a 10 percent index should be created.

If an indexer suspects that an index will need more space than has been assigned, it is the indexer's duty to bring this matter to the editor's attention as soon as possible so that the production department will have the lead time to consider changing the layout of the index pages. The indexer would do well to keep a running tally of entries per page as the work progresses.

To summarize, before indexing begins, the indexer must determine what major sections of the text will be indexed and which sections, if any, will not. The publisher's style requirements must be clearly understood. The indexer must have at least a general notion of the space that will be available for the index.

# Chapter Four

**STRUCTURE OF ENTRIES**

I ndexes are everywhere—we find them in reference books, in school books, in computer manuals, and in policy and procedures manuals. Although the presentation of an index may vary from book to book, we always seem to recognize one when we come across it.

One reason we recognize indexes so readily is that indexes are highly structured documents. The structure of an index is by design; it is not happenstance. Index writers who have a sound understanding of the interrelation of the parts of an index to its whole will be in a good position to write indexes that are cohesive, indexes that work. In this chapter we shall examine the external and internal structure of an index.

## External Structure

The sequence of entries in an index follows a particular order. In the case of an alphabetic index, the entries follow the order of the alphabet, beginning with $A$ and ending with $Z$. In a numeric index, the sequence followed is that of the value of numbers, beginning with lower values and progressing in ascending numeric order.

Superficially, the order of main headings appears linear. $A$'s are followed by $B$'s, which are followed by $C$'s, and so on. There is indeed a linear progression from one main heading to another as determined by the ordering sequence. As noted earlier, though, an index can be viewed as a network. Although main headings are arranged as individual nodes in a particular order, these nodes are often related to one another through the use of cross-references. The cross-references form interrelationships in the index network that help users to identify and to locate all relevant information about a topic.

The linear nature of an index is truly superficial and relates only to the external structure of the index. The ordered, linear sequence of main headings provides the index writer with a convenient way to guide the reader to distant portions of the index.

Although printed book indexes are presented in a linear format, they are not used in a linear fashion. Indexes are not meant to be read from beginning to end. Readers jump around in an index seeking the location of the information they want. Internal guideposts in the index may send readers to another part of the index. Readers go directly to that other portion of the index; they do not read the material in between the two points.

The text of the index itself can be described as a hypertext. Many of the nodes are linked through cross-referencing that leads users to related information in the index document. An index that is arranged in one of the formats described later in this chapter allows readers to browse the index network. One of the benefits of structured browsing is serendipity. While the primary focus here is on the presentation of indexes in a printed medium, many of the same principles are applicable to the presentation of indexes in an electronic medium.

## Internal Structure

Internally, the index structure is hierarchical. Within a complex index entry—that is, an entry composed of a main heading, subheadings, and, possibly, sub-subheadings—there is a hierarchical relationship between the various elements of the entry. The subheadings present more specific aspects of the main heading; the sub-subheadings present more specific aspects of the main heading and subheadings.

An index entry has four structural elements: the main heading, subheadings, reference locators, and cross-references. These four elements will be discussed in this chapter. The arrangement, or presentation order, of entries will be discussed in the next chapter.

### Introductory Note

An *introductory note*, also called a headnote or explanatory note, precedes index entries whenever the index deviates from standard index presentation formats or when the scope of indexing is not complete. Certain situations automatically trigger the necessity of an introductory note: the presence of more than one index, special handling of reference locators, nontraditional arrangement of index entries, use of special abbreviations, or limitations on the scope of indexing. Following are some sample notes for these situations.

Multiple indexes: "Two indexes are provided: a name index followed by a subject index."

Special reference locators: "All page numbers appearing in bold type refer to locations in the text where terms are defined." Or, "Page numbers appearing in italic type refer to pages that contain illustrations."

Nontraditional arrangement of entries: In a product number index for a microprocessor book the following note appeared: "Devices are listed under their root number without prefixes, except when the prefix is an integral part of the number (e.g., Z80)."

Abbreviations: "Throughout this index the abbreviation *WF* will be used to indicate references to William Faulkner."

Scope limitation: "None of the information contained in footnotes has been indexed." Or, "Material in the appendixes has not been indexed."

Introductory notes are necessary whenever there is a possibility that readers will not understand the arrangement or presentation of information in the index. The note will clearly and concisely explain any special devices used in the index.

### Main Headings

The main headings in an index are the primary access points for readers. When looking for information about a topic, readers will attempt to locate the topic at the main heading level. Thus, the terms selected as main headings are crucial to the overall access to information within the index. The nature of main heading terms also determines the nature of subheading terms. For example, a main heading that is very general may be followed by not only subheadings but also sub-subheadings. In some indexes, such broad main headings will be eliminated and the subheadings will become main headings themselves to provide more useful access points within the index.

■ *Choice of headings.* It is always important that the indexer provide main heading terms that reflect the concepts in the text and terms that readers will be likely to look up. Main headings are often nouns, or nouns preceded by an adjective. A main heading should never be composed of an adjective or adverb standing alone. The structure of the following entry is not correct:

> public
>   affairs policy, 56
>   health, 33
>   information services, 43
>   speaking, 98

These subheadings, taken from a course catalog, are not related to each other. They have been forced into a hierarchical relationship based on the adjective *public*. The subheadings should appear as main headings, separate and distinct from one another.

> public affairs policy, 56
> public health, 33
> public information services, 43
> public speaking, 98

Indexers should refrain from creating inappropriate relationships between terms. When a hierarchical relationship emerges in an index through the use of subheadings, the indexer must carefully evaluate the nature of the relationship. Artificial relationships are misleading to readers and unfair to the text.

In the previous chapter, term specificity was discussed in relation to exhaustivity and depth of indexing. Recall that Gerard Salton wrote that "term specificity refers to the degree of breadth or narrowness of terms" (Salton 1988, 277). In regard to the choice of headings in an index, examination of the breadth or narrowness of terms leads naturally to a discussion of classification. A classification scheme is often presented in a hierarchical form with broad terms subdivided into narrower terms. We often see such arrangements in the natural sciences, where genus-species relationships cascade down a list from very broad to very narrow terms. The Dewey decimal system is another well-known classification scheme.

Indexers have been instructed to avoid classification in book indexes. Wellisch issues such a warning when he writes:

> Classification is in many respects fundamental to indexing as well as to any other information retrieval technique, but it ought not to be employed in the arrangement of topical index headings. The main reason for this is that, however "logical" or "natural" a classified arrangement in hierarchical form may seem to be to the classifier, it may not be so to other people who are not privy to the principles of division and subdivision employed by the maker of the classification. (Wellisch 1995, 70)

Classification schemes are often used in periodical and database indexing. One purpose of such schemes is to ensure some level of vocabulary control when indexing large, and often open-ended, collections of material. Bella Hass Weinberg (1988, 3) writes, "The predetermined lists of subdivisions in subject catalogs and periodical indexes do not permit exact specification of the aspect or point-of-view of the topic." While it is possible to identify what a document is about in a general sense, Weinberg argues that "indexing which is limited to the representation of aboutness serves the novice in a discipline adequately, but does not serve the scholar or researcher, who is concerned with highly specific aspects of or points-of-view on a subject" (3). Weinberg's article offers an excellent description of what we should not find in book indexes.

Main headings should be specific; they should be directly related to the concepts in the text. In a book about twentieth-century transportation, a discussion about automobiles and trucks is best represented by using the entries *automobiles* and *trucks*, instead of *vehicles*. Surely this book will be filled with references to many types of vehicles. If *vehicles* were chosen as a main heading, undoubtedly there would be a long list of subheadings accompanied by some sub-subheadings. For example,

> vehicles
>   automobiles
>     diesel-powered autos
>     four-door autos
>     four-wheel-drive autos
>     station wagons
>     two-door autos
>   buses
>   mopeds
>   motorcycles
>     with four-stroke engines
>     with two-stroke engines
>   trucks
>     with double trailers
>     flat beds
>     height restrictions and
>     refrigerated trailers
>     with twin axles
>   vans
>     commercial use of
>     private use of

The main entry, *vehicles*, is not specific. While it can be argued that *vehicles* is a general term or broader term for the various subheadings, it is not the job of an indexer to classify information by applying an external taxonomy to the language of the text. In a classified listing such as the one above, the subheadings can be located only if the reader first looks up *vehicles*. There is no direct access to *automobiles, buses,* or *trucks*. These subheadings are buried under the broad term *vehicles*. If readers do not understand the classification scheme, they will not be able to locate relevant information.

When choosing main headings, indexers must always consider the reader and the nature of the text. Generally speaking, when index entries become extremely complex, going down to sub-subheading and sub-sub-subheading levels, it is a sign that the main heading lacks specificity. For a thorough and entertaining discussion of classification and classified headings, see G. Norman Knight's book *Indexing, The Art of* (1979, 96–100).

Despite the history of admonishment against classification in book indexes, it is important to maintain a reasonable perspective about this matter. There are those who would have indexers eliminate any index entry that has the appearance of classification, that is, any entry that embodies a genus-species relationship. Some of the entries used as examples in this book would be candidates for elimination, such as:

> dogs, 10–18; beagles, 75–83; collies, 1122–29; coonhounds, 243–49; English setters, 35–42; Gordon setters, 282–89; Great Danes, 1541–49; Irish setters, 700–712; poodles, 342–56. *See also* American Kennel Club

This entry is composed of a broad term as the main heading (*dogs*) and narrow terms as the subheadings (types of dogs). If the only entry for *Gordon setters* were here, under *dogs*, I too would argue that this is not a helpful way to present the information in the index. It would be best if each of the subheadings also appeared as a main heading in the index. That way the reader looking up *Gordon setters* would find the entry in the *G*'s. But to suggest that the types of dogs be entered only as main headings and that the entry above be eliminated because of its classified nature is quite shortsighted.

Remember that the BS 3700 encourages the indexer to "group together information on subjects that is scattered by the arrangement of the document." Gathering together related information will sometimes result in the development of headings that appear to be classified. It is not difficult to imagine a context where the *dogs* entry above could prove very useful. For example, someone reading my autobiography might know that dogs played an important role in my life. If the *dogs* entry were eliminated from the index, the reader would have to know exactly what breeds of dogs to look for. Lacking this knowledge, the reader would be unable to locate any information about my dogs.

Imagine another book, whose subject is using personal computers in a small business. We might find the following classified headings in the index:

> operating systems
> Apple Mac OS
> Microsoft Windows
> Red Hat Linux

Again, we will assume that all the subheadings above also appear as main headings. These classified headings gather together related information for the readers. If these entries were eliminated, readers would have to read the entire book to find out which operating systems were discussed, or they would have to scan the entire index and locate the programs by name.

Stauber (2004, 151–153) refers to classified subheadings as "subtopic categorical subheadings."

Is one kind of subheading more valuable or correct than another? Here we have hit upon a major source of debate among indexers. One common idea is that subtopic categorical subheadings are always unacceptable. The reasons I have heard for this prohibition are that readers:

- should be able to go directly to the specific topic
- should not have to go to the topic they want via a broader topic
- should not have to guess where the indexer has placed a topic in a hierarchy

These are all important priorities. But they are not good reasons for banning subtopic subheadings. Subtopic subheadings do not imply an organizational structure for the entire index. They do not prevent specific topics from having their own access points, nor require that they only be found in deep levels of classified arrays. Subtopic subheadings are simply one of several ways that subheadings can be related to the main heading. Instead of worrying about whether you are breaking a "rule" against classification in indexes, I recommend that you think about whether your choice of subheadings breaks up the main heading information in a useful way, and whether each topic has its own access point. (153)

To blindly follow the rule that insists that there be no classified entries in indexes is not only shortsighted, it is often a disservice to the users of indexes. While an index should not rely solely on classified arrangements, the needs of readers must always come first. The thoughtful indexer will provide a balanced mixture of broad and narrow terms in the index.

At the main heading level, readers should be able to locate references for all the major topics in the document. Within the index structure, main headings are the primary access points. The choice of words and phrases as main headings will be informed by the language of the text and the anticipated language of the readers. Specific aspects of major topics are often treated at the subheading level, which will be discussed shortly.

▌ *Double-posting.* Given the importance of the main heading, the indexer must consider the need to provide multiple access points for the same information. Again, the needs of readers are crucial. It is reasonable to assume that readers may look up a topic in more than one way. While one reader may look up *automobiles,* another reader may be just as likely to look up *cars.* The indexer may decide to double-post the information by using both terms:

        automobiles, 55–60
        cars, 55–60

The phrase *double-post* is borrowed from bookkeeping. In a double-entry accounting system it is necessary to post account information twice, as a debit and as a credit. In this sense, *post* means to enter in the correct form and place—not always an easy task in accounting or indexing!

When case law is cited in an index, it is often double-posted. The reason is that one reader may remember the defendant's name in a case, while another may remember the plaintiff's name. When double-posting a case law citation, retain the correct placement of the names so that the inversion makes clear who is the plaintiff and who is the defendant:

        *Roe* v. *Wade,* 78
        *Wade, Roe* v., 78

Double-posting of index entries may take the form of direct inversions:

        **book contracts**
            **of trade publishers, 34–39**
        **trade publishers**
            **book contracts of, 34–39**

Sometimes the double-posted information is not a direct inversion of terms; instead, it is more subtle.

        **concatenation of files**
            **COPY command parameter for, 56–59**
            **printing concatenated files, 93**
        **COPY command, 12–14, 56–59**

In the example above, specific information (the COPY command parameter) about the COPY command has been double-posted at the subheading level and at the main heading level.

The advantage of double-posting information is that it gives readers multiple access points for information. But there can be disadvantages as well. First, double-posting of entries may take up too much space in an index. Second, when an entire entry is double-posted, both entries must contain the same information; the reference locators and subheadings must be the same. While it may be easy to maintain this consistency when double-posted terms appear only once, as in the *automobiles/cars* entry above, it can be difficult for the indexer to remember to double-post all the cited information scattered throughout the text.

In the early stages of writing an index, many indexers do not double-post terms. Instead they create a *See* cross-reference at the main heading level, as in "automobiles. *See* cars." Later, during the editing stage, the indexer may decide to double-post information rather than use a *See* reference. It is best to double-post entries when doing so does not take up more space than a *See* reference.

Here, the important thing to keep in mind is that the main heading level is what provides the primary access to information in the index. The choice of main heading terms should be guided by the text of the document and by the anticipated needs of the index users.

## Subheadings

A main heading followed by a lengthy sequence of page numbers should be broken down into subheadings. Generally, when there are more than five reference locators for a heading, subheadings should be added to enhance the usability of the index. The following main heading is in need of subheadings:

> **wildlife losses from pesticides, 83–85, 87, 88, 100–** > **107, 114–117, 118–120, 121–122, 125–129**

Without subheadings, readers will spend far too much time attempting to locate the information they seek. The index should provide quick and easy access to information. It should not place an excessive burden of locating specific information about a topic on the readers. The index should help readers narrow their search in order to retrieve information from the text quickly.

Subheadings are always related to the main heading they modify. Often the subheadings represent subdivisions or more specific aspects of the main heading. The entry above can be easily broken down as

> **wildlife losses from pesticides, 83–85** > **Dutch elm disease spraying, 100–107** > **in England, 114–117** > **forest spraying, 121–122, 125–129** > **Japanese beetle spraying, 87, 88** > **in rice fields, 118–120**

Subheadings can be action-oriented, as in the following example:

> **files** > **copying, 52** > **creating, 10–12** > **deleting, 43** > **editing, 35–38** > **moving, 88**

Subheadings frequently present related aspects of the main heading. The purpose of subheadings is to filter information about a topic further so readers can perform a more refined search for information. The following example shows subheadings as filters that present specific information about the main heading:

> **Title page**
>     **author's name on,** 1.11, 1.13, 19.47
>     **content of,** 1.9–13, 1.29
>     **copyediting,** 2.111
>     **placement of,** 1.1, 1.9
>     **type specifications for,** 1.9–11, 19.47

Subheadings can be overdone, however. As noted earlier, space in an index is a precious commodity. The usefulness of subheadings must be carefully evaluated. A list of subheadings, all with the same page number, should be condensed. The following entry from a college course catalog is an example of an overdone list of subheadings:

> **accounting courses**
>     **advanced,** 14
>     **beginning,** 14
>     **intermediate,** 14

These subheadings provide no substantive information. In this case the main heading, "accounting courses, 14," would have been sufficient. An index is not intended to be an outline of the entire contents of the document. The indexer's job is to present useful and efficient access points to information in the text. Readers should not have to sort through and read excessively long lists of subheadings that overanalyze the heading they modify.

Do Mi Stauber (2004, 149–158) identifies five types of subheadings: categorical subheadings, subtopic categorical subheadings, relational subheadings, descriptive-aspect subheadings, and feature subheadings. Stauber's discussion of this typology provides guidance for correctly handling the tricky relationship between a main heading and subheadings.

### Form of Main Headings and Subheadings

Main headings and subheadings are usually nouns, nouns preceded by adjectives, or gerunds. They should be as succinct as possible without sacrificing clarity. Because most indexes are alphabetized, it is important to pull the crucial term in a phrase forward so that it can be alphabetized.

  ■ *Inversion.* When personal names are cited in an index, the name is often inverted so that the surname will be the keyword for sorting. If we wish to index Virginia Woolf, we invert the name, as in *Woolf, Virginia.* This way the important portion of the phrase, "Woolf," is pulled forward for alphabetizing. Other types of terms are also often inverted. For example, the text may refer to a "holographic will." In the index this term may appear as *wills, holographic.*

The following example, taken from Microsoft Press's *Running MS-DOS* (2nd ed., 1985), illustrates the problems that arise when the important term in a phrase is not pulled forward for alphabetizing:

**Some Advanced Features**
**Some Important Keys**
  **Alt**
  **Backspace**
  **Break**
  **Ctrl**
  **Shift**
**Some More Useful Batch Files**
**Some Useful Batch Files**
**Some Useful Commands**

It is unlikely that someone looking for information about batch files will think of looking up *Some More Useful Batch Files* or *Some Useful Batch Files* in the *S*'s. All the information about batch files should be gathered together under the heading *batch files.*

▎ *Singular versus plural.* A question that often arises is whether headings and subheadings should be expressed in singular or plural form. Those nouns that we can count numbers of and ask "how many?" of are often expressed in plural form:

**books**
**dogs**
**mice**
**politicians**
**rocks**

Those nouns that we do not count individual numbers of, but of which we ask "how much?" are generally expressed in the singular form:

**air**
**fertilizer**
**pepper**
**tea**
**wine**

One should avoid the use of the plural form attached in parentheses to the noun, for example, *CD(s)* or *bicycle(s)*. In both of these, we can ask "how many?" so the plural form should be used. Excessive use of punctuation in an index can make the index look busy and dense when printed and thus more difficult to use.

Consistency within the index is important to maintain. If the indexer uses *CDs* as an entry, then *DVDs*, not *DVD*, would be used to ensure consistency. Consistent handling of singular/plural forms of entries is one aspect of parallel construction. Indexers who resolve problems with singular versus plural forms of entries during the initial term selection process will find that there will be less editing needed later. Also, it is good to remember that singular and plural forms of terms not only are a matter of style but also can denote different meanings:

> **writing (an activity)**
> **writings (artistic works)**

The use of parenthetic plurals is common, however, in cookbook indexes. This is an important exception. Thérèse Shere (2004, 7–8) points out:

> And one last quirk of cookbook index style: parenthetic plurals are commonly used for main headings which are names of ingredients or recipe categories, so that subheadings which delete a word "read" properly whether the deletion is singular or plural. Look at each main heading to see whether this is necessary; don't do it if the deletions are all singular or all plural.

> Peach(es)
>   cobbler
>   crisp
>   poached in vanilla syrup
>   upside-down cake
> *but*
> Peaches
>   Melba
>   poached in vanilla syrup
>   spiced

> Cake(s)
>   about
>   chocolate
>   polenta pound cake
>   poppyseed
>   yeasted sugar cake

> Cake
>   angel food
>   chocolate
>   polenta
>   poppyseed

> Notice that some subheadings repeat the main heading word anyway, where deletion might be confusing (*polenta pound* or *yeasted sugar* as subheadings for *Cake[s]*). This practice can get a bit ugly—you will see headings like *Strawberry(ies)* and *Anchovy(ies)*.

> If recipe titles are always given in full, parenthetic plurals aren't necessary—these main headings are given in the plural:

> Peaches
>   Peach Cobbler
>   Peach Crisp
>   Peaches Poached in Vanilla Syrup
>   Peach Upside-down Cake

■ *Parallel construction.* Throughout the index it is desirable to maintain parallel construction within entries. If gerunds are used in most of the subheadings, a participle would look out of place.

> Words
>   capitalizing
>   dividing
>   hyphenated
>   spelling

The subheading *hyphenated* should be *hyphenating* in order to maintain parallel construction within this entry. Parallel construction can, of course, be overdone. An index is not an outline or other type of list. Parallel construction within entries is desirable, but one should be careful not to interfere with the meaning of subheadings by forcing parallel construction.

■ *Homographs.* Homographs are terms that have the same spelling but different meanings. If there is any chance that readers may misinterpret the meaning of a homograph, the indexer can add a qualifying phrase to the term. Such phrases are called *parenthetical qualifiers*, or simply, *qualifiers.* But do note that capitalization can clear up some misinterpretations.

> bourbon (an American whiskey made from corn)
> Bourbon (a European ruling family)
> bow (a device for shooting arrows)
> bow (front part of a boat or ship)
> perch (a fish)
> perch (a resting place, often for birds)
> rubber (slang for condom)
> rubber (tropical tree latex)
> turkey (the bird)
> Turkey (the country)

■ *Multiple terms in an entry.* There is no prescribed limit on the number of terms in a heading or subheading. Although entries should be as succinct as possible, additional terms are often needed for clarity. Frequently, two distinct topics are discussed in tandem, and it may be appropriate to combine the terms and use a cross-reference.

> replace operations. *See* search-and-replace operations
> search-and-replace operations, 56–60
>
> crime and punishment, 69
> punishment. *See* crime and punishment

■ *Adjectives and adverbs.* Generally, an adjective or adverb should not stand alone as an index entry. An exception to this rule is when the term itself is the subject, as in a usage or style guide. Adjectives are often combined with nouns to form main headings and subheadings in an index. These noun phrases are referred to as *compound headings.*

> Indian names
> lodgepole pine
> medical training
> metropolitan newspapers
> Ponderosa pine

The indexer must decide how readers are likely to look up information. In a general book about western pine trees, the indexer can reasonably assume that readers will look up the types of trees by their common names, which usually begin with an adjective.

■ *Function words: Articles, prepositions, and conjunctions.* At the main heading level, articles, prepositions, and conjunctions, frequently referred to as *function words*, are not used as the first term in a common phrase. The only time they do appear as the first word is when they are part of a formal name, as in a book title or geographic name. In the next chapter the alphabetizing rules for function words will be discussed.

A casual review of a variety of indexes reveals that articles, prepositions, and conjunctions are heavily used as the first term in subheadings in some indexes and not used at all in other indexes. Clearly, there are two schools of thought regarding the use of these terms.

It was noted earlier that subheadings must have a direct relationship with the main heading they modify. This relationship can be described as a *logical relationship*. The following entry is an example in which the subheadings could be described as subsets of the main heading. Thus, there is a direct logical relationship.

> breed groups
> herding, 75–80
> hound, 38–43
> nonsporting, 25–30
> sporting, 132–37
> terrier, 90–95
> toy, 50–55
> working, 110–15

All subheadings must be logically related to their main headings. However, there are some who feel that the subheadings must have a *grammatical relationship* with their main headings as well. The idea here is that the main heading and the subheading can be read as a complete phrase. The following example from the index of *The Chicago Manual of Style* (1982) illustrates subheadings that have a grammatical relationship with the main heading.

Indention
  in bibliographies
  of block quotations
  of chapter openings
  of footnotes
  in indexes
  marking for
  with poetry
  after subheads
  in tables

Notice how each subheading can be combined with the main heading to form a sensible phrase: "indention in bibliographies," "indention of block quotations," "indention of chapter openings," and so on. Those favoring the logical approach would very likely structure the same entry in this way:

Indention
  bibliographies
  block quotations
  chapter openings
  footnotes
  indexes
  marking for
  poetry
  subheads
  tables

Proponents of the logical style would argue that the relationships expressed with the leading prepositions are implied and do not need to be formally included in the subheadings. Anyone looking at the entry above would *know* that the *bibliographies* subheading refers to indention in bibliographies; this does not need to be stated explicitly.

If we compare the two *Indention* entries, we notice that the sorting order of the subheadings is the same. The leading prepositions have not been alphabetized in the first example. This alphabetizing oddity is another reason, some argue, that there is no need to impose grammatical relationships on subheadings. Alphabetizing will be discussed in more detail in the next chapter.

A more pedestrian concern is the space used by leading prepositions, articles, and conjunctions in subheadings. When an index is printed in narrow columns, a leading preposition may create a line that is too long for the column width; the line will break and carry over to another line. It can be argued that this will add unnecessary length to an index—a particular concern when space is limited.

An uncritical use of leading prepositions can easily lead to unsightly lists of the same preposition being repeated in each subheading.

> recipes
>   for beef
>   for chicken
>   for fish
>   for pork
>   for shellfish
>   for turkey
>   for veal
>   for vegetables

It is important to remember that function words may be necessary as the leading term in a subheading for clarity. When the lack of a preposition creates an ambiguous subheading, the preposition should be included even if entries appear to be unparallel. In the example below, the subheadings clearly have two different meanings.

> management
>   by computers
>   of computers

Heated discussion goes on in indexing circles about leading articles, prepositions, and conjunctions in subheadings—see Wellisch's argument in favor of alphabetizing function words (1995, 387–391). We must not lose sight of the important role that these parts of speech can play to clarify meaning. The trouble with these terms is primarily related to whether or not they should be alphabetized. Indexers wishing to sidestep this problem should consider using leading articles, prepositions, and conjunctions in subheadings only when absolutely necessary for clarity. Lastly, when possible, put the function word at the end of the subheading. For example,

> oak trees
>   and irrigation

can be changed to

> oak trees
>   irrigation and

## Reference Locators

A locator is defined as "the part of an entry in an index that indicates the location of the documentary unit to which the entry refers" (Wellisch 2000, 42). In printed media a reference locator can take many forms: a page number, a section number, a line number, and so on. In electronic media a reference locator might be a file name, a physical pointer to the actual text, a set of coordinates, or a file name/screen number/line number sequence.

Regardless of the type of locator, long series of undifferentiated locators after an entry are not desirable. The general rule is that if there are more than five locators, the entry should be further qualified with subheadings or sub-subheadings.

Locators indicate the beginning and end of the discussion. Indexes that cite only the beginning of a discussion eliminate a useful reference device. The entry below does not allow the reader to discern where the main discussion of this topic occurs.

> **voodoo**, 13, 22, 38

Far more helpful is the following entry:

> **voodoo**, 13, 22–29, 38

■ *Page numbers as locators.* Many books are numbered sequentially with arabic page numbers (1, 2, 3, . . . ). Often the front matter is numbered with sequential roman numerals (i, ii, iii, . . . ). The locators for a term should be presented in ascending numeric order with roman numerals preceding arabic numbers. For example,

> **glaciers**, iv, 45–52, 134, 140–42

■ *Continuous discussion of a topic.* Continuous discussion of a topic that traverses two or more pages is indicated by a *page range*: 23–29. Often the page range concatenator, the character between the page numbers, is the typographic symbol known as an en dash. An en dash is slightly longer than the hyphen used within a word and shorter than the em dash.

Whenever possible, page ranges should be expressed in full; that is, all digits should be used. Page ranges expressed in full leave no doubt regarding the numbers indicated. However, as we know by now, many editors are concerned about space requirements for the index. Expressing three- or four-digit page ranges in full can take up considerable space.

Many style guides request that page ranges be compressed or elided. There are various rules regarding which digits in a page range are repeated and which digits are dropped. The most common set of rules are those found in *The Chicago Manual of Style* (2003, 18.13):

| First Number | Second Number | Examples |
|---|---|---|
| 1–99 | Use all digits | 3–10, 71–72, 96–117 |
| 100 or multiples of 100 | Use all digits | 100–104, 1100–1113 |
| 101 through 109, 201 through 209, etc. | Use changed part only | 101–8, 1103–4 |
| 110 through 199, 210 through 299, etc. | Use two or more digits as needed | 321–23, 498–532, 1087–89, 11564–615, 12991–13001 |
| | *But* if three digits change in a four-digit number, use all four | 1496–1504, 2787–2816 |

*The Oxford Guide to Style* (Ritter et al. 2002, 7.1.4) prefers the most succinct elision possible:

> For a span of numbers generally, use an en rule, eliding to the fewest number of figures possible: *30–1, 42–3, 132–6, 1841–5.* But in each hundred do not elide digits in the group 10 to 19, as these represent single rather than compound numbers: *10–12, 15–19, 114–18, 214–15, 310–11.*

∎ *Noncontinuous discussion of a topic.* When discussion of a topic is not continuous, but scattered throughout a range of pages, a page range is not generally used. *The Chicago Manual of Style* states, "Scattered references to a subject over several pages or sections are usually indicated by separate locators" (2003, 18.12) The locators for noncontinuous discussions are separated by commas.

> Scotch whisky, 33, 34, 35

If passing mention of a topic spans many pages, some publishers allow the use of *passim* (meaning "here and there"). For example,

> Scotch whisky, 33–42 passim

Do keep in mind that most publishers discourage the use of *passim*, and many forbid its use. Trivial passing mentions of a topic are generally not indexed. However, if the scattered references are deemed indexable and use of *passim* is allowed, it is a convenient alternative to a long string of page numbers. It also helps distinguish a truly continuous discussion from slighter mentions of a topic. In the example above, had *passim* not been used, the entry would have been quite lengthy:

> Scotch whisky, 33, 34, 35, 37, 39, 40, 41, 42

*The Oxford Guide to Style* suggests "Avoid *passim* ('throughout') unless there are a large number of general references to a person or topic in one section of a book" (16.5.2). *The Chicago Manual of Style* allows the use of *passim* in certain circumstances: "The term *passim* may be used to indicate scattered references over a number of not necessarily sequential pages or sections (e.g., 78–88 passim). Trivial mentions are best either ignored or, if needed for some reason, gathered at the end of the entry under a subentry 'mentioned'" (2003, 18.12).

One of the main complaints about the use of *passim* is that it lacks precision, and indexers by nature desire precision. Although the use of *passim* in an index is discouraged, there are times when its use may indeed provide additional and appropriate information. In 1992, André

De Tienne, an editor at the Peirce Edition Project, offered the following argument in favor of *passim* use during a discussion on the INDEX-L electronic conference.

> Many claim the primary problem with the use of passim in an index is the lack of precision. How far this is a real shortcoming is worth studying, since it is mainly a matter of interpretation. If passim is affixed to a big group of pages, like "25–60 passim," very little help is indeed given to the reader, no matter the meaning of the term. If, however, passim is affixed to a small cluster of pages, like "25–30 passim," the word becomes useful, because it gives to those page numbers a different tone, and thereby increases the information given to the reader.
> Another problem often cited about the use of passim is that passim means different things to different people. Well, this is a truism. Any word can be understood and used differently by different people, be they index-makers or index-users. The point is that no matter how varying the meaning is, it will retain a common core, "here and there throughout," or some such. It may lack precision, but in a way that's exactly what the word is about: "the entry is worth looking up on pp. 25–30, but please know, dear reader, that it is not the central topic of discussion—its various occurrences lack definite precision." Adding passim to hyphenated numbers, in this regard, amounts thus to an increase of information, since it tells the reader that pages 25–30 are worth looking at, though they don't deserve the same degree of expectation as regular page numbers.

André De Tienne reminds us that we can add additional meaning to a reference locator with the judicious use of *passim*. Indexers often add additional information value to reference locators with the use of annotations or different type enhancements such as bold or italic. However, without a doubt the use of *passim* is discouraged by many publishers. Unfortunately, as we try to make indexes more user-friendly, we often abandon some of the finer details of the art of indexing.

It is not always easy for the indexer to distinguish continuous and noncontinuous discussion of a topic. The problem can be exacerbated by poor book editing. An experienced book editor will see to it that discussion of tangential matters does not interfere with the continuous presentation of a topic. The careful editor will remove such material, thus ensuring that information is provided in a cohesive manner.

It has become common at some presses not to make any distinction between continuous and noncontinuous discussion of a topic on consecutive pages. It is thought that using a page range for an entire discussion is an aid for the readers because a page range is easier than a string of separate page numbers to read. Although indexers may find this practice disturbing because of its lack of precision, it is an important element to look for in a publisher's style guide. If no mention is made in the style guide of the distinction between continuous and noncontinuous discussion on consecutive pages, the indexer is safe to assume that a page range can be used for noncontinuous discussion on consecutive pages.

▮ *Multipart page numbers.* Some documents are paginated with multipart page numbers rather than consecutive page numbers. A common example is the separate pagination of chapters in a document. Each chapter begins with a page 1. The actual folio is a combination of the chapter number and the page number. Page 3 in chapter 5 may be paginated as 5-3.

This type of pagination is often found in documents that are frequently revised—for example, a software manual. When future changes in the software affect only one chapter of the manual, the changes can be made to that one chapter without affecting the pagination (and indexing) of the remainder of the manual.

When chapter–page number pagination is used, the correct way to indicate a page range is by use of the concatenator *to.* If an entry cites discussion on pages 10 through 15 of chapter 3, the page range should look like this:

> directory structure, 3-10 to 3-15

Notice that a hyphen, not an en dash, is used between the chapter number and the page number. Unfortunately this locator format takes up a lot of space. Although some may be tempted to change the format to something like

> directory structure, 3.10-15,

this is not permissible because the locators must be in the same format as that used in the text. Designers of documents with nonconsecutive pagination should consider what impact their pagination scheme will have on the index, but all too often this matter is not considered during the design process.

Multipart page numbers may be alphanumeric. Instead of numbered chapters or sections, there are letters. Appendixes are commonly numbered in this way. A document may have four appendixes, A through D. The pagination for the appendixes is of the form A-1, B-1, and so forth.

Such references follow the same format as the numbered chapters above. If there is an entry that contains locators for both a numbered chapter and a lettered appendix, the appendix locators follow the chapter locators.

**directory structure, 3-2, B-7 to B-10**

In this example, the order of the locators follows their order in the document. Matters become more complex when alphanumeric pagination in a document is not in ascending alphabetic order. Take another software manual that has three sections: "Getting Started," "General Reference," and "Utilities." The following pagination is used for the first page of each section.

**Getting Started: STR-1**
**General Reference: REF-1**
**Utilities: UTL-1**

The problem with this type of pagination arises when an entry has locators from more than one section. A sorting order has to be chosen. There is a tendency to sort multiple references alphabetically regardless of their order in the document:

**file conversion, REF-10, STR-23, UTL-4**

Sorting these locators alphabetically implies that the STR-23 reference will be found after the REF-10 reference in the document. This is, of course, not correct. The "Getting Started" section precedes the "General Reference" section. Readers looking up a series of references should be able to work from the front of a document to the back without the need to flip back and forth in the document. Alphanumeric locators should be sorted in the sequence of their appearance in the text.

There are many other complex variations on the handling of multipart locators. See chapter 6, "Special Concerns in Indexing," for a discussion of locator format in multivolume works.

∎ *Annotated page numbers.* An index often points out illustrative material in a book. One way to accomplish this is to add an annotation to the locator. In an architecture book that contains many photographs and drawings, distinguishing a discussion of a building from the page number of an illustration may be helpful:

**Palace of Fine Arts, 32–38, 35fig, 75–78**

Note that in the example above, the reference locators are in ascending numeric order based on the first number in the series. Some publishers may require that annotated locators appear at the end of regular locators.

    **Palace of Fine Arts, 32–38, 75–78, 35fig**

Rather than using an annotation like *fig.*, some editors ask the indexer to make page references to illustrative material italic. This technique saves space and reduces the density of the reference locator.

Books with a variety of illustrative materials often distinguish annotations for photographs, maps, and tables. A scheme like the following may be used.

    **References to photographs: 45(ph)**
    **References to maps: 45(map)**
    **References to tables 45(t)**

In a heavily illustrated book, say, one that contains photographs, maps, and tabular material, the use of annotated page references can create a very dense and visually busy index. Instead of using annotated page references, descriptive subheadings can convey the same information more clearly:

    **Palace of Fine Arts, 32, 38**
    **architectural drawing of, 35**
    **photographs of, 75–78**

Pages that contain several illustrative items may be cited. If the items are numbered, the number may be added to the annotation. For example, reference to table 12 on a page that contains three other tables may be expressed as

    **gross national product, 56(t12)** *or* **56t.12** *or* **56t12**

A similar format is followed when a footnote has to be referenced by number. A reference to footnote number 13 on page 68 can be cited as 68n13 or 68n.13. Endnotes, whether at the end of the chapters or the end of the book, are always cited by note number; otherwise, they would be difficult to find because there are many notes on one page.

When there is more than one note cited by number on a page, the note numbers are separated by a comma. Some publishers require that the *n.* annotation be changed to *nn.* when multiple notes are referenced. For example,

    **Gordon setters, 55nn 23, 27** *or* **55nn. 23, 27**

One might consider the use of parentheses in such a situation, as it is not hard to imagine a note number in the above format being confused with a page number. For example,

    **Gordon setters, 55(nn 23, 27)** *or* **55(nn. 23, 27)**

or the *n.* can be repeated and attached to each note reference:

> **Gordon setters, 55n23, n27** *or* **55n.23, n.27**

If there is only one footnote on a page, it is not necessary to include the footnote number as part of the reference locator. The addition of an *n* (with no period) is sufficient:

> **web presses, 45, 84n**

Endnotes can pose a problem regarding context of a discussion. Let's suppose we find the following in the body text of a book on page 135:

> Several studies[18] have found that the kiwi fruit is an excellent source of vitamin C. As a matter of fact, the kiwi contains twenty-six times the amount of vitamin C per ounce as the orange.

Then in the endnotes section on page 387, we find note 18:

> [18] Perhaps the best-known study of the vitamin C content of kiwi fruit is that of Mary Smith, "Vitamin C and Kiwis," *Journal of Nutrition* 15, no. 4 (1987): 234–47. Smith found that a 76-gram kiwi contains 57 mg of vitamin C and .85 mg of vitamin E.

The problem for the indexer is that Mary Smith is mentioned by name only in the note reference on page 387. If the only reference to Mary Smith is "Smith, Mary, 387n18," there is no convenient way for readers to locate the context where Mary Smith is actually discussed. The following reference would be misleading:

> **Smith, Mary, 135, 387n18**

Mary Smith's name does not actually appear on page 135. Unless readers ascertain that note 18 refers to Mary Smith, they would likely be unable to discern the relevant context.

One solution to this vexing problem evolved during correspondence between Hans Wellisch and myself (Wellisch 1995, 185–186). To provide readers with the context of a referenced name that does not appear verbatim in the text, use a special locator format for the page number. Using the *Mary Smith* example above, and adding a few additional page references, such a format would look like:

> **Smith, Mary, 45–49, [135n18], 228, 387n18**

An introductory note would explain the use of square brackets: "Page references enclosed in square brackets indicate textual references to endnotes." This format clearly indicates to readers that note 18 on page 135 references Mary Smith even though her name does not appear in the text.

The indexer, in consultation with the production editor, should devise a scheme for handling visually complex references in a way that will be readable. When choosing a format for annotated reference locators, it is best to work with a sample entry that contains both annotated references and regular references. It is worth the effort to take a little time before indexing begins to choose a format that will be easy to read. The problems that arise with reference locators that include table numbers or note numbers may become apparent when sample entries are formatted for review. For example,

> Gordon setters, 23, 55nn 23, 27, 135
> Gordon setters, 23, 55(nn 23, 27), 135
> Gordon setters, 23, 55n23, n27, 135
> Gordon setters, 23, 55nn23, 27, 135
>
> gross national product, 35, 56(t12), 121
> gross national product, 35, 56t.12, 121
> gross national product, 35, 56*t*12, 121
> gross national product, 35, 56T12, 121

As we can see in the first sample entry for *Gordon setters*, multiple note references attached to the same page number pose problems. The second note reference (note 27 on page 55) is not visually attached to the page reference; it floats on the line and could easily be mistaken for a page reference. It is always best to keep the reference locator as simple as possible, using minimal punctuation or type changes. But clarity is also important. The entirety of a locator should be unambiguous. Often it is only through trial and error, trying out different formats, that we can arrive at the best solution.

As we have seen, many variations are possible in annotated page references. For example, some publishers drop the period following *n.* and *nn.* (*n* and *nn*); some use italic for annotated page references while others do not. Regardless of which scheme is used, the format should be clearly explained to readers in an introductory note.

❚ *Column or quadrant identifiers.* In large-format books, such as encyclopedias, adding a column or quadrant identifier to the locator may be helpful. For example, a book with large pages and two columns of text per page may benefit from a quadrant identifier. Each page would be divided into four imaginary quadrants, identified by letters. Quadrant *a* would be the upper left quadrant, *b* would be the lower left quadrant, *c* would be the upper right quadrant, and *d* would be the lower right quadrant. A reference to 235b would refer to text that appears on page 235 somewhere in the lower left section of the page.

Column identifiers are used when there are multiple columns of usually dense text. In a book with three columns of text per page, an identification scheme could start with column *a* on the left side and run to column *c* on the right side of each page.

This type of reference locator lends itself fairly well to the use of page ranges that indicate a continuous discussion of a topic. To indicate a discussion that begins on page 40, column *a*, and ends on page 43, column *b*, the page range would be 40a–43b.

It is also important to keep in mind that this type of notation can become quite confusing if other alphabetic identifiers are used for footnotes or illustrations.

The use of column or quadrant identifiers requires mention in the introductory note for the index. Readers must be clearly told what scheme is being used, particularly when the locator includes imaginary elements that are not discernible by looking at a page of text.

▌ *Locators that are not page numbers.* The primary benefit of using locators that are not page numbers is that they are not tied to the pagination of the document. Usually this means that indexing can begin before page proofs have been produced. At other times, this locator format is chosen because extensive revision of the document is anticipated. These revisions will change the pagination. However, if the locators are not tied to the original pagination, the impact on the index entries will be minimized.

*Section or paragraph numbers.* In many reference books, paragraphs within each chapter are numbered. Most of the index entries are tied to the paragraph numbers. This scheme enables index users to quickly find the particular piece of text that is referenced. This numbering scheme works well in reference books in which the content is presented as discrete units.

Legal books are commonly indexed by section number. Sometimes the section numbering is quite straightforward. The first section in each chapter or division begins with the chapter/division number expressed in hundreds. For example, the first section in chapter 2 will be §200; the first section in chapter 6 will be §600; and so on. In some legal material the numbering scheme is more elaborate. It may begin with a roman numeral article number and move down several levels using both arabic numbers and letters. A complex legal reference locator may look like "IV:2.3.1(a)." Such detailed numbering schemes are also common in engineering reports.

When reference locators are lengthy and complex, the index will appear dense. Sometimes there is nothing one can do about this. However, the indexer should not hesitate to suggest a more compact locator format if it is feasible. Small changes can go far to increase the usability of an index. For example, many legal indexes are by their nature dense. They often are composed of entries that are several subheading levels deep. The index can be lightened a bit by simply omitting the section number symbol (§) as part of the reference locator.

*Line numbers.* In some documents every line of text is numbered. The line numbering may be consecutive throughout the document, as in a legal brief. In other documents the line numbering may be consecutive throughout a chapter or division. Or the line numbering may start anew on each page. When the line numbering is not consecutive throughout the document, another locator will have to be added to the line number locator.

In the case of line numbering that is consecutive through each chapter, the chapter number will precede the line number in the reference locator. One way to reference line 435 in chapter 2 would be to cite it as 2:435.

If line numbering starts again on each page of text, the page number will have to be part of the reference locator. This format defeats the goal of not tying reference locators to final page proof pagination, but it may prove useful in text that is very dense.

*Electronic media.* Indexers working with electronic, book-length material will find that they must deal with a very different locator system than that which has already been discussed. While file structuring and pointer formats are outside the scope of this book, a few general comments may be helpful.

Electronic documents present the same indexing challenges as printed media documents. The indexing process and principles described in this book can be applied to online documents. The presentation of a structured index in an electronic document provides users with a familiar and useful gateway to information contained in the text.

The electronic index will very likely look like a printed index with or without the familiar reference locators. Users will be able to select the index terms and be taken directly to the referenced text. Indexers working with electronic material may physically mark the beginning and end of the discussion of a topic. In some systems, the pertinent discussion will appear highlighted, distinguishing it from surrounding text.

The demands on the indexer for exact and detailed reference locator assignments are potentially much greater in the electronic environment. However, the same guidelines we use when working with printed media documents apply here as well. More information about indexes for electronic media can be found in chapter 6 ("Single-source Indexing"), chapter 8 ("Electronic Display of Indexes"), and chapter 10 ("Embedded Indexing Software").

## Cross-references

Unlike main headings and subheadings, which provide access to locations in the text, *cross-references* are internal navigation guides within the index. Cross-references are a vital part of any index. They are the links between various nodes in the index network. Proper use of cross-references greatly enhances the usability of an index.

There are four types of cross-references used in book indexes:

> *See*
> *See under*
> *See also*
> *See also under*

This chapter discusses the use of cross-references. Their format and placement within the entry will be discussed in chapter 8, "Format and Layout of the Index."

❚ *See* and *See under.* The primary function of the *See* cross-reference is vocabulary control. A *See* cross-reference directs users from a term not used in the index to the term that is used as a heading. *See* cross-references serve three important functions:

> They *control* the scattering of information in an index.
> They *anticipate* the language of index users.
> They *reconcile* the language of the document with the users' language.

A *See* cross-reference is used whenever it may be reasonably assumed that a reader will look up a topic using terminology that is not used in the index. The text may use several different terms to describe the same thing—this is especially true in multiple-author works such as a collection of research papers. The indexer must choose one term or phrase as an entry. *See* cross-references are used to guide the readers from the terms not chosen to the chosen term. The *See* cross-reference can also relate synonymous terms or nearly synonymous terms:

> **American Civil War.** *See* **Civil War**
> **War between the States.** *See* **Civil War**

A *See* cross-reference can merge antonyms into one phrase:

**unemployment.** *See* **employment and unemployment**

*See* cross-references are often used to handle slang or other popularized terms:

**grass.** *See* **marijuana**

*See* references lead the reader to organizational names used in the text:

**Catholic Church.** *See* **Roman Catholic Church**

Or they direct a reader from an abbreviation or acronym to the spelled-out version of the term:

**ABA.** *See* **American Bar Association**

*See* references are commonly associated with geographic names. The judicious use of this type of cross-reference is particularly important when place names have changed. For example,

**Burma.** *See* **Myanmar**
**McKinley National Park.** *See* **Denali National Park**

Personal names often require the use of *See* cross-references. When an individual has been mentioned under a pen name or pseudonym, it is good practice to cross-reference from the individual's real surname:

**Clemens, Samuel.** *See* **Twain, Mark**

Western women's names pose particular problems because the surname often changes with marriage. The text will most likely indicate to the indexer which name to use in the index. If the discussion in the text refers to a woman after she has married, then her married name is the likely choice for the index. But the indexer should provide a cross-reference from the woman's maiden name to the married name.

**Rodham, Hillary.** *See* **Clinton, Hillary Rodham**

Conversely, if a woman is better known by her maiden name than by her married name, the indexer should use the maiden name. The situation becomes even more complex when a woman has been married more than once. It is the indexer's job, through the use of cross-references, to tie the various names together.

**Burton, Mrs. Richard.** *See* **Taylor, Elizabeth**
**Warner, Mrs. John V.** *See* **Taylor, Elizabeth**

When a *See* cross-reference refers to a term that is a subheading, some indexers use the phrase *See under* followed by the main heading. Using the example below, we might find the cross-reference "silver coins. *See under* currency" in the index. The use of "under" indicates that the term will be found explicitly as a subheading below the main heading indicated. This convention may save space in the index because the indexer need not repeat the entire main heading and subheading.

> **currency**
> **dollar bills**
> **silver coins**

Alternatively, a cross-reference to a subheading may take the form of "silver coins. *See* currency, silver coins." This format repeats the main heading and the subheading text in full. When the subheading is included, *The Chicago Manual of Style* requires a colon after the main heading (2003, 18.18), as in:

> **silver coins.** *See* **currency: silver coins**

While *See* references are a vital part of an index, they can be overdone. Although many terms have synonyms, it is not the indexer's job to anticipate each and every one of them. To prevent an index from becoming cluttered with directional signs that send the reader back and forth in the index, the indexer must exercise common sense and anticipate terms that readers are likely to look up. The text may provide hints for possible cross-references. Such a hint may take the following form: "Introductory notes, also known as headnotes or explanatory notes, play an important role in complex indexes." The following cross-reference would be appropriate:

> **headnotes.** *See* **introductory notes**

The indexer must look carefully for such hints in the text. Many authors will provide synonymous terminology when a topic is first introduced and indicate which is the preferred term. Synonymous terms should be cross-referenced. However, the indexer must often go beyond the text and consider other ways that readers may look up information. Authors will not always provide the terminology.

*See* cross-references should be evaluated in terms of their usefulness. It can be irritating for readers to be sent from one place in the index to another only to pick up one or two page references. It is often kinder to provide quick access to information by double-posting a term rather than using a *See* cross-reference. For example, instead of using "cars. *See* autos" the indexer may decide to provide both terms because there are so few page references:

> **autos, 54, 89**
> **cars, 54, 89**

Double-posting information can save the index user time. But if *autos* were followed by subheadings, posting the information one place and cross-referencing it from the other term would save space. Frequently, the indexer will not know the complete form of an entry until the entire text has been indexed. To maintain term consistency, the indexer may decide initially to use a *See* reference. Later, during the editing phase of the index, the indexer can make a final determination on the benefit to the readers of double-posting the terms instead.

▮ *See also* and *See also under.* The primary function of a *See also* cross-reference is to guide users to related and additional information at another heading, as in the following example:

> **drug trafficking.** *See also* **narcotics**
> **narcotics.** *See also* **drug trafficking**

*See also* cross-references may be "two-way" as above. The indexer uses *See also* cross-references when users may be expected to miss additional and related information. The important word to keep in mind here is *additional.*

> **diskettes**
>   **care of, 12**
>   **formatting of, 18–20**
>
> **FORMAT command**
>   **for floppy disks, 18–20**
>   **for hard drives, 35–39**
>   **parameters summarized, 42**
>   *See also* **diskettes**

In the example above there is no additional information about the FORMAT command under the *diskettes* heading. The time of readers who look up *diskettes* for new, related information will have been wasted. Thus, the example above is an inappropriate use of the *See also* device.

Within an index there will be many related topics. It is not the indexer's job to make all these relationships explicit. In many situations it is fair to assume that readers have enough savvy to discern obvious relationships. A woodworking book most likely does not need a cross-reference like "hammers. *See also* nails." Indexers must be careful not to clutter the index with condescending cross-references. The indexer's good judgment will anticipate related information that readers might miss if a cross-reference is lacking.

*See also under* may be used to refer readers to a subheading that appears verbatim. For example,

> sudden oak death
>   discovery of
>   testing for
>   *See also under* coastal live oak

At the *coastal live oak* main heading there is a subheading for *sudden oak death*.

▌ *General cross-references.* While there is no hard-and-fast rule about the number of *See also* cross-references that may be associated with a particular entry, an excessive number suggests a structural problem with the entry itself. In such cases, the main heading is often too general or vague. In other situations the indexer needs to refer readers to an entire class of terms without naming each and every term. Here a general cross-reference can be used. For example,

> commands
>   error messages associated with, 135–41
>   parameters, 28
>   syntax, 25–27
>   *See also individual command names*

or

> dogs
>   breeding of, 75–80
>   feeding of, 35
>   registration rules, 90
>   whelping of, 81–83
>   *See also breed names*

In both of the examples above the indexer has guided readers to specific types of entries without listing them individually. In a book on dogs where more than 120 breeds are discussed, the indexer can avoid listing each and every breed ("*See also* Afghans; cocker spaniels; collies; . . .").

Note that the words that form the general cross-reference are set in italics. The use of italics in this situation indicates to the reader that the terms referenced are general in nature; they are not specific terms that will be found in the index. For instance, there will be no entries in the *I*'s for "individual command names." *The Chicago Manual of Style* (2003, 18.22) recommends:

> When generic cross-references accompany specific cross-references, the former are placed last, even if out of alphabetic order.
>
> > dogs, 35–42. *See also* American Kennel Club; shelters; *and individual breed names*

General cross-references are very useful devices. In the *commands* entry above, the indexer has chosen to post all the commands as main headings rather than list them as subheadings under *commands*. In a technical index such as a computer manual, where one is likely to find many commands discussed, the usability of the index will be enhanced by posting individual commands as main headings. Most users wanting information about a particular command will look up that command by name. A user looking for *FORMAT command* will likely go to the *F*'s before going to the *C*'s. The use of the general cross-reference allows the indexer to post general information that applies to all commands under the *commands* entry. The *See also* cross-reference neatly guides readers to more specific information.

■ *Completeness of cross-references.* The form that cross-references should take has fueled much debate among indexers and editors. Should the heading pointed to be cited in its complete form? The complete form includes all punctuation and all parenthetical phrases that may be associated with the term. The argument in favor of complete citation is that there will be absolutely no ambiguity regarding the term referred to. However, in the case of a lengthy main heading, one must exercise some common sense. For example, "labor unions. *See also* AFL-CIO" is no less clear than "labor unions. *See also* AFL-CIO (American Federation of Labor and Congress of Industrial Organizations)." Providing this cumbersome cross-reference in full adds unnecessary length to the entry.

Clarity, however, should never be sacrificed to succinctness. Given the sample entries below, a cross-reference such as "*See* LIST" would be inappropriate. The parenthetical phrase is needed so that the readers will know exactly which term is being referenced.

> **LIST (command)**
> **LIST (text tag)**

Because there is disagreement on whether cross-referenced terms can be shortened, the indexer would be wise to check with the publisher before shortening cross-references.

■ *Directness of cross-references.* Cross-references should always provide direct access to information. They should be one-step links. They should not send the reader on a cross-reference trail, as in "hunting dogs. *See* Gordon setters," only to find "Gordon setters. *See* setters." In this case, the *hunting dogs* reference should direct the reader to *setters*.

■ *Multiple cross-references.* When more than one term is referred to in a cross-reference, it is necessary to separate the terms with semicolons.

books. *See also* reference books; trade books

A comma is never used to separate two referenced terms. However, a comma may be used to reference a subheading. For example,

whelping. *See* dogs, whelping of

Here, *whelping* of is a subheading under the main heading *dogs*. Remember that *The Chicago Manual of Style* requires a colon after the main heading, not a comma (2003, 18.18): "whelping. *See* dogs: whelping of." This format is an alternative to "whelping. *See under* dogs."

■ *Blind and circular cross-references.* The indexer should make sure that there are no cross-references that refer to terms that do not exist in the index. These are called blind cross-references; they send the reader nowhere. "Chicken. *See also* poultry" would be a blind cross-reference if there were no entry for *poultry*.

Of equally bad form is the circular cross-reference. These are *See* cross-references that reference each other, resulting in no information being found. For example,

autos. *See* cars
cars. *See* autos

■ *Reference locators and cross-references.* A cross-reference never has a reference locator associated with it. Remember that the cross-reference is a navigation guide around the index itself. The purpose of a cross-reference is not to send readers to a particular location in the text. The main headings and subheadings are the access points to the text.

# Chapter Five

## ARRANGEMENT OF ENTRIES

The *arrangement of entries* refers to the order in which the entries are presented. In most indexes this order is alphabetic. However, there is more than one way to get from *A* to *Z*. There are two alphabetic orders, word-by-word and letter-by-letter. Main headings are alphabetized following one of these sorting orders. Although subheadings generally follow the same alphabetizing scheme as the main headings, there are exceptions, which will be discussed shortly.

When as children we all learned to sing the so-called alphabet song, we were surely left with the impression that the order of the alphabet was a straightforward matter. Not so when it comes to alphabetizing index entries! The problem is that terms in an index often include elements that are not letters of the alphabet:

> **Woolf, Virginia**
> **New York City**
> **!du command**
> **War of 1812**

All four terms include spaces. The first and third terms have punctuation marks, the comma and the exclamation point. The last term includes numbers. Any sorting scheme must take nonletter characters into consideration. For the purposes of this discussion, each separable entity in a term will be referred to as a character. Characters include letters, numbers, symbols, and spaces.

The most cogent discussion of arrangement schemes is found in *NISO TR03: Guidelines for the Alphabetical Arrangement of Letters and Sorting of Numerals and Other Symbols* (1999). I will use *NISO TR03* as the normative reference for discussion of word-by-word versus letter-by-letter alphabetizing. It is important that arrangement schemes are able to be integrated into the programming of indexing software. In the past, this has not always been the case. Some rules were based on usage rather than logic. As we will see, *NISO TR03* is clear and concise. Indexers can set up their indexing programs to conform to the NISO recommendations. Later in the chapter we will look at the alphabetizing rules of *The Chicago Manual of Style*, Columbia University Press, and *ISO 999* in relation to *NISO TR03*.

## Order of Characters

The order of characters in *NISO TR03* (3.) is as follows: "spaces; symbols other than numerals, letters, and punctuation marks; numerals (0 through 9); letters (A through Z)."

Further, *NISO TR03* establishes the following rules:

> (3.1) A space precedes any other character in alphanumeric arrangement.
> (3.2) The hyphen, dash (of any length), or slash is to be treated as a space.

Let's look at an example:

> **TYPE-ADF command**
> type font
> type foundry
> type metal
> Type/Specs Inc.
> typeface
> typeset

Notice that the first and fifth terms include punctuation described in 3.2. The hyphen and the slash are treated like a space.

In section 3.3 *NISO TR03* defines other punctuation marks that are ignored:

> The following punctuation marks should be disregarded for arrangement purposes: period (full stop), comma, semi-colon, colon, parentheses, square brackets, angle brackets, braces (curved brackets, wigglies), apostrophe, quotation marks (single or double), exclamation mark, question mark. They are *not* to be treated as spaces

Here is an example that applies the rules from section 3.3:

> **New, Agnes**
> **New Jersey**
> **New, Thomas**
> **New York**
> **"New York Dining"**
> **New York (NY)**
> *New York: Visitor's Guide*

*NISO TR03* continues this discussion with recommendations for handling symbols and other types of alphanumeric characters. Please see chapter 6 for details about such characters in index entries.

Now, let's look at a series of terms arranged in the basic order specified by *NISO TR03*.

New, Agnes
New Jersey
New, Thomas
New York
"New York Dining"
New York (NY)
*New York: Visitor's Guide*
Newark (NJ)
TYPE-ADF command
type font
type foundry
type metal
Type/Specs Inc.
typeface
typeset

Before moving on to the differences between word-by-word and letter-by-letter alphabetizing, here is a summary of the basic rules regarding the order of characters.

1. Space precedes any other character.
   a. hyphen treated as a space
   b. dash treated as a space
   c. slash treated as a space
2. These punctuation marks are ignored:
   a. period/full stop .
   b. comma ,
   c. colon :
   d. parentheses ( )
   e. square brackets [ ]
   f. angle brackets ‹ ›
   g. braces { }
   h. apostrophe '
   i. quotation marks " "
   j. exclamation mark !
   k. question mark ?
3. Symbols other than numerals, letters, and punctuation marks precede numerals and letters.
4. Numerals precede letters.
5. Letters follow numerals.

It is important to understand that these rules are offered as normative rules because they make sense and they can be implemented in computerized sorting routines. These rules also provide a basic framework for discussion of variance from the rules.

## Word-by-Word Alphabetizing

If the rules above are applied, particularly rule 1, then the arrangement order is known as word-by-word alphabetizing. *NISO TR03* describes word-by-word arrangement in this way (4.1.2.1):

> Application of the rule in section 3.1 (spaces precede all other characters) results in what is known as word-by-word arrangement. This method is preferred, because it keeps together headings beginning with the same word (or words). The word-by-word method has always been used in library catalogs as well as in many indexes.

Although there are some variations in the details, both *NISO TR02* (Anderson 1997, 9.3) and *ISO 999* (8.2) recommend word-by-word arrangement of index entries. *NISO TR02* acknowledges the problem with various interpretations of the basic rules regarding arrangement:

> Two de facto standards widely used in libraries and databases in the United States are the American Library Association (ALA) and the Library of Congress (LC) filing rules. The guidelines for alphanumeric arrangement in *The Chicago Manual of Style* are used as a de facto standard by many publishers. These three codes of alphanumeric arrangement are, however, incompatible with each other. (Anderson 1997, 9.1)

## Letter-by-Letter Alphabetizing

The letter-by-letter method distinguishes itself by ignoring rule 1 (spaces precede all other characters). When the spaces and all other punctuation are ignored, the alphabetizing continues across the entry as though all letters are run together. For example,

> **TYPE-ADF command**
> typeface
> type font
> type foundry
> type metal
> typeset
> **Type/Specs Inc.**

The argument in favor of this type of arrangement is that different spellings of the same term are kept together. For example, *on line files, on-line files,* and *online files* would all appear in the same place in the arrangement.

Here is a comparison of word-by-word and letter-by-arrangement as specified in *NISO TR03*. The difference between the two is whether rule 1 is followed.

| Word-by-Word | Letter-by-letter |
|---|---|
| New, Agnes | New, Agnes |
| New Jersey | Newark (NJ) |
| New, Thomas | New Jersey |
| New York | New, Thomas |
| "New York Dining" | New York |
| New York (NY) | "New York Dining" |
| *New York: Visitor's Guide* | New York (NY) |
| Newark (NJ) | *New York: Visitor's Guide* |
| TYPE-ADF command | TYPE-ADF command |
| type font | typeface |
| type foundry | type font |
| type metal | type foundry |
| Type/Specs Inc. | type metal |
| typeface | typeset |
| typeset | Type/Specs Inc. |

At this point the two forms of alphabetizing must seem very straight-forward. If the recommendations of *NISO TR03* were followed, the two alphanumeric arrangement schemes would be very clear. However, when we look at various publishers' style guides, we will see that some of the five rules are violated.

## Basic Rules Affecting Both Alphabetizing Orders

Almost every rule that follows has significant exceptions that will be discussed in chapter 6. These rules, however, can be followed for many indexes that do not include the use of specialized terminology.

When arabic or roman numerals appear in entries either at the beginning of the entry or within the entry, and are sorted numerically, they are sorted in ascending numeric order. Arabic and roman numerals within entries are interfiled according to their numeric order. Guidelines for choosing between arranging numerals in numeric order or as though spelled out are discussed in chapter 6. Entries beginning with numbers are generally placed before the alphabetic listing of entries:

> 5th Avenue
> *XX Century Gazetteer*
> *2001: A Space Odyssey*

Symbols in an index, if they are few, may be sorted as they are spelled. But if there are many symbols, it may be preferable to arrange them in accordance with special rules (see chapter 6).

Diacritical marks are usually ignored in alphabetizing; a *ü* sorts as a *u*. When possible, letters with diacritical marks are sorted like their English equivalents.

An introductory note will be necessary if the indexer has chosen to use a nontraditional arrangement sequence. The note will explain any convention used by the indexer that might confuse users of the index.

## Other Alphabetizing Guidelines
### The University of Chicago Press
*The Chicago Manual of Style* makes clear that the preference is letter-by-letter alphabetizing; however, they may accept word-by-word arrangement (2003, 18.56). Here is how the two systems are described:

> **18.57** *The letter-by-letter system.* In the letter-by-letter system, alphabetizing continues up to the first parenthesis or comma; it then starts again after the punctuation point. Word spaces and all other punctuation marks are ignored. Both open and hyphenated compounds such as *New York* or *self-pity* are treated as single words. The order of precedence is one word, word followed by a parenthesis, and word followed by a comma, number, or letters. The index to this manual, in accordance with Chicago's traditional preference, is arranged letter by letter.
>
> **18.58** *The word-by-word system.* In the word-by-word system, alphabetizing continues only up to the end of the first word (counting hyphenated compounds as one word), using subsequent words only when additional headings begin with the same word. As in the letter-by-letter system, alphabetizing continues up to the first parenthesis or comma; it then starts again after the punctuation point. The order of precedence is one word, word followed by a parenthesis, word followed by a comma, word followed by a space, and word followed by a comma, number, or letters.
>
> **18.59** *The two systems compared.* In both systems a parenthesis or comma interrupts the alphabetizing, and other punctuation marks (hyphens, slashes, quotation marks, periods, etc.) are ignored.

Applying these rules results in this type of arrangement:

| Letter-by-Letter | Word-by-Word |
|---|---|
| New, Agnes | New, Agnes |
| New, Thomas | New, Thomas |
| Newark (NJ) | New Jersey |
| New Jersey | New York |
| New York | New York (NY) |
| New York (NY) | "New York Dining" |
| "New York Dining" | *New York: Visitor's Guide* |
| *New York: Visitor's Guide* | Newark (NJ) |

In this example, the only difference in the two arrangements is the placement of Newark (NJ). This arrangement method modifies rules 2(b) and 2(d) in that the comma and parentheses are not ignored, but interrupt the alphabetizing. Additionally, in the Chicago form of word-by-word alphabetizing, rule 1(a–c) is discarded; hyphens, dashes, and slashes are ignored rather than treated as a space.

### Columbia University Press
Like the University of Chicago Press, Columbia University Press (2002) prefers letter-by-letter arrangement. Their form of letter-by-letter alphabetizing is not the same as the Chicago style.

> Main entries (and alphabetized subentries) should be arranged dictionary style, in which each letter is the controlling unit, and not in phone directory style, in which each word is the controlling unit. (Have you ever tried to find Acme Coyote Costumes in the A section of your phone book, or, worse, Acmemiskov, Arcady?) However, letter-by-letter indexing works only up to a punctuation mark, not beyond it. (31–32)

Here is how the sample entries would be arranged when following Columbia's letter-by-letter rules:

> **New, Agnes**
> **New, Thomas**
> **Newark (NJ)**
> **New Jersey**
> **New York**
> **New York (NY)**
> *New York: Visitor's Guide*
> **"New York Dining"**

Note that the entry *New York: Visitor's Guide* comes before "New York Dining" because Columbia stops the sorting after a punctuation mark, in this case the colon. This arrangement method ignores rules 1, 1(a), and 2(a–k). Additionally, Columbia introduces a rule based on usage: hyphens used in compound words are ignored; other hyphens stop the sorting. Indexers following this method of arrangement must pay attention to the types of hyphens that appear in index entries.

### *ISO 999*
Section 8 of *ISO 999* defines the arrangement of entries in indexes. Following are excerpts and their references.

> (8.1) All characters and symbols normally have a filing value.
> Punctuation symbols used to distinguish types of index heading may be given special values in order to sort the headings in the order required.

The value given to a blank space will depend on whether letter-by-letter or word-by-word order is required.

(8.2) Index headings consisting of more than one word should be filed by the word-by-word method, in which a space files before a letter.

An alternative arrangement, letter-by-letter, disregards such characters as the space and dash.

(8.5) Index headings beginning with the same terms should be filed in the following sequence:

term with or without subheadings;

term with qualifier;

term as first element of longer term.

Example:

> milk
> > cows'
> > goats'
> *Milk* (report)
> milk allergies
> Milk Marketing Board

The ISO preference is for word-by-word alphabetizing. However, like the University of Chicago, ISO allows for special treatment of entries that include qualifiers in parentheses. Here is how the word-by-word sample entries would look:

> New, Agnes
> New Jersey
> New, Thomas
> New York
> New York (NY)
> "New York Dining"
> *New York: Visitor's Guide*
> Newark (NJ)

## Summary of Arrangement Preferences

For a summary of the alphabetizing practices preferred by *NISO TR03*, the University of Chicago Press, Columbia University Press, and *ISO 999*, see table 5.1.

## Nonalphabetic Arrangement in Indexes

Readers expect indexes to be arranged in alphabetic order. The decision to arrange entries in a nonalphabetic order should not be made lightly. The important factor to consider is whether the nonalphabetic arrangement will make entries easier for readers to locate. Generally, main head-

Table 5.1. Summary of arrangement preferences

| NISO TR03 | University of Chicago Press | Columbia University Press | ISO 999 |
|---|---|---|---|
| New, Agnes | New, Agnes | New, Agnes | New, Agnes |
| New Jersey | New, Thomas | New, Thomas | New Jersey |
| New, Thomas | Newark (NJ) | Newark (NJ) | New, Thomas |
| New York | New Jersey | New Jersey | New York |
| "New York Dining" | New York | New York | New York (NY) |
| New York (NY) | New York (NY) | New York (NY) | "New York Dining" |
| New York: Visitor's Guide | "New York Dining" | New York: Visitor's Guide | New York: Visitor's Guide |
| Newark (NJ) | New York: Visitor's Guide | "New York Dining" | Newark (NJ) |
| TYPE-ADF command | TYPE-ADF command | TYPE-ADF command | TYPE-ADF command |
| type font | typeface | Type/Specs Inc. | type font |
| type foundry | type font | typeface | type foundry |
| type metal | type foundry | type font | type metal |
| Type/Specs Inc. | type metal | type foundry | typeface |
| typeface | typeset | type metal | typeset |
| typeset | Type/Specs Inc. | typeset | Type/Specs Inc. |

ings are arranged in the alphabetic sequences noted above. Nonalphabetic arrangements occur at the subheading levels.

### Function Words: Articles, Prepositions, and Conjunctions

By far the most common nonalphabetic arrangement encountered in indexes is when leading articles, prepositions, and conjunctions in subheadings are not alphabetized. Instead, the word following the article, preposition, or conjunction is sorted.

> **books**
>> **for adult readers**
>> **the autumn market for**
>> **mass market sales of**
>> **and movie options**
>> **in production during May**

The best way to handle leading articles, prepositions, and conjunctions in subheadings is a subject of debate. Many publishers' style guides instruct the indexer not to alphabetize these terms. Here are some arguments on both sides of this issue.

Those in favor of not alphabetizing these function words argue that the attention of the index user should be on the important keyword that follows the introductory term. Readers should not be burdened with figuring out which, if any, introductory term an indexer may have used to begin the entry. Furthermore, ignoring these terms has been standard practice in alphabetizing for years, so readers are familiar with it.

Those in favor of alphabetizing the introductory terms point out, quite correctly, that we alphabetize everything else in the index and that readers expect index entries to be alphabetized. They remind us that these structural terms should not be used frivolously in the index. They should be used only when absolutely necessary for clarity. So, the argument goes, if the terms are necessary, why not alphabetize them?

Clearly, both schools of thought have strong arguments. Wellisch (1995, 387–391) offers a detailed analysis of the various ways of handling prepositions. He concludes, "Clearly, strict alphabetization of every word in a heading or subheading, long or short, 'important' or 'unimportant,' is the only sensible procedure, and indexers should insist on it (even though a struggle over this issue with ossified editors may, alas, often end in defeat)."

In regard to legal indexing, Moys (Moys et al. 1993, 51) points out that alphabetizing on function words can provide clear guidance to readers.

She provides the following example, which actually highlights the function words:

Appeals
  against
    penalties
    planning permission
  from
    arbitrators
    Magistrates' courts
  to
    Crown courts
    House of Lords

Chances are that your publisher will not want the introductory terms alphabetized when they appear in subheadings. The rules regarding these terms in main headings are much clearer.

When articles, prepositions, or conjunctions appear as the first term in a main heading, the phrase is probably a title of a book, an article, a play, or a painting. If the first term is an article, such as *A* or *The,* the term is not alphabetized. For example, the book title *A Tale of Two Cities* would appear in the *T*'s, sorted on *Tale.* The actual entry could appear in the *T*'s in one of three ways:

*Tale of Two Cities, A,* or
*A Tale of Two Cities,* or
*Tale of Two Cities*

In the last example above, the *A* has been dropped entirely from the entry. This practice is common and preferred when it is necessary to economize on the length of index entries. The absence of the article does not compromise the meaning of the entry. Unlike in a bibliography, it is not required that titles in an index be entered in their complete form.

If the first term in a main heading is a preposition or conjunction, the term is alphabetized. For example, the book title *Of Mice and Men* appears in the *O*'s, sorted on *Of.*

If an article, preposition, or conjunction appears in any other position besides as the first term in an entry, it is always alphabetized. The *and* in the phrase "dogs and cats" is alphabetized.

### Words That Are Spelled Alike
Some style guides recommend that terms that are spelled alike be arranged in the following sequence: person, place, and thing. Other style guides go one step further: they require filing a title after a thing (see *The*

*Oxford Guide to Style,* Ritter et al. 2002, 581). This arrangement results in a listing such as

> London, Jack
> London, England
> *London, an Antique Shopper's Guide*

The major problem with this odd rule is that most index users have no idea that it exists. Readers looking at the list above will probably think that the indexer made an alphabetizing mistake. And in a lengthy index, readers may miss index entries entirely because the entry they are looking for is not in alphabetic order. This type of arrangement is not recommended by *NISO TR03* or *ISO 999*. The fifteenth edition of *The Chicago Manual of Style* specifically recommends (2003, 18.60) that

> when a person, a place, and a thing have the same name, they are arranged in normal alphabetical order:
>
> | hoe, garden | London, England |
> | Hoe, Robert | London, Jack |

Words that are spelled alike are to be arranged in alphabetic order like all other entries in the index. If there are two words that are spelled alike but have different meanings, a qualifier must be added to distinguish the two entries.

## Chronological/Page Number Order for Subheadings

In some books readers may be aided by subheadings arranged in a chronological order. In the biography of a naval officer the following type of subheadings might be helpful, for example:

> military career
>   ensign
>   lieutenant
>   lieutenant commander
>   commander
>   captain
>   admiral

Subheadings in a geology book might be arranged in the order of geologic epochs:

> sedimentary strata
>   Pleistocene
>   Pliocene
>   Miocene
>   Cretaceous

But all too often, chronological order is confused with page number order. A handful of publishers require all subheadings to be sorted in page number order. Apparently the assumption is that the narrative of a text unfolds in chronological order. But as the example below will demonstrate, this is not always the case. This entry is taken from the book *China Builds the Bomb* (Stanford, CA: Stanford University Press, 1988). As originally published, the entry was in run-in style. Indented style is used here because it is easier to read. Also, only the first few page number sequences have been included in the excerpt.

> Tests, 234, 244–45
> arms control negotiations and, 1, 12
> first atomic bomb (Oct. 16, 1964), 1–2, 182–89
> U.S., 18, 20
> plutonium bomb (Dec. 27, 1968), 113, 114n
> atomic bomb detonation process (Nov. 20, 1963; June 6, 1964),
> 156–60
> "cold," 201
> "fundamentals of a thermonuclear explosion" (Dec. 28, 1966),
> 201
> hydrogen bomb "booster" (May 9, 1966), 201
> DF-2 missile (Oct. 27, 1966), 202–3, 209
> hydrogen bomb (June 17, 1967), 205–6, 267
> weapon, 207, 290
> air-dropped atomic bomb (May 14, 1965), 208
> liquid-fueled missile (Nov. 1960), 212
> DF-3 missile (Dec. 1966), 213
> underground, 285
> British, 290
> French, 290
> Soviet, 290

Because the indexer has included dates as part of some of the subheadings, we are able to analyze the order of the entries. Moving down the list, which is in page number order, the first date is 1964, the next date is 1968, the following date is 1963, and so on; the dates are not in chronological order. Moreover, like items ("hydrogen bomb," for example) are separated. The reader must read the entire list because of the nonalphabetic arrangement. Without a doubt, the usability of an index arranged in this manner is severely compromised.

Hazel Bell (1989, 169, 170) makes a strong case, however, for chronological arrangement in subheadings in the indexes of biographies:

It seems generally agreed that alphabetical arrangement of subheadings should give way to chronological for biographies. For one thing, alphabetical arrangement is helpful only if you know what the entries are likely to be: climate/history/population of a country. But it is at best confusing, at worst ridiculous, to list for a person:

death, dental problems, divorce, marriage, meets future wife, schooldays

and chronological arrangement will coincide roughly with the events of the book, producing a minor narrative in itself, easy to follow.

Bell clearly acknowledges the problems of arranging entries in simple page number order when she writes:

> Some take the easiest way of all to arrange entries—in order of occurrence, no messing. This will not help the reader who does not know where to look for them; nor where entries occur where one would not expect them—the funeral of the character anticipated in the introduction, for instance—even his entire career there summarized.

Bell goes on to suggest other ways of collating entries in the index of a biography. Biographies challenge the indexer in a most demanding way. Indexers wishing to index biographies will benefit from consulting Hazel Bell's *Indexing Biographies and Other Stories of Human Lives* (2004).

In books other than biographies, page number order for index entries can be difficult to use. In order to access specific information, readers must possess a good amount of knowledge about when the information might have appeared within the particular time spectrum for the book. The less specialized the knowledge required of index users, the greater will be the access to information in the index for a greater number of readers.

When subheadings are sorted in page number order, the demand for clear and structured term selection disappears. Since the entries will not be sorted alphabetically, the wording of the entries is less important. The subheadings still must convey a clear sense of the material cited, but the demand on the indexer to pull the most important term forward for sorting is eliminated. But the demand on the reader, who must stumble through often long lists of subheadings, is greatly increased.

## How to Choose an Arrangement Order

Ideally, every index will be arranged in such a way that readers can easily and quickly locate information. The indexer cannot conclude that one way of alphabetizing is always better than another way of alphabetizing.

The easiest way to decide on an alphabetizing scheme is to view the index in word-by-word order and also in letter-by-letter order. Thanks to dedicated indexing software, this is an easy task.

Here are some general guidelines for determining which alphabetic order may be most applicable to certain types of documents. If an index has a lot of names, word-by-word alphabetizing may be the best way to keep groups of similar names together. In disciplines in which many entries will be related multipart phrases, word-by-word alphabetizing may be the best way to keep groups of these terms together. Legal and medical indexes are frequently sorted this way.

Many technical indexes will benefit from a letter-by-letter sort. This is particularly true in fields in which the language is not standardized. Take the following terms as examples:

> data base
> database
>
> on line
> on-line
> online

Of course, a given index would not contain all these variant spellings. In the text, one of the spellings would be used consistently, it is hoped. But a reader might easily assume that the term is spelled differently from the usage in the text. These terms will all be sorted in the same location if a letter-by-letter sort is used. However, a word-by-word sort will place the variant spellings in quite different locations. This certainly can be an issue in a lengthy index.

Remember that advocates of word-by-word order argue that this scheme gathers like terms together. Those in the letter-by-letter camp suggest that readers are more familiar with letter-by-letter sorting because it is used frequently in dictionaries, encyclopedias, and directories.

In many indexes there will be little, if any, discernible difference between the two alphabetizing orders. But if the indexer or editor feels that an entry is out of place, it is time to consider sorting the index in a different way.

The decision to arrange subheadings in a nonalphabetic sequence should be made thoughtfully. Common sense will be the best guide in this matter. If a true chronological listing is desired, do not confuse chronological order with page number order for subheadings.

An indexer can do an excellent job of isolating concepts that need to be in an index; however, if the arrangement of entries is not sensible, readers will have a difficult time. Whatever arrangement is selected, the selection should be based on the needs of the readers.

# Chapter Six

## SPECIAL CONCERNS IN INDEXING

This chapter is a collection of disparate topics that require special consideration in indexing. Even in the most straightforward text, indexers sometimes confront oddities they are not quite sure how to handle. This chapter offers some guidance to those who strive to present a systematic (and sensible) arrangement of index entries.

## Abbreviations and Acronyms

Quite often lengthy names of organizations and companies are referred to in the text in a shortened form. The indexer must decide whether to post information at the shortened form or at the spelled-out form of the term. The general rule is that shortened forms that are "widely known" should be entered in the index (*The Chicago Manual of Style 2003*, 18.46). Undoubtedly we can agree on certain abbreviations and acronyms that fall into this category—such as NATO or UNICEF. Such terms can be entered in the index without cross-references from the spelled-out versions of the names.

As we deal with more specialized texts, the question "widely known to whom?" arises. Then it becomes very important that the indexer have a good sense of the audience for the book. The indexer must decide not only which form of a term to use for the entry in the index but also whether cross-references are necessary. Inserting cross-references for every abbreviation or acronym in the index can add a great deal of length to the index and possibly cause space problems. The indexer must decide how much cross-referencing is appropriate for the audience.

An introductory book about computer programming may refer to terms such as ASCII, AWK, BASIC, and XML. When the terms were introduced in the text, the author undoubtedly provided the spelled-out versions from which the acronyms and abbreviations were derived. However, a complete list of cross-references such as those below is not necessary. It would add length to the index out of all proportion to the other important concepts included in it.

> American Standard Code for Information Interchange. *See* ASCII
> Aho, Weinberger, and Kernighan. *See* AWK
> Beginner's All-purpose Symbolic Instruction Code. *See* BASIC
> eXtensible Markup Language. *See* XML

The decision on whether to provide cross-references does not rest solely on whether a term is widely known. We may not be able to make that assumption about the reader of an introductory programming book, who may have never heard of XML. But XML is a term the readers of this book will learn; they will be likely to look it up as XML, not as eXtensible Markup Language.

Some acronyms have enjoyed wide usage, and the original meanings of the terms have been forgotten by most readers. Such acronyms should be entered directly in the index. There is no need for cross-referencing from the spelled-out version of the term.

> modem, *not* MOdulator DEModulator
> laser, *not* Light Amplification by Stimulated
> Emission of Radiation

An index that posts information at abbreviations or acronyms may benefit by including the spelled-out version of the terms after the shortened version.

> SLA (Special Libraries Association)
> SLA (Symbionese Liberation Army)

This way readers can be certain that they have indeed located the term desired.

In a book that contains many shortened forms of names, the indexer's job will be made slightly easier if the author has provided the indexer with a list of these names in both shortened and spelled-out forms. Indexers not blessed with such an organized author can pick up the full form of a shortened name when it is first introduced. The full name may not be mentioned for another two hundred pages, and it is quite time-consuming to return to the text in order to locate it later.

As with any type of multiple postings, all information should be gathered in one place or else completely double-posted. The indexer must decide the exact form of the organization name entry and use it consistently. Do not split references between more than one form of the entry.

Abbreviations and acronyms should be alphabetized in the same way as the other entries in the index, whether letter-by-letter or word-by-word. They are not usually alphabetized as if they were spelled out. An exception that many publishers allow is that the abbreviation U.S. may be alphabetized as though spelled out. This allows a term like *U.S. Bureau of Reclamation* to interfile with other U.S. entries such as *United States Coast Guard.*

## Uppercase and Lowercase Letters

The case of letters in an entry is generally disregarded when entries are sorted. An uppercase *A* has the same sorting value as a lowercase *a*. However, in certain odd situations entries may be the same except for case. In the twenty-fourth edition of *Stedman's Medical Dictionary* we find the following two entries in this order:

> **M.u. Abbreviation for Mache unit**
> **m.u. Abbreviation for mouse unit**

It would seem from this example that uppercase precedes lowercase when the entries are the same except for case. Given the widespread use of computers, such a sorting precedence would make sense (see chapter 10 for a discussion of computers and sorting). But one must decide whether uppercase or lowercase has precedence and apply the rule throughout the index when two entries are spelled the same except for case.

## International Characters

In English-language indexes, terms that are derived from languages using the Latin alphabet are sorted according to their English equivalents. For example, *à* sorts as *a*, *ç* sorts as *c*, and *ü* sorts as *u*. Many languages do not use the Latin alphabet. Some of these languages are transliterated, that is, converted to the Latin alphabet. "These languages include Arabic, Chinese, Hebrew, Japanese, Russian, and other living languages as well as ancient languages such as Greek and Sanskrit" (*The Chicago Manual of Style* 2003, 10.89). Once words are transliterated, or romanized, their characters are sorted according to their English (Latin) equivalents. For more information about various transliteration schemes, see "Languages Usually Transliterated (or Romanized)" in *CMS* (2003, 10.89–129), Wellisch (1995, 421–429), and *ALA-LC Romanization Tables: Transliteration Schemes for Non-Roman Scripts* (http://www.loc.gov/catdir/cpso/roman.html).

Indexers working with languages that are based on a non-Latin alphabet and are not transliterated must obtain guidance regarding arrangement of entries from the publisher. W. Eliot Kimber and Joshua Reynolds (2002) discuss some of the interesting issues surrounding sorting of non-Latin languages in their paper "Internationalized Back-of-the-Book Indexes for XSL Formatting Objects." For example, they point out that

"Arabic has very complex collation [sorting] rules that depend on word roots rather than simply word spelling, significantly complicating the collation algorithm for Arabic. . . . Japanese is collated based on phonetic pronunciation. . . . Thai has no well-defined notion of 'word'" (2). While Kimber and Reynolds do not deal with the nuances of alphabetization as described in chapter 5, their paper does present a good starting point for the arrangement of non-Latin languages.

## Numerals, Symbols, and Other Nonalphanumeric Characters in Entries

Frequently nonalphabetic characters appear within index entries, as in *War of 1812*. Some scholarly publishers require that numbers be alphabetized as though spelled out. Many style guides and even indexing standards offer little or no guidance regarding the arrangement of symbols in entries. Indexers who work with technical material will surely have entries that contain symbols as terms—for example, the *!mv command*. To ensure efficient access to entries containing nonalphabetic characters, a consistent sorting procedure must be adopted.

### Numerals in Entries

❚ *Arrangement of numerals.* Numerals may appear in any position within an entry. When an entry begins with a numeral, the filing sequence is of greater importance because of the reader's need to find the main entry. There are two ways to sort numerals. One approach is to sort them as though spelled out. The second method is to arrange the numerals in ascending numeric order.

As noted above, some scholarly publishers, like Oxford, require that numerals be alphabetized as though spelled out (*Ritter et. al 2002*, 16.3.3). For example:

> *1984* (Orwell) (alphabetized as *nineteen eighty-four*)
> 10 Downing Street (alphabetized as *ten downing street*)

Chicago recommends that headings beginning with numerals be alphabetized as though spelled out only when there are very few entries of this kind (2003, 18.63).

The *ISO 999* (8.3a) suggests that "in indexes where few headings begin with numerals, they may be arranged as if spelt out in words in the appropriate language." The following examples are provided:

> *1984* (alphabetized as *nineteen eighty-four*)
> 1:30 a.m. (alphabetized as *one thirty*)

> *1001 nights* (alphabetized as *one thousand and one*)
> *1066 and all that* (alphabetized as *ten sixty-six*)
> *xx century cyclopedia and atlas* (alphabetized as *twentieth*)

*ISO 999* qualifies the suggestion to arrange the terms as though spelled out only when there are "few headings" that being with numerals. This is sensible advice. When there are many terms beginning with numerals, the indexer should consider arranging the terms in ascending numeric order. *The Chicago Manual of Style* also suggests a numeric arrangement when there are many such entries (2003, 18.63). *NISO TR03* recommends, "All headings beginning with a numeral should be arranged ahead of any heading beginning with a letter, *not* as if spelled out" (3.4). Furthermore, *TR03* states that "headings beginning with numbers written in arabic numerals should be sorted in ascending arithmetical order before headings beginning with a letter sequence" (6.1).

It is important to keep in mind that the "alphabetize-as-though-spelled-out" rule can create rather strange sorting sequences when consistently applied to entries.

> **Route 66** (alphabetize as *Route Sixty-six*)
> **Route 33** (alphabetize as *Route Thirty-three*)
> **War of 1812** (alphabetize as *War of Eighteen Twelve*)
> **War of 1037** (alphabetize as *War of Ten Thirty-seven*)

Sorting sequences can become even stranger when a term can be spelled in a variety of ways. The following term is the name of a CPU chip for a computer:

> **80486 CPU**

How should this term be spelled out? There are several options:

> **eight oh four eight six CPU**
> **eight zero four eight six CPU**
> **eighty-four eighty-six CPU**
> **eighty thousand four hundred eighty-six CPU**

Then what does one do about the common nomenclature? This chip is commonly referred to as the "486" (four eighty-six).

The alphabetize-as-though-spelled-out rule is fraught with problems when more than a handful of entries contain numerals. A more sensible approach is to arrange numerals in ascending numeric order and, if there are only a few of these entries, to provide either double-posted entries or cross-references at the spelled-out version of the terms.

Entries that begin with numerals and are sorted in ascending numeric order are placed at the beginning of the index before the *A*'s (*The Chicago Manual of Style* 2003, 18.63; *NISO TR03*, 6.1).

When numerals are sorted in ascending numeric order, the rule applies to all numerals within an entry, regardless of their placement within the entry. It is important to note that unsophisticated computer sorting programs will not sort numbers in correct ascending order. The following is likely to result from sorting by these programs:

80486 CPU
8088 CPU

The indexer must be prepared to remedy such incorrect arrangements.

When numbers are sorted numerically, a decimal point is treated as a decimal point, not as a period. When a comma is used as a visual aid in large numbers, it should not be sorted.

5 version
5.01 version
5.12 version
5.2 version

10 widgets
100 widgets
1,000 widgets
10,000 widgets

There are occasions when the indexer may choose to arrange numeric entries by size, which may not follow a strictly numeric order. For example, the following list of memory chips is arranged by size:

16 Kb DRAM
64 Kb DRAM
256 Kb DRAM
1 Mb DRAM
4 Mb DRAM
64 Mb DRAM
1 Gb DRAM

This arrangement begins with the smaller unit of measurement, kilobytes, then continues with megabytes and gigabytes. Notice that within each category the entries are sorted in ascending numeric order.

▪ *Roman and arabic numerals.* When numbers appear in both arabic (1, 2, 3) and roman (I, II, III or i, ii, iii) form, and the entries are sorted in numeric order, the arabic and roman numerals should be interfiled and sorted by their numeric values (*NISO TR03,* 6.4; *ISO 999,* 8.3a).

test 2
test III
test 5
test X

∎ *Subscripts and superscripts.* Subscript and superscript numbers that occur in index entries are sorted by numeric value with numbers preceding letters. *NISO TR03* provides the following example (3.7):

> **49 best short stories**
> **49$_{Ca}$ accumulation**
> **a$^2$ + b$^2$ = c$^2$**
> **H$_2$0**
> **H$_2$SO$_4$**
> **Hamburg**
> **HO-scale**

∎ *Numbers as prefixes in chemical names.* When a number forms the prefix to a chemical name, the number is at first ignored.

> **cadmium**
> **4-chlorophenol**
> **CO**
> **CO$_2$**

If there are two chemical compound names that are identical except for the numeric prefix, the prefix is taken into consideration after the alphabetic portion of the term is sorted. For example:

> **3-chlorophenol**
> **4-chlorophenol**

(See the discussion below for information on Greek letters and other symbols as prefixes in chemical names.)

## Symbols in Entries

What is meant here by a symbol? On a very basic level, in this discussion, a *symbol* shall mean anything that is not a letter or number. Symbols come in such a variety of forms that dealing with every possible symbol would be impossible. Symbols will be discussed in terms of their function or use: as punctuation, as representations, as literals.

∎ *Symbols as punctuation.* Indexes frequently contain symbols that are used as punctuation within an entry. For example, the comma in *Smith, Mary* is used as punctuation. Commas are also used to separate a main heading from a subentry; for example, *horses, nutritional requirements of.* As we saw in the previous chapter, the word-by-word and letter-by-letter sorting methods guide the sorting of the space character, the hyphen, and the diagonal slash. All other punctuation marks are ignored in the alphabetization of entries. Such marks include the following:

apostrophe                Harry's Diner
colon                     *The Geography of Strabo: Books I–II*
comma                     Woolf, Virginia
double quotation          "Crisis at Noon"
exclamation point         On! Corporation
semicolon                 books. *See also* media; publishing

■ *Symbols as representations.* Symbols are often used to represent words; the ampersand (&) is a good example. Frequently such symbols are arranged in the index as though spelled out:

> **business & management programs**
> **business law**

In this example the ampersand is sorted as if spelled *and*.

In medical or chemistry indexing it is common to encounter terms that begin with Greek letters, such as alpha (α) or beta (β). Sometimes such prefixes are not sorted, but the keyword following the prefix is sorted. Other times the prefix is sorted as though spelled out as the name of the letter. If the prefix is sorted in this way, the following would result:

> **α-dog**
> **β-cat**

The arrangement of medical and chemical terms is not a straightforward matter. Often the same term is spelled in different ways by different authors. While it is the indexer's job to provide the most direct access to a term through sensible arrangement of the index, that task can become quite complex in medical texts. Furthermore, terminology can change over time.

For example, α-fetoprotein frequently used to be indexed in the *F*'s as *fetoprotein*. Nowadays this protein is widely known by its abbreviation, AFP. Today's indexers, as a result, generally file the term in the *A*'s, as if spelled *alpha-fetoprotein*.

A common rule is to produce an entry in the index just as it is provided in the text. If the Greek letter is used in the text, the Greek letter is used in the index. The interpretation of the Greek letter is of little consequence if the Greek letter is ignored and the sorting begins with the keyword that follows. However, the indexer must be very careful when interpreting the meaning of such symbols. For example:

> **μ (mean daily motion in astronomy)**
> **μ (micro)**
> **μ (micron)**
> **μ (mu, the twelfth letter of the Greek alphabet)**

The indexer must know that "µg" will sort as *microgram*, whereas "µ circuit" will sort as *mu circuit*. It is beyond the scope of this book to explore the nuances of the arrangement of entries in medical, chemistry, or engineering books. These specialized disciplines have various conventions that the index must follow. Companies that publish material in these disciplines will have indexing style guides that resolve some questions regarding the sorting of entries that contain symbols. There are also subject-area dictionaries that may help the indexer understand the nomenclature. But all too often the indexer will be confronted with terms that appear in neither the publisher's style guides nor the special dictionaries. This is when the experienced indexer's judgment is so crucial.

In many texts names are followed by the trademark, service mark, or registered mark symbol.

**Widgets To Go ®**

Generally such terms are entered in the index without the symbol. If an editor wishes to have the symbols present in the index, a generic code will have to be used to represent them, because there is no standard font for representing these symbols reliably. Generic coding is discussed in chapter 8.

▌ *Symbols as literals.* In many texts, especially in computer documentation, symbols are intended to be used quite literally. As noted above, we often treat commas, hyphens, or diagonals as punctuation. But when these symbols are used in a literal sense, we must apply a standardized sorting sequence to them. For example, let's say we have the following entries in a technical index:

**mv command**
   **-p parameter**
   **/p parameter**

The hyphen and the diagonal above are characters that the user would actually type as part of the command; they are used literally. The indexer must decide which comes first, the hyphen or the diagonal. Luckily, we can to turn for guidance to a standard that assigns a decimal code value to 128 characters. The decimal code value is understood by a great many computers, enabling the exchange of information among those computers. For our purposes, the decimal codes provide an ordering sequence; they start at 000 and end at 255. This standard is called the American Standard Code for Information Interchange, better known as ASCII (pronounced "as-key").

Following is a partial ASCII table that includes the characters we would be most likely to encounter when indexing computer documentation.

| Decimal Code | Character |
|---|---|
| 032 | (space character) |
| 033 | ! |
| 034 | " (quotation mark) |
| 035 | # |
| 036 | $ |
| 037 | % |
| 038 | & |
| 039 | ' (apostrophe) |
| 040 | ( |
| 041 | ) |
| 042 | * |
| 043 | + |
| 044 | , (comma) |
| 045 | - (hyphen) |
| 046 | . (period, decimal point) |
| 047 | / |
| 058 | : |
| 059 | ; |
| 060 | < |
| 061 | = |
| 062 | > |
| 063 | ? |
| 064 | @ |
| 091 | [ |
| 092 | \ |
| 093 | ] |
| 094 | ^ |
| 095 | _ (underscore) |
| 123 | { |
| 124 | \| (vertical bar, logical OR) |
| 125 | } |
| 126 | ~ (tilde) |

If you refer back to the example of the *mv command*, you will see that the subentries appear in the correct order. The hyphen, used in the *-p parameter* subentry, has an ASCII value of 045 while the diagonal, used in the */p parameter* subentry, has an ASCII value of 047.

ASCII provides a sorting order for some symbols, upper- and lowercase letters *A* through *Z*, and numbers. This is actually a very limited set of characters. To meet the needs of an increasingly interconnected world a new standard was developed, the *Unicode Standard* (2003).

The Unicode Standard is the universal character encoding scheme for written characters and text. It defines a consistent way of encoding multilingual text that enables the exchange of text data internationally and creates the foundation for global software. . . .

While modeled on the ASCII character set, the Unicode Standard goes far beyond ASCII's limited ability to encode only the upper- and lowercase characters A through Z. It provides the capacity to encode all characters used for the written languages of the world. . . .

The Unicode Standard specifies a numeric value (code point) and name for each of its characters. In this respect, it is similar to other character encoding standards from ASCII onward. (1)

Version 4.0 of the *Unicode Standard* contains 96,382 characters. "The unified Han subset contains 70,207 ideographic characters defined by national and industry standards of China, Japan, Korea, Taiwan, Vietnam, and Singapore. In addition, the Unicode Standard includes punctuation marks, mathematical symbols, technical symbols, geometric shapes, and dingbats" (2003, 2). All in all, Unicode provides room for the encoding of over one million characters.

When indexes contain symbols that are used literally and fall outside of ASCII-defined order, the *Unicode Standard* can be used to ascertain a sorting rank for the symbol. Because of the massive scope of Unicode, indexers must be careful when assigning values to symbols. In version 4.0 of the standard, sixteen different characters appear in a table titled "Unicode Dash Characters" (2003, 156). The list includes familiar dashes such as the en dash, em dash, hyphen, and minus sign. Also included are the Armenian hyphen, figure dash, and swung dash. Current information about Unicode is provided by the Unicode Consortium (http://www.unicode.org).

When an entry begins with a symbol as a literal character, these entries should be placed at the beginning of the index, preceding any entries that begin with numbers or letters. When there are only a few such symbols, the indexer may wish to double-post the entry—as a symbol and also in the spelled-out version:

> \* (asterisk), as a wildcard character, 56
> ? (question mark), as a wildcard character, 57
> asterisk (\*), as a wildcard character, 56
> question mark (?), as a wildcard character, 57

When these symbols appear within an entry, the sort order precedence is the same as when they appear at the beginning of an entry. That is, symbols precede numbers, which precede letters:

> Control-!, 67
> Control-\*, 35
> Control-1, 89
> Control-9, 45
> Control-A, 76
> Control-C, 55

In technical documentation different entries may be preceded by the same symbol. For example, in some programs all commands are preceded with a "control" character, as in ^B or ^C. When there will be many entries of this type in the index, the indexer may decide to ignore the special character when sorting the entries. This way an entry such as ^B *command* would appear in the B's and ^C *command* in the C's. In this case, an introductory note at the beginning of the index should explain the sorting method.

It is commonplace that indexers working with technical material must cope with several types of symbols in entries. Often the symbols are ignored and the entries are sorted in a letter-by-letter sequence. This type of arrangement may not require an explanatory note, since the interfiling of entries with and without symbols is immediately obvious to the index users. The 1992 edition of the *Microsoft Windows Resource Kit for Operating System Version 3.1* contains an index where entries often begin with or contain various symbols. In the following example, note how the indexer has interfiled these types of entries:

Default
_DEFAULT.PIF
Deleting files
DLL (dynamic-link library)
DLL filename extension
Network Assistant
Networks and Windows 3.1
[Network] section
[Network_Specific] section
[Network_Version] section
[New.groups] section
NewSpace
Nonmaskable interrupts (NMI)

Readers scanning this index will quickly ascertain the arrangement used by the indexer.

### Other Nonalphanumeric Characters in Entries

Many disciplines use special symbols and signs that have particular meaning within the discipline. In astronomy we find symbols for the sun, moon, and planets. There are special symbols that represent the signs of the zodiac and aspects and nodes of stellar objects. While these special characters may appear in the index, they are unlikely to appear as the first character in an entry. They probably would appear in parentheses after their names in the index. The key here is that they all have names. The name would be used as the alphabetizing term in the index.

For more information about the indexing of stellar object names, see the *Deep-Sky Name Index 2000.0,* by Hugh Maddocks (1991). As with registered marks, service marks, and trademarks, special symbols of this type will need a generic code if they are going in the index (see the discussion of generic coding in chapter 8).

The graphical user interface (GUI) that has become so prevalent in computer software poses special problems for the indexer of GUI documentation. Software with a graphical interface is characterized by the presence of icons that represent particular functions or tasks.

Before discussing icons, we should note a rather important characteristic of computer documentation in particular and technical documentation in general. A computer software manual, for instance, is part of a larger package that includes the program itself. In this sense the manual does not exist in and of itself; rather, it exists in relation to the software product. Many software manuals are intended to be used for reference purposes. Instead of reading them from front to back, readers turn to the manuals for information about particular aspects of the program. The software manual and its index attempt to provide a path from the program, or what is seen on a monitor, to specific information in the text.

When programs were character-based rather than graphically oriented, many functions had a name that appeared on the monitor. The technical writer would use that name in the documentation, and the indexer would include the name in the index. It was quite simple; for example, the *Edit Fields command* would appear in the index in the *E*'s.

Today, however, we find that GUI-based software often presents users with images on their monitors that have no names. Some of these images, or icons as they are called, suggest their own names. But the names of many of the icons are impossible to figure out by just looking at them. The technical writer will undoubtedly write about how to use the icon and will use the icon name in the text. The challenge for the indexer is to provide access to the discussion about the particular icon when the readers may have no idea what the icon is called.

While some have suggested that the icons appear as small graphic representations in the text of the index, this still does not solve the problem of how to help readers locate them. If the icon appeared immediately after its name, for example, we still would have the problem of readers not necessarily knowing its name. If the icons appeared at the beginning of the index, how would we order them? If there are only a few icons, the order may not make much difference since the short list can be easily scanned.

But some of the more complex programs have many, many icons. It would not be easy to scan such a long list.

One solution used by some software publishers is to provide an appendix that includes all the program's icons along with their names. The appendix is a functional overview of the program—broken down by menus—then the commands, then icons associated with various modes of the program. Once the users know the name of the icon, they can look up information about the icon in the index. Another solution that is far more efficient is to provide a way for users to get the name of the icon while using the program.

The bottom line is that readers need to know the icon name. The index in a printed book is text-oriented. Users of indexes look up words. Technical writers and technical indexers use words. Users of GUI-type software need to be provided with a way to access the words used by the writers and indexers.

## Multiauthored Works

Multiauthored works come in a variety of forms. From an indexing perspective, the easiest type of multiauthored book to work with is one on which the authors have collaborated closely with an editor to help make the text a seamless, one-voice discussion. Working with a book of this type is similar to working with a single-authored text.

Far more indexing challenges are posed by books that contain submissions by multiple authors in which content editing has not been performed on the book as a whole but, instead, the individual submissions have been edited for internal consistency. Such books are fairly common in specialized subject areas. Often collections of papers are solicited on a specific topic and published as graduate-level textbooks. Another common example is the publication of proceedings from a conference as a collection of papers.

The primary problem for the indexer with this type of multiauthored publication is vocabulary control. Even when the collection of writings is about a narrow subject, multiple authors will use a variety of terms in writing about the same topic. The indexer will need to identify synonyms carefully and gather related information together under one term. Without careful vocabulary control, information in the index will be scattered.

As an example, different authors may refer to a hard disk drive in a computer in different ways. The indexer must decide on a term of choice, post all relevant information at that term, and cross-reference to the preferred term from the other terms. The following example illustrates scattered information:

> **hard disk drives, 34–37**
> **rigid disk drives, 125**
> **Winchester drives, 223**

A reader looking up *hard disk drives* would miss the information on pages 125 and 223. A better method would be for the indexer to consolidate the entries in the following way:

> **hard disk drives, 34–37, 125, 223**
> **rigid disk drives.** *See* **hard disk drives**
> **Winchester drives.** *See* **hard disk drives**

Often the content of multiauthored works is dense. Given the need for vocabulary control, the indexer should postpone extensive double-posting of information until the editing stage. When the indexer anticipates a vocabulary control problem, it is best to focus on gathering together related information rather than run the risk of scattering information. Making decisions about double-posting will be far easier when one can assess what has emerged from the text after it has been indexed.

Collections of papers are frequently highly technical. Such collections often represent cutting-edge work in a field. New theories and new terminology will often be introduced. Ideally, the indexer will be fluent in the language of the discipline and able to cope effectively with such technical material.

Some editors offer to send the indexer author-highlighted page proofs. Authors highlight the terms in their papers that they think should go in the index. Earlier in the book there was discussion of author highlights in general, with a single author highlighting terms in the text. Multiple-author highlights are generally not very helpful because of the absence of vocabulary control. Some authors will be far too detailed, while others will highlight only a few terms, not wishing to be involved in the process at all.

These days many conference proceedings are available at the time of the conference. Papers are submitted months in advance of the conference dates. While it is still rare for such proceedings to contain an index, more and more proceedings are appearing with alphabetical subject listings in the back. Authors are asked to submit index terms along with their papers; then these terms are collated and matched with the appropriate page numbers. This type of author-selected topic index is probably better than nothing and certainly provides ample evidence of the need for proper subject indexing in multiauthored works.

## Multivolume Works

A range of books may appear in multivolume editions: biographies, histories, technical manuals, and so on. Sometimes the volumes are published one at a time, with several years in between; other series are released all at once. It is common for individual volumes to be indexed individually. Then a cumulative index, or master index, is issued for the entire series after all volumes have been published.

The indexing of multivolume works can be manageable (at best) or a dreadful nightmare (at worst). The worst-case scenario is the collection that has missed every production deadline; instead of taking five years to publish, it has taken fifteen years. Each volume was indexed by a different person. None of the indexers were given much guidance regarding term selection and vocabulary control. And now it's time to produce a cumulative index to the series. The editor in charge of the cumulative index believes that the individual volume indexes can be merged and gently massaged by an index editor in a short time. The resulting cumulative index is a hodgepodge of scattered information with cross-references that go in seemingly endless loops.

Diane Ullius, formerly copy chief at Time-Life Books, managed the production of many of the Time-Life Books series. Each series generally averaged twenty volumes. The average length of each volume was approximately 160 pages, or around 60,000 words. During the production life of the series, a volume was produced every two months. With few exceptions, an index was produced for each volume, and some of the series did have a cumulative index, which typically appeared about two months after the publication of the final volume. Ullius points out that the ideal arrangement was to contract with a single indexer for an entire series.

> An individual indexer is more likely to maintain consistent terminology and a consistent conceptual approach to the index. The problems we discovered when multiple indexers worked on a series were more than differences in term selection. There were also significant differences in the depth of indexing and the conceptual design of the indexes.

Not all Time-Life series have a cumulative index. Ullius feels that the amount of topical overlap between the volumes is the key determinant of the need for a cumulative index. Volumes that are arranged in discrete topical or chronological units may not benefit from the production of a cumulative index.

Once the decision to produce a cumulative index has been made, Ullius points out,

> it's not just a matter of merging the individual volume indexes. We put as much time and effort into a 160-page index as we put into a 160-page narrative book. Work on the cumulative index begins long before the last volume in the series has been published. It is extremely important to budget an adequate amount of time for editing the cumulative index. Even if a single indexer has produced all the individual indexes, there will still be term consistency problems that must be resolved during the editing phase. Ideally, the indexer will be heavily involved with the preparation of the cumulative index. However, even with the best of planning it's still a challenge. (Personal communication, 1999)

Three tenets to keep in mind when dealing with multivolume indexes are (1) planning for indexing is necessary, (2) your plans will be incomplete, and (3) every step will take longer than anticipated.

Multivolume works, even when written by one author, pose some of the same vocabulary control problems that we find in multiauthored works. The maintenance of term consistency is crucial in multivolume works. It is important to identify any type of terminology that can be standardized. For example, in a ten-volume series about plants, there should be a uniform set of guidelines about how to post plant names.

When a large series of volumes is being indexed by a team of indexers, the team will work best with a formalized vocabulary. Preindexing activities may include the development of a thesaurus for indexing. The use of a classified set of terms may result in more consistent indexing. For more information about thesaurus and taxonomy design see *NISO Z39.19-200x, Guidelines for the Construction, Format, and Management of Monolingual Controlled Vocabularies.*

The indexing team needs a leader—one person the indexers can turn to for guidance and resolution of indexing problems. Ideally, the index project manager/editor will be involved in the crucial planning stages as well. It is folly to believe that eight competent indexers working independently without supervision will produce eight indexes that will cumulate flawlessly.

Even if a cumulative index for a series is not being produced, the individual-volume indexes need to be as consistent with each other as possible, because readers will use indexes from various volumes. Readers should be able to look up the same topic in the same way in each index. Readers will be frustrated if they must rethink how a term might be posted as they move from one index to another.

### Reference Locator Format for Cumulative Indexes

Often the reference locator format for cumulative indexes is not as straightforward as the format for a single-volume index. If each volume in a series begins pagination anew, the volume number and page number for each entry will need to be identified. Each volume is likely to be numbered, with the number visible on the spine of the book. Whatever numbering system is used by the publisher to identify the volume should also be used in the cumulative index. If a publisher has used roman numerals for the volume numbers, roman numerals should be used in the cumulative index. A reference for page 35 of volume II and page 78 of volume V may look like the following:

>     term, II:35; V:78
>     term, *II*:35; *V*:78
>     term, (II)35; (V)78
>     term, *II* 35; *V* 78

The design of the reference locator format should be kept as simple as possible. Cumulative indexes tend to be dense and lengthy. A simple locator format that provides readers with the necessary information should not add significantly to the density of the index text.

When planning the locator format, it is important to consider how continuous discussions in the form of page ranges will be handled. Will it be necessary to repeat the volume number?

>     term, II-35 to II-39

Or can the locator be designed in such a way that the volume number is not repeated? The latter alternative will save space.

>     term, II:35–39

In the case of multiple references from the same volume, will the volume number be repeated?

>     term, II:35–39, II:68, II:235

Ideally, the volume number should not be repeated, as it is in the example above. This format takes up a lot of space and will surely create more turnover lines. However, we must also assume that there will be entries with not only multiple references from the same volume but also multiple references from multiple volumes. Readers need to be able to distinguish references from various volumes without becoming confused. Repeating the volume numbers with each locator is perhaps the most accurate approach. But careful design of the locator can provide accurate results while producing an easily read line of text:

term, *II:*35–39, 68, 235; *V:*78, 123; *VIII:*78–85, 97
term, *II* 35–39, 68, 235; *V* 78, 123; *VIII* 78–85, 97

Notice that in the examples above, commas are used to separate references from the same volume while semicolons are used to separate references from different volumes. If bold or italic typefaces are used in the text of the index, one should be careful about using such typefaces in the reference locators. Index pages that are dense and cluttered with various typographical elements are difficult to use.

### Are Cumulative Indexes Necessary for All Multivolume Works?

Just because a group of books form a series it does not necessarily follow that a cumulative index for the entire series will be useful or worth the time and expense of producing it. When the individual components of a series stand on their own, quite independent of other titles in the series, a cumulative index is probably not necessary. Let's take the example of a nature series that includes titles such as *Rocks, Mammals, Plants,* and *Climate.* Readers interested in locating information about hurricanes will turn to the index in the *Climate* book. Likewise, readers interested in bears will probably go immediately to the *Mammals* book. Such readers are unlikely to need the cumulative index to find the proper volume. Assuming that each volume has its own index, most readers will find the use of a cumulative index a cumbersome extra step.

On the other hand, when the individual books in a series are closely interrelated, a cumulative index to the series may prove extremely useful. A five-volume collection of a writer's diary entries would be enhanced by a cumulative index to all five volumes. Undoubtedly there will be people and places that are referred to in all five volumes. A cumulative index will save readers time by gathering together all these related references. Without a cumulative index, readers will have to look up particular entries in five separate indexes.

### Multiple Indexes

Most books are published with a single index, whose primary benefit is that readers need look in only one place for information. In some situations, though, the readers' needs may be better served by multiple indexes. In legal works, for instance, the subject index is frequently preceded by a table of cases.

Multiple indexes can be useful when there are discrete types of entries that can stand alone in their own index. Quite often a secondary index is a specialized subset of the general subject index. The different indexes are designed for different types of users, with one group having more specialized subject knowledge than the other group.

A subject index and a command index might be appropriate for a computer software manual. The subject index contains entries for the "plain English" version of the commands. The command index contains entries for the commands themselves. For example, the subject index may have an entry *saving a file*, while the command index may cite the same information as ∧*KD* (*save a file*) and *Alt-F7* (*save a file*).

Entries for plant names in a gardening book may appear in their vernacular form in the subject index, while a separate botanical name index cites the formal names.

| Subject Index | Botanical Name Index |
|---|---|
| English ivy | *Hedera helix* |
| redwood | *Sequoia sempervirens* |
| scrub oak | *Quercus dumosa* |

When a book has references to many people, a separate name index can help make a subject index easier to use because it is not cluttered with names. In the same vein, a book that contains many references to authors and titles of works may benefit from the inclusion of a separate index of authors and titles cited.

The decision to provide multiple indexes should not be made lightly. As Pat Booth (2001, 19) points out, "Before deciding to make separate sequences of headings, the indexer should be certain that this arrangement will be the best for the user, remembering always that separation has the disadvantage of requiring the user to understand the distinction and to find the required sequence. As always, each case must be decided on its merits."

If there is more than one index, each should be titled in a clear manner so as to distinguish it from the other. It is good practice to reference the other index in the introductory note: "Following the subject index is a command index." And "Preceding the command index is a general subject index."

The decision to provide multiple indexes is ideally made before indexing begins. The indexer will need to maintain multiple sets of entries. While this is not very difficult to do, it is best done right from the start.

Another matter to keep in mind in regard to multiple indexes is that they are more difficult to revise in the future than are single indexes. If a book and its index will definitely be revised in the future, it is best to approach multiple indexes for this type of text with some caution. During the index revision process, revising a single group of index entries will be much easier than revising multiple groups of entries.

## Translations

As the publishing industry becomes increasingly global, many more books will be translated from one language to another. There will arise the matter of what to do with the index. There are two options: translate the original index, or index the translation.

Because a properly written index is so intimately tied to the language of the audience, the most viable solution would seem to be to index the translated text. A simpleminded, word-by-word translation of the index could easily result in a loss of nuance. For example, the double-posting of synonymous terms that make sense to an American audience may make no sense to a German audience. An index that anticipated the vocabulary needs of an American audience may appear chauvinistic to a French audience if translated verbatim. Another argument in favor of indexing the translation is that the process will probably take no more time than translating an existing index and changing the page numbers to match the new text.

*The Oxford Guide to Style* clearly recommends that the index be translated (Ritter et al. 2002, 13.11.1.9):

> It is a translator's duty to translate all main and subordinate entries in the index, and to put them in English alphabetical order. Since, from a publisher's point of view, you will count as the author of that edition of the work, normal practice makes you responsible for inserting, or causing an indexer to insert, the correct page numbers from the proofs. If this is unacceptable, please raise the matter when the contract is drawn up. Notify the editor if the original index is so unsatisfactory that a new one must be provided.

Aside from the problems inherent in translating an index, most translators, like most authors, lack indexing experience. See chapter 2 for an overview of the problems faced by authors writing their own indexes.

In the United States there has been significant growth in Spanish-language publishing. Many titles are translated into Spanish, while others are originally written in Spanish. In a 2003 interview, Janet Perlman of Southwest Indexing had this to say:

> An area that has taken prominence in my business recently is Spanish-language materials. In the past few years I have seen a tremendous upswing in demand for indexers of Spanish materials, and I've been happy to continue to add clients in this area to the point where it now makes up between a third and a half of my business. (Mulvany 2003b, 2)

There are far more indexers with multilanguage skills than there are translators with indexing skills. The various professional indexers' societies maintain listings of indexers with language skills.

## Single-source Indexing

The globalization of business has greatly impacted the technical documentation community. Today there is enormous pressure to provide product documentation in multiple formats and languages, all with a simultaneous release date. Let's use the example of a word-processing program. The documentation for this program will be provided in multiple formats. For example,

printed manual
electronic manual on a CD
online help
Web-site knowledge base files

Additionally, the program will be released simultaneously throughout North America, South America, and Europe. Release throughout the rest of the world will follow within a month. The multiple formats listed above will need to be localized for the various foreign markets.

> To many people, localization sounds like "just a linguistic process" identical or similar to translation. However, while translation plays an important role in the localization of all text-based products, the process of localization is actually much broader that this. The Localization Standards Association (LISA) defines localization as "the process of modifying products or services to account for differences in distinct markets." (Lommel 2003, 13)

In 2003 LISA reported that "enterprises may be localizing products regularly into 60 or more languages (and sometimes in excess of 170)" (Lommel 2003, 17). When properly executed, localization is a complex process. In 2003, LISA estimated "the total size of the localization world-wide at a minimum of USD 3.7 billion per annum, with a likely figure around USD 5 billion (some estimates put it as high as USD 15 billion). . . . To give a comparison: recent figures for the size of the translation industry range from 'between USD 11 billion and USD 18 billion' (American Translators' Association) to USD 30 billion (European Commission)" (Lommel 2003, 18–19). It is evident that the localization and translation of text is a large industry that will continue to experience great growth.

In the word-processing program example, the four formats would be localized and translated into at least twenty languages. *Single-sourcing* refers to the creation of a single set of documentation files that will eventually be converted to multiple formats and localized for various global markets. Ann Rockley sums up the impact of single-sourcing on technical communicators in this way:

> Typically, writers have been responsible for creating the content, formatting the content, and "publishing" the content in a variety of formats. These roles have meant that writers have had to become tools experts—oftentimes "jacks of all trades and masters of none." Single sourcing separates the creation of content from the output. As a result, the writer is responsible for content, and the information technologist is responsible for handling all aspects of the output. (Rockley 2001, 193)

In regard to software documentation, the goal of single-sourcing is to create a basic documentation set (or *single-source document*) that can be output in multiple formats, including translation into other languages. The index entries are embedded in the single-source document. (For the many problems with embedded indexing software, see chapter 10.)

In her paper, "Single-source Indexing," Jan C. Wright points out:

> As more and more people try to get one index to work in all the content they produce from a base set of files, whether print or online, it becomes evident that indexes are not just another piece of content to be converted to another format. Since they function as search tools, they should change their functionality to best utilize the interface they are residing in.
>
> Indexes, by their very nature, are not straightforward pieces of content. They have a database nature to their construction that is often not considered until they undergo a conversion process. (Wright 2001, 208)

Wright also notes, "Every single-sourcing project uses different tool sets, different conversion methods, and different compilers. Tools are chosen to meet a variety of output needs, and sadly sometimes the index isn't considered when the choices are made" (2001, 211). Indexers working on single-source projects would benefit from a thorough reading of Wright's article. She identifies potential problems for various situations, offers solutions, and provides a checklist of issues to consider.

Indexers of single-source documents must be aware of the functional limitations of the software tools that are used to produce the various other formats. Additionally, there are many issues to address in writing for an international audience. The Sun Microsystems' *Style Guide for the Computer Industry* offers this general advice (Sun 2003, 135):

> More and more business transactions and communications occur over the World Wide Web, which is an international medium. Writing documentation that can be easily translated into other languages and delivered to audiences in other countries is becoming a mandate for the computer industry. Fortunately, the guidelines that you need to follow when writing for an international audience also apply to good technical writing in general.

Guidelines for writing an index that will be translated do not differ greatly from those for index writing in general. The single-source indexer must work with the terminology present in the text. However, there are situations when the indexer's discretion can be helpful to translators.

Consistency in index term selection is extremely important. Synonymous terms are often used in technical documentation. While double-posting such terms can be a user-friendly technique in an English-language index, it can cause serious problems in a translated index. For example, the translator may not understand that the two index entries are synonymous; in fact, when translated, the two entries may have entirely different meanings. Instead of double-posting this type of information, it is better to gather it in one place and use *See* cross-references from the other terms.

When an index will be translated, consistency and precision in term selection are extremely important. When an index will be produced in multiple formats, indexers must be aware of the technical limitations of the tools that will be used.

> When I do single-sourcing, I always index to the least competent of the environments the index will be displayed in, which is the online component. The print indexes always look off, not fully featured, because of that process. (Wright 2003, 8)

# Chapter Seven

## NAMES, NAMES, NAMES

At first glance, names in a text might seem to be easily handled. The first time I was asked to produce a separate name index for a book, I thought it would be a simple task. The book, which was about the Italian section of San Francisco, contained many Italian names, with amazing combinations of vowels. The task proved to be quite tedious. There were the usual typos, making it difficult to discern who was who. Many of the women mentioned in the text were married, and therefore their names had changed. Various devices had to be used to distinguish two people with the same name. This first experience with a name index made me suspicious of future requests from editors to "throw together a simple name index."

One of the problems with names is that they often change. This is true not only of personal names but also of organization names and geographic names. The rule of thumb regarding names is to post the entries in the way that readers are most likely to look them up. Keep this important rule in mind as we discuss the nuances of personal names, geographic names, organization names, and names of works.

Noeline Bridge (2002) identifies six patterns of name problems:

1. order in which to enter names
2. length or brevity of names
3. one-word names
4. distinguishing between names that are similar
5. names that change
6. spelling of transliterated names

These are indeed issues that every indexer will face at some time or another. While it is not necessary or practical for the working indexer to know every rule for every situation, it is important to know where to turn for authoritative guidance.

The American Library Association's *Anglo-American Cataloging Rules* (2002) is a primary reference source for personal names. Particular references to this tome will be cited as follows: *AACR2* (section number). One of the most comprehensive sources of reference information is Hazel Bell's *Indexing Biographies* (2004); chapter 15 addresses printed reference works, and the appendix prepared by Noeline Bridge discusses Internet resources. Noeline Bridge's article "Verifying Personal Names on the Web" (2003) includes useful online sources, some of which are cited below.

## Personal Names

Many Western names are composed of at least two elements: a forename (first name) and a surname (last name). Such names are inverted in the index so that the surname is the element that is first alphabetized. Thus, *Virginia Woolf* is entered in the index as *Woolf, Virginia*.

The way names are presented in the text will often determine how they are presented in the index. If an author discusses *John F. Kennedy*, the name should be indexed as *Kennedy, John F.*, not as *Kennedy, John Fitzgerald*.

It is not uncommon in texts or scholarly works to find a name given only as a surname. When only a surname is given, it may be that the individual is well enough known within the context of the book that no forename need also be given. For example, we often see references to Freud or Columbus or, in a book about indexing, to Knight. In situations like this, when the author has provided only a surname, the indexer must add the forename or initials to the surname when posting the entry. It is very bad form to have a surname standing alone as an entry. The examples above would be posted as

> **Columbus, Christopher**
> **Freud, Sigmund**
> **Knight, G. Norman**

Indexers who expect to encounter personal names in their work will benefit from having reference sources at hand. In the United States the primary authority for entry format of names is the Library of Congress catalog (http://catalog.loc.gov/). If the name cannot be located there, library catalogers are apt to look up how the name is handled in *The New Encyclopaedia Britannica* (http://www.britannica.com), *Academic American Encyclopedia (1990)*, and *The Encyclopedia Americana (1990)*. If the name is entered the same way in all three of these sources, then that is the form used. If the form varies in these sources, the form in *The New Encyclopaedia Britannica* generally takes precedence. Another useful resource is the

*Columbia Encyclopedia* (2000), also made available online by Columbia University's Project Bartleby (http://www.bartleby.com/65/).

For general purposes another reference choice is *Merriam-Webster's Biographical Dictionary* (1995). *The Librarians' Index to the Internet* (http://lii.org) has a "People" section that lists biographical dictionary Web sites. There are also many specialized references for different fields, such as the *Who's Who* series, the *New Catholic Encyclopedia* (2003), *Encyclopaedia Judaica* (1972), and *The Oxford Classical Dictionary* (Hornblower and Spawforth, 2003), to name a few. The Getty Research Institute provides the *Union List of Artist Names* (1994) online at: http://www.getty.edu/research/conducting_research/vocabularies/ulan/. The Web sites of the Canadian and American indexing societies (see appendix B) also contain useful lists of online resources.

In a book that contains many references to individuals, the indexer may be able to find in the bibliography the full names of the people mentioned in the text by their surnames only. For this reason, indexers should always request a copy of the bibliography, even though the actual contents of the bibliography are not being indexed. Make it clear to the editor that you need the bibliography for reference. It need not be typeset; manuscript copy is better than nothing!

There is some debate regarding how far the indexer should go to provide a complete, full citation for a name. Let the treatment of the name in the text and common sense be your guide. In the case of Columbus, if the author has made reference to the explorer's Spanish name, Cristobal Colon, or the Genoese name, Cristoforo Colombo, the indexer should provide cross-references.

> Colombo, Cristoforo. *See* Columbus, Christopher
> Colon, Cristobal. *See* Columbus, Christopher

But if the author has made no reference to Columbus's other names, there is no need for the indexer to insert these lesser-known variations in the index.

### Pseudonyms

Often pseudonyms are pen names used by authors or stage names used by actors. Or, as Knight points out, a pseudonym might be used "to court obscurity after disgrace, as Oscar Wilde ended his days in Paris under the name of Sebastian Melmoth" (1979, 66–67).

Whatever the reason for the use of a pseudonym, if the text does not make mention of the real name, the indexer need not provide a reference to it. For instance, a book about American authors that discusses Mark Twain with no mention of his given name, Samuel Clemens, needs only an entry for *Twain, Mark*.

If the text provides both the real name and the pseudonym, both variations must be in the index. Whichever form is predominantly used in the text is the form in which the entries should be posted. A discussion of George Orwell that includes an initial reference to the writer's real name would be handled in this way:

**Blair, Eric Arthur.** *See* **Orwell, George**

All the index entries for George Orwell would be gathered together under *Orwell, George*. Likewise, if most of the discussion in the text refers to a real name, the pseudonym would provide a cross-reference.

**Cross, Amanda.** *See* **Heilbrun, Carolyn G.**

It may be helpful in some indexes to add the pseudonym in parentheses after the real name. Such a descriptor may assure readers that they have indeed located the proper reference.

**Heilbrun, Carolyn G. (pseudonym: Amanda Cross)**

The addition of such descriptors, however, should be left to the discretion of the indexer. An entry for as well known a writer as Samuel Clemens would not necessarily need such a descriptor. As with any entry, name entries are best kept as short as possible without sacrificing clarity.

## Names That Change

Personal names can change for a variety of reasons. An individual entering a religious order may replace a secular name with a religious name: a woman named Mary Jackson, say, becomes Sister Anthony. Some individuals may legally change their names: Delbert Hodgepuss, say, petitions the court to change his name to Mack Turner. Many immigrants to the United States changed their names so that they would sound less foreign: Bohimer Veverka changes his name to Bruce Vevera, for example. By far the most common instance of name changing in patriarchal societies occurs when a woman marries and takes on her husband's surname.

In any situation in which a name has changed, the indexer must decide whether it is necessary to provide a cross-reference from an earlier name to the name currently used. The text of the document often provides guidance in this matter. If the author has referred to a name that is not currently used, then the indexer must provide a cross-reference.

Bouvier, Jacqueline. *See* Onassis, Jacqueline
Kennedy, Jacqueline. *See* Onassis, Jacqueline

The matter of cross-referencing is very much determined by the text. The index should not be a vehicle for the indexer to demonstrate prowess in tracking down the genealogical roots of every individual mentioned in a text. Nor should the index attempt to compensate for less than thorough research by the author. On the other hand, through the use of simple devices, the indexer can add depth to an entry. In historical or genealogical works indexers may include a woman's maiden name in parentheses and provide a cross-reference to her married name:

Agee, Victoria (Powers)
Powers, Victoria. *See* Agee, Victoria

## Compound Names

Names that are composed of three or more name elements, sometimes with the last two joined by a hyphen, are compound names. Do note that a distinction is made between a compound surname and a surname that includes articles or prepositions. Ascertaining which element to use for alphabetizing can be difficult.

If there is a preferred or commonly known form of a compound name, it should be alphabetized under the preferred element. For example, the paternal surname for David Lloyd George is "George." However, he is known as "Lloyd George" and is entered in the index in that manner:

Lloyd George, David

Knight's discussion (1979, 69) of the alphabetizing of Sir Winston Spencer Churchill is another example of using a preferred form. The name was originally presented as Spencer-Churchill. But most readers, and indeed Sir Winston himself, would expect and prefer references at *Churchill* instead.

Again, hints from the text can guide the indexer. If the element preceding the last surname element is usually presented as an initial, this is an indication that the abbreviated element should not be used for alphabetizing. If Mary Daley Stanton is commonly referred to as Mary D. Stanton, then *Stanton* is the element used for indexing.

Familiarity with the subject matter is of course a great asset. Someone indexing material that is not her specialty may easily misinterpret a reference to the English composer Vaughan Williams. Instead of entering the name as *Vaughan Williams, Ralph*, the indexer may post it in the *W*'s, which would be incorrect. Referring to a biographical dictionary would be wise in situations like this. When there is doubt about which element to alphabetize first, the indexer should pay careful attention to the way the author has handled the name. Of course, the name may not be used again until much later in the book. However, the careful indexer will maintain a query list so that sorting problems such as these can be resolved. As a last resort, the book editor can be consulted. But indexers should keep in mind that it is their job to solve such problems, and only particularly troublesome name problems should be referred to the book editor.

When a compound surname is hyphenated, the name is alphabetized under the first element:

> **Dalton-Smith, George**
> **Hills-Fenworth, Alice**

When a name appears in compound form without hyphenation, the indexing task becomes more difficult. The indexer must then decide how to enter the name in the index. Again, the first place to turn for guidance is the text. Let's say that Thomas Parsons Brinkerhoff is formally introduced using the complete name and later is referred to as "Parsons Brinkerhoff." The indexer would pick up this clue from the text and enter the name in the index as

> **Parsons Brinkerhoff, Thomas**

Unfortunately, the indexer is not always provided with such guidance in the text. The next recourse for the indexer is to check the reference sources mentioned earlier in this chapter. If the name cannot be located in reference sources, and the person's language is English or one of the Scandinavian languages, *AACR2* (22.5C6) recommends entry under the last part of the name:

> **Davenport, Susan Grissom**
> **Eklund, James Swann**

Married women's names sometimes take the form of compound surnames composed of a maiden name and a husband's surname. The husband's surname is the element generally recommended for entry. For example,

> **Stowe, Harriet Beecher**

Frequently it is assumed that the maiden name precedes the husband's surname in a married woman's name, and indeed, this is often the case. But the arrangement of a married woman's compound surname is not always predicated on the "maiden name first, husband's surname last" rule. These days the names may be arranged on the basis of aesthetics, on which arrangement sounds better or looks better. Let's say that Susan Smith marries Harry Jackson; she decides to be called Susan Jackson Smith because to her that arrangement sounds better. The indexer who may know nothing of the marriage can safely enter the name in the index as *Smith, Susan Jackson*. The indexer can dispense with the patriarchal rule regarding husband's surname first and instead follow the guidance in *AACR2* (22.5C6) and enter the name under the final element.

Note that if the compound surname is Czech, French, Hungarian, Italian, or Spanish, *AACR2* (22.5C5) recommends that the first element of the compound be used as the entry element.

### Names with "Saint"

Some publishers' style guides recommend that personal names in the form of a saint's name be alphabetized as if the "St." were spelled out as "Saint." However, the names retain their original spelling, whether "Saint" or "St." This rule results in alphabetized lists such as

> **St. Albans, Marie**
> **St. George, Francis**
> **Saint Thomas, Claire**

Sorting abbreviated "St." names as if they are spelled out is yet another quirk that has become common practice. Anytime an alphabetic list is not sorted alphabetically we must take pause. We must consider the users' needs. Is it likely that index users intuitively know that names with "St." will not be sorted as they are spelled? It should be noted that the fifteenth edition of *The Chicago Manual of Style* recommends that "a family name in the form of a saint's name is alphabetized letter by letter as the name is spelled, whether *Saint, San, St.*, or however" (2003, 18.73). The three names above, when alphabetized as they are given, would appear as

> **Saint Thomas, Claire**
> **St. Albans, Marie**
> **St. George, Francis**

### Christian Saints

The names of Christian saints are not alphabetized in the *S*'s with the word "Saint" preceding their names. Instead, they are entered under one of the other elements of the name. The *New Catholic Encyclopedia* (2003) is a good reference for the form of name entries for saints and popes.

> **Francis of Assisi, Saint**
> **Gonzaga, Luigi, Saint**
> **Teresa of Avila, Saint**

### Names with "Mac," "Mc," or "M'"

As with names with "Saint," some publishers' style guides recommend that abbreviated forms of "Mac," that is, "Mc" and "M,'" be alphabetized as if spelled out as "Mac." Such a recommendation results in lists such as

> McBain, Sally
> McDougal, Jeremy
> Macintosh, George

We have here another situation in which entries are arranged out of alphabetic order. *The Chicago Manual of Style* recommends that "names beginning with *Mac* or *Mc* are alphabetized letter by letter, as they appear" (2003, 18.71). *ISO 999* recommends that contractions "should be filed as given, not as if spelt out in their fullest form" (7.3.6). Knight rightly points out that "with African names the prefix M' is not a contraction for Mac. Thus the township of M'Baiki would have to be listed between, say, Mazgirt (Turkey) and Mbala" (1979, 121).

In regard to the abbreviated forms of "Mac" and "Saint," the primary reason one might wish to sort these names as if they are spelled out is to gather these similar names together in one place. Most people, though, expect an index to be arranged in alphabetic order. Thus, names that are not arranged in alphabetic order can be confusing. Certainly, forms of names with "Mac" and "Saint" are not the only names that sound alike but are spelled differently. It is not unreasonable to ask how far we might go with this type of alphabetizing quirk. Should all names that sound like "Harrison" be placed in the same location in the index, including Harison, Harrisson, and Harisson? Pat Booth and Mary Piggott, authors of *Choice and Form of Entries* (1988, sec. 4.1.1.1, p. 27), offer a sensible solution.

> Where names that sound alike may be spelled differently, a reference from one form to the other will be necessary. If the name is of a single person or family, a *see* reference should be made, as Ussher *see* Usher. If more than one family's name appears in the index and alternative spellings could be overlooked, *see also* references should be made between the alternatives.
>
> > fford *see also* Ford
> > Ford *see also* fford
> > Philips *see also* Phillips
> > Phillips *see also* Philips

The Booth and Piggott recommendation ensures that the index will remain in alphabetic order and that readers will be guided to alternative spellings of homophonous names.

## Titles in Names

Titles preceding names come in a variety of forms: Mr. John Smith, Dr. Lisa Jones, Msgr. Joseph Reilly, Lady Jane Maddocks, Capt. Marcia Miller. While there is disagreement about whether to retain a title in the index, one general rule can be discerned. If two entries are identical, a title can be used effectively to distinguish between the two.

> Smith, John
> Smith, John (Capt.)

Some indexers place the title before the forename, as in *Smith, Capt. John*. However, the title is not used as a secondary sort field. The entry for Capt. Smith would still be adjacent to the other John Smith entry.

Some style guides require that clerical titles be retained in the index while others suggest that they be dropped. One problem with many titles, including clerical titles, is that they can indeed change during the course of discussion. For example, when Joseph Reilly is introduced on page 35, he may be a monsignor. But by the time we reach page 278, Reilly may be an archbishop. If there is more than one Joseph Reilly in the index, then it will be necessary to distinguish one from the other. In a case like this, the highest ranking title should be used:

> Reilly, Joseph (Archbishop of Kensington)

If there is only one Joseph Reilly in the index, the title may be safely dropped without grave consequences.

Titles of nobility present a tangled web indeed for indexers living in societies lacking a formal tradition of peerage. Indexers who must deal with titles of nobility should consult appropriate reference sources. Section 22.12 in *AACR2* provides a simple overview. In regard to British titles, Booth and Piggott (1988) provide useful examples that may meet the needs of many indexers. These authors also recommend the following references: the current edition of *Who's Who* and Valentine Heywood's *British Titles* (1951).

Though British titles of rank are complex, a simple overview, drawn from Booth and Piggott, can offer guidance. Titles are often retained in the index entry; however, the placement of the title within the entry can vary. The recommendation regarding "Dame," "Sir," "Lord," and "Lady" is to place the title in front of the forename:

> Maddocks, Lady Jane
> Shelton, Sir James

Note that the "Lord" and "Lady" above are used as courtesy titles. The handling of the title is different when the wife of a knight or baronet is given the title "Lady." In this situation, the title is placed after the fore-name:

> **Hunt, Mary, Lady**

But if the woman is also the daughter of a duke, duchess, marquess, marchioness, earl, or countess, the title is placed before the forename. The daughter of a countess would be entered in this way:

> **Hunt, Lady Mary**

If an individual has a title of honor, but does not use the title, the title should be omitted:

> **Christie, Agatha,** *not* **Christie, Dame Agatha**

Booth (2001, 92) sums up the situation in this way: "Some British names with titles follow rules that are not part of common knowledge and if they are to be indexed it can be time-consuming to check the necessary background." Among other guides to British peerage and aristocracy, Hazel K. Bell (2004, 88) recommends *Burke's Genealogical and Heraldic History of the Peerage, Baronetage, and Knightage* (n.d.) and *Debrett's People of Today* (n.d.). David Lee's article (1991), "Coping with a Title: The Indexer and the British Aristocracy," is also recommended.

*AACR2* provides suggestions for handling names of persons who acquire new titles or disclaim titles (22.6B3). *The Chicago Manual of Style* recommends, "Princes and princesses are usually indexed under their given names. Duke, earls, and the like are indexed under the title" (2003, 18.38). Furthermore, it is suggested that "Lord," "Lady," "Sir," and "Dame" not be included in the index entry unless the title is necessary for identification. If they are used in the index, these titles are ignored in alphabetizing.

Titles of nobility are not restricted to British names. Indexers working with names of nobility from other countries should consult appropriate references.

### Names Followed by Abbreviations

When names are followed by abbreviations for degrees, such as "PhD" or "MD," the abbreviation is not retained in the index. If a name includes an abbreviation like "Jr." or "Sr." or "III," the abbreviation is retained in the index but placed after the forename.

> **Roosevelt, Theodore, Jr.**
> **Tittwillow, James R., III**

Not only can people whose names have titles and abbreviations be troublesome; animals can also pose problems. Take the example of a 350-page book that chronicles the history of a particular breed of dog. The indexer will undoubtedly be confronted with hundreds, if not thousands, of dog names. Many of these names will be composed of titles, both preceding and following a kennel name. Also, many of the dogs will be best known by their "call names" (the name they are called at home). The indexer may need to devise an unorthodox arrangement. For example, the introductory note to the index may point out that the designation "Ch." for "Champion" that precedes many names will not be alphabetized and that names in parentheses following kennel names indicate the call names. If the "Ch." preceding the name were sorted, there would be hundreds of names listed in the *C*'s. However, it is important to retain the "Ch." in the name, and, because other titles are placed after the kennel name, the "Ch." must remain in front. The name index for this dog book may contain entries in the following order:

> Ch. Aberlon's Catch the Hawk, CD, JH, WD (Gavin)
> Ch. Aberlon's Catch the Wind (Macy)
> Ch. Aberlon's Daring Dazzler, CD, JH (Daz)
> Afternod Ember of Gordon Hill
> Ch. Afternod Robena of Aberdeen
> Ch. Afternod Yank of Rockaplenty, CD
> Ch. Blackthorn's Thistle of Kymry, CD (Tulip)
> Hacasak Grand Ute
> Ch. Harvest Going in Style (Questor)
> Hugh's Sir Gordie of Windy Hill
> Ch. Loch Adair Kate
> Ch. Rockaplenty Hang Em High
> Rockaplenty Inherit the Wind
> Ch. Torrance of Ellicot

An important point to remember about names is that there is often more to the arrangement of names than at first meets the eye. Whatever devices an indexer uses, they must be used consistently. And decisions regarding the arrangement of names must be guided by the needs of the readers. Even though, in the kennel name listings above, the names are not in strict alphabetic order, a consistent method has been used to arrange the names so that dogs with the same kennel name are gathered together. Furthermore, the indexer will have placed a headnote to the index explaining the arrangement conventions.

## Names with Only a Forename

A name that does not include a surname can be indexed under the given name. Include modifying phrases that help distinguish the name from other names that are the same.

> Charles II, King of France
> Charles II, King of Great Britain
> John, the Baptist
> John XXIII, Pope

## Roman Names

*AACR2* recommends that a Roman living before AD 476 be entered under the part of the name that is most commonly used (22.9):

> **Cicero, Marcus Tullius**

If the text is unclear or there is any doubt regarding the element to use for entry, the recommendation is to enter the name in uninverted order:

> **Martianus Capella**

## Obscure Names

Sometimes a text makes reference to an individual by only a forename or a surname. If such references are indexable and the full name cannot be ascertained, the name is entered as given in the text and further identified by a qualifying phrase:

> **Sarah (Lady Jane's handmaid)**

## Names with Particles

Complete information regarding the nuances of indexing all types of names is beyond the scope of this book. It is hoped that enough information is presented here to guide the indexer through casual encounters with non-Anglo names. Far more detailed reference sources should be sought when the indexer confronts more than a handful of such names. The primary reference for this section is *Anglo-American Cataloging Rules (2002) (AACR2)*.

## General Rules

If a surname contains articles or prepositions or a combination of the two, the portion of the name most commonly used should be the basis for alphabetizing. The author's use of the surname in the text will guide the indexer. If the use of the name in the text is not clear, the indexer may wish to refer to an appropriate biographical dictionary. If the name cannot be located in a reference source, the following rules for handling articles and prepositions in surnames, adapted from *AACR2* (22.5D1), may be consulted. *AACR2* differs greatly in some instances from the rules used in Merriam-Webster's biographical dictionaries, particularly in relation to particles in European names. The *AACR2* rules are presented because of their growing acceptance around the world. But regardless of how a name is posted in the index, if there is any doubt about readers' ability to locate a name, the indexer must provide cross-references from alternative posting locations.

## Afrikaans

The Afrikaans name should be entered under the prefix.

> Du Plessis, Menán
> Van der Post, Christiaan Willem Hendrik

Also see the helpful information provided by Cynthia Bertelsen in *Issues in Cataloging Non-Western Materials: Special Problems with African Language Materials* (1996).

## American and English

American, Australian, Canadian, or British names should be entered under the prefix.

> De Havilland, Sir Geoffrey (British aeronautical engineer)
> de la Roche, Mazo (Canadian novelist)
> De Peyster, Abraham (American merchant and shipowner)
> Van Buren, Martin (American president)
> Van de Graff, Robert J. (American physicist)

## Dutch

In Dutch names, if the prefix is *ver,* enter under the prefix. Otherwise enter under the name following the prefix.

> Brink, Bernhard ten
> Hertog, Ary den
> Roos, Sjoerd Hendrik de
> Ver Boven, Daisy

## French

If the prefix in a French name consists of an article or a contraction of an article and a preposition, the prefix should be used for alphabetizing. If the prefix is a preposition, the part of the name following the preposition should be used.

> Aubigné, Théodore Agrippa d'
> Du Bos, Charles
> Du Guesclin, Bertrand
> La Fontaine, Jean de
> Musset, Alfred de
> Toulouse-Lautrec, Henri de

In the case of a compound French surname, *AACR2* recommends that the name be entered under the first element (22.5C5).

## German

Enter German names under the prefix when the prefix consists of an article or a contraction of an article and a preposition. Otherwise, enter under the name following the prefix.

> Am Thym, August
> Beethoven, Ludwig van
> Goethe, Johann Wolfgang von
> Richthofen, Manfred von
> Zur Linde, Otto

## Hungarian

Many indexing guides (*The Chicago Manual of Style 2003*, 18.77) direct that Hungarian names be presented with the surname first, followed by a forename. The name is entered in the index in the same form, with a comma inserted after the surname. Thus, the text reference for Molnár Ferenc is cited in the index as

> Molnár, Ferenc

Section 22.15B2 of *AACR2* advises, "Include the enclitic *né* attached to the names of some Hungarian married women." Additionally, in the case of a compound Hungarian surname, *AACR2* recommends that the name be entered under the first element (22.5C5).

## Italian

Modern Italian names are entered under the prefix.

> De Martini, Luigi
> Della Piane, Giovanni
> Di Maggio, Giuseppe
> Lo Schiavo, Fiorello

If the name is of medieval origin, the indexer must determine whether the prefix is part of the name. According to *AACR2* (22.5D1), "*De, de', degli, dei*, and *de li* occurring in names of the period are rarely part of the surname." For example, Lorenzo de' Medici is entered as *Medici, Lorenzo de'*.

In the case of a compound Italian surname, *AACR2* recommends that the name be entered under the first element (22.5C5).

## Portuguese

The prefix of Portuguese names is not alphabetized, and the name is entered under the element following the prefix.

## Romanian
The prefix of Romanian names is used for alphabetizing, with the exception of *de*. In that case, use the element following the *de* for alphabetizing.

## Scandinavian
If the prefix is of Scandinavian, German, or Dutch origin, alphabetize under the name following the prefix. If the prefix is the Dutch *de* or is of other origin, however, enter the name under the prefix.

## Spanish
If an article is the only element in the prefix of a Spanish name, it should be used for alphabetizing:

> **Las Heras, Manuel Antonio**

Other names are entered on the element following the prefix.

> **Figueroa, Francisco de**

In the case of a compound Spanish surname, *AACR2* recommends that the name be entered under the first element (22.5C5). Delfina Molina y Vedia de Bastianini is entered as

> **Molina y Vedia de Bastianini, Delfina**

The *Chicago Manual of Style* (2003, 18.82) adds,

> In Spain and in some Latin American countries a double family name is often used, of which the first element is the father's family name and the second the mother's birth name (*her* father's family name). The two names are sometimes joined by *y* (and). Such compound names are alphabetized under the first element. . . .
>
> > Ortega y Gasset, José

## Non-European Names
Languages of non-European origin are not written in the Roman alphabet. Scholarly texts that include personal names and other terms from non-Roman alphabets will very likely indicate what transliteration system has been used. Problems arise for the indexer when the text uses more than one type of transliteration. For example, some books about China may contain both Wade-Giles and pinyin usage. The indexer should post names in the way that the author has cited them. Cross-references to alternative forms of a name should be provided when the author has used them in the text. It is not the indexer's job to impose a consistent transliteration system on the index when such consistency is lacking in the text.

For more information about various transliteration schemes see "Languages Usually Transliterated (or Romanized)" in *The Chicago Manual of Style* (2003, 10.89–129), Wellisch (1995, 421–429), and *ALA-LC Romanization Tables*.

Many names of non-European origin are composed of several compound elements. As Knight says in regard to Arabic names, "These can present some difficulty" (1979, 77). This is an understatement at best. Often with no guidance from the text, the indexer must determine which portion of the name should be used for alphabetizing purposes.

Readers are cautioned that the guidelines that follow are very, very general. Indexers confronted with a multitude of non-European names are urged to consult reference sources for the appropriate language. The applicable sections of *AACR2* are cited with the various language groups. For more detailed treatment of names in other languages, *AACR2* refers readers to *Names of Persons: National Usages for Entry in Catalogues* (IFLA 1996).

### Arabic

> Most Muslim names are of Arabic origin. Islam originated in Arabia and in only half a century spread over a large part of the world. . . . We find that the names of Muslims living in one country are different in form and style from those of Muslims in other countries. For instance, Iranian, Turkish and Indian Muslim names differ from each other. (Akhtar 1989, 156)

Even though many Islamic names are derived from Arabic, it is important for the indexer to understand that geography may play a critical role in the structure of the name. With this caveat in mind, some general guidance can be offered about the entry element in Arabic names.

Modern Arabic names often consist of two elements presented as a forename and a surname. These names should be inverted for alphabetizing.

> **Arafat, Yasser**
> **Hussein, Saddam**

The *AACR2* rules in section 22.22 apply to names that do not contain a surname or an element acting as a surname. Many names are preceded with an article, often *al-* or *el-*. Wellisch (1995, 372) reminds us that the "initial article . . . , joined to a name by a hyphen, is a part of that name and is not transposed but is disregarded in alphabetization." For example, Muhammad Hamid al-Jamal is entered as al-Jamal, Muhammad Hamid

Remember that the *al-* and *el-* are not alphabetized.

There are prefixes that indicate relationships, such as *Abd, Abu, Bin,* and *Ibn.* These are integral parts of the name that should not be transposed and should be alphabetized. Here are some examples:

Abd-al-Nasir, Jamal
bin Laden, Osama
Ibn al-Muqaffa, Abu Muhammad
al-Jamal, Muhammad Hamid
Salah, Ahmad

Likewise, the founder of Saudi Arabia is known (and alphabetized) as Ibn Saud, whereas his son is entered under his forename, Faisal. As should be evident, there is nothing straightforward about the indexing of Arabic names. The treatment of the name in the text should guide the indexer. Lacking guidance from the text, the indexer may turn to *AACR2* (22.22), *The Encyclopaedia of Islam* (Gibb 1960), or *Concise Encyclopedia of Islam* (Gibb and Kramers 2001). Online resources that may be helpful include Columbia University Library's Middle East and Jewish Studies Web site (http://www.columbia.edu/cu/lweb/indiv/mideast/cuvlm/) and the Middle East Virtual Library (http://ssgdoc.bibliothek.uni-halle.de/vlib/html/).

### Burmese

Surnames are not used in Burmese. Occasionally a Western name precedes the Burmese name. If this is the case, the Western name should be moved to the end and the Burmese name used for the entry element. A term of address is often included in the name, quite often the term of respect *U*. These terms are retained in the index listings. The indexer must be careful to distinguish terms of address from the same words used in a name:

Chit Maung, Saw (term of address)
Nu, U
Mya Sein
Than Tun, Walter
Thant, U
U Shan Maung, Maung (term of address)

### Chinese

Chinese names are usually presented with the surname given first. In the index, these names are presented as given, without inversion. No comma is used between the elements:

>> Cheng Shifa
>> Li Keran

If the name has been Westernized—that is, the surname is given last, preceded by the given name—the name should be inverted in the index:

>> Tsou, Tang
>> Wong, Thomas

Today the pinyin romanization system is used for the Chinese language. However, some books may contain both pinyin and Wade-Giles spellings. Indexers should follow the format of the name in the text. Cross-references from one format to the other may be helpful. For example:

>> Tseng Yu-ho. *See* Zeng Youhe

### Hebrew

In *Indexing from A to Z,* Hans Wellisch (1995, 373) gives the following advice: "Hebrew names of Jews living in Palestine since about 1880 and in Israel since 1948 generally consist of one or two forenames followed by a surname and are treated like Western names." Thus, the name Shemuel Yosef Agnon would appear in the index as

>> Agnon, Shemuel Yosef

Wellisch goes on to explain that "Hebrew names of Jews who lived before the early 19th century have almost always the pattern: forename(s), followed either by a patronymic or by an epithet or both; they are indexed by forename" (373–374).

>> Akiba ben Joseph
>> Benjamin of Tudela."

### Indian

Modern Indian names generally appear with the surname last. In the index these names are inverted. Mohandas Karamchand Gandhi is indexed as

>> Gandhi, Mohandas Karamchand

*AACR2* points out exceptions found in Kannada, Malayalam, Tamil, and Telugu names that do not contain surnames (22.25B2). In these cases, the recommendation is to enter under the given name. The given names in these languages are often preceded by a place name, sometimes by the father's given name, and sometimes by a caste name. It is important for the indexer to keep this arrangement in mind when attempting to ascertain the given name. For example, Tittai Kirusna Ayyankar would be entered as

**Kirusna Ayyankar, Tittai**
(given name = Kirusna)
(caste name = Ayyankar)
(place name = Tittai)

*AACR2* recommends that persons living before the middle of the nineteenth century be entered under the first element of their personal name (22.25A1).

## Indonesian

Javan names consist of only a personal name and should be indexed in that manner:

**Suharto**
**Sukarno**

Other Indonesian names frequently consist of more than one element. They are often entered under the last element of the name. For example, Idrus Nasir Djajadiningrat is entered as

**Djajadiningrat, Idrus Nasir**

There are many exceptions to this rule. Some names include elements that denote filial relationships plus the father's name; others include initials or abbreviations as the last element; still others include titles or honorifics. Sometimes these names are entered under the first element rather than the last. Indexers should see *AACR2* (22.26C–22.26F) for further discussion. Additionally, Indonesian names may include titles and honorific words in the text. Indexers can consult *AACR2* (22.26, note 20) for listings that may help distinguish a title from a given name.

## Japanese

Generally, two elements form a Japanese name. The surname is given first, followed by the forename. These names are entered in uninverted format. However, some authors present a Japanese name in Western order: forename first, followed by surname. If a Japanese name is presented in this fashion, it must be inverted in the index. The indexer must make certain which portion of the name is the surname.

If a name is presented in traditional format in the text, such as Yoshida Shigeru, it appears in the index uninverted:

**Yoshida Shigeru**

## Malay

The general rule for Malay names is to enter the name under the first element of the name unless the person uses another element as a surname:

A. Samad Said
A. L. Bunggan
Rejab F. I.

See section 22.27 in *AACR2* for a more detailed discussion of Malay names. Note that *AACR2* provides a list of Iban titles of honor, titles of office, and religious titles (22.27, note 24).

## Russian

"Russian names consist of three elements: forename, patronymic, and family name" (Wellisch 1995, 371). The entry format for Russian names is family name, forename and patronymic. The name Ivan Petrovich Smirnov would appear in the index as

**Smirnov, Ivan Petrovich**

Wellisch adds this caution, however: "The standard form of address is the forename and patronymic but not the family name. Thus, Ivan Petrovich Smirnov is addressed as Ivan Petrovich; if this form appears in a text, its second element should not be mistaken for a family name and indexed as *Petrovich, Ivan,* and an effort must be made to ascertain the family name" (371).

## Thai

Although surnames are used in Thai names, the general rule is to use the forename as the entry element because most people are generally known by and addressed by this name. In the text the Thai name is usually presented with the forename first, followed by the surname. Thus, the name Dhanit Yupho is entered in the index as

**Dhanit Yupho**

*AACR2* provides recommendations for the citing of Thai royalty, nobility, Buddhist monastics, ecclesiastics, and supreme patriarchs. See *AACR2* (22.28B –22.28D3) for further discussion.

## Vietnamese

Vietnamese names are usually composed of three parts, with the surname given first. What causes confusion with Vietnamese names is that persons are usually referred to by their forenames. For example, General Vo Nguyen Giap is referred to as General Giap. But the name is entered in the index as

**Vo Nguyen Giap**

A cross-reference can be provided from the more familiar part of the name for those individuals better known by their forenames.

Many Cambodian and Laotian names follow the same pattern of usage and citation as Vietnamese names.

## Geographic Names

More frequently than not, geographic names that appear in the text are indexable. Like personal names, geographic names can have various spellings and some do change over time. The way the name appears in the text should help the indexer determine the form of the name in the index.

### Preliminary Expressions: Geographic Features

It is important to distinguish between a place name, such as the name of a town, and a name for a geographic feature, such as a mountain or lake. When a geographic feature is preceded by a preliminary expression such as "Mt." or "Lake," the name is placed in the index in inverted format. For example, Mt. Shasta appears in the index as *Shasta, Mt.*

But if the preliminary expression is part of a place name, the expression is retained in uninverted form in the index. Mount Vernon, Virginia, would appear in the index as *Mount Vernon (VA)*. The indexer must determine whether such a reference is to a town or to a mountain peak. Careful examination of the context of the reference in the text generally clears up any ambiguity.

On this distinction between preliminary expressions that refer to a geographic feature and those that are parts of place names, Wellisch (1995, 383–384) remarks:

> There is no good reason for this procedure other than perhaps to avoid an accumulation of too many entries beginning with the same word, and it is probably due to the practice of inversion of many compound terms in a misguided attempt to bring the "more important" term to the fore. Since, however, geographical terms in foreign languages, such as Golfe, Lac, Lago, Mare, Mont, or Monte, are never inverted, the practice of inversion in English place names is quite incongruous and inconsistent (Is the Isle of Man to be so entered or is the name to be inverted to Man, Isle of?).

Although the rule for inversion of preliminary expressions seems clear-cut, there are exceptions. When citing the rule, many style guides include the "Cape of Good Hope" example. One style guide tells us to index this term as *Good Hope, Cape of,* while another style guide presents the term in uninverted form. *Merriam-Webster's Geographical Dictionary* (1997) provides the most sensible resolution to the "Cape of Good Hope problem," posting the information at *Good Hope, Cape of* and providing a *See* cross-reference from *Cape of Good Hope.* It is always important to keep the readers' needs in mind. When it appears likely that readers may look up a term in a form not used in the index, provide a *See* cross-reference to the preferred term.

There are times when one and the same index must distinguish between an actual cape and "cape" as part of a place name. For example, a book about the Outer Banks of North Carolina may make reference to Cape Hatteras and Cape Hatteras National Seashore park. Strictly speaking, these two terms would appear in the index in the following order:

> **Cape Hatteras National Seashore, 38**
> **Hatteras, Cape, 28, 30, 35–42**

In a moderately lengthy index, these two entries may be separated from one another by several pages. Readers could look in the *C*'s and, finding only the reference for the park, assume that the cape itself is not discussed. These readers would miss all the references found at the *Hatteras, Cape* entry. In such a situation, it is quite reasonable for the indexer to insert a pointer (a cross-reference) to the actual *Cape Hatteras* entries. The entries might then appear as

> **Cape Hatteras.** *See* **Hatteras, Cape**
> **Cape Hatteras National Seashore, 38**
> **Hatteras, Cape, 28, 30, 35–42**

In the entries above, the indexer has handled the references correctly and at the same time has provided a reasonable cross-reference for readers who may not know the posting rules.

### Preliminary Expressions: Articles and Prepositions

There are place names that begin with articles. A common example is The Dalles in northern Oregon, an exciting spot where the Deschutes River joins the Columbia River. Another well-known example is The Hague in the Netherlands. In both cases, the article *The* is part of the name. These names appear with the article on maps. Since the article is part of the formal name, the names are entered in the index in uninverted form, sorted on *The.* It might be helpful to readers to supply cross-references, as in

Dalles. *See* The Dalles
Hague. *See* The Hague
Thebes
The Dalles
Thedford
The Hague

Likewise, if the name begins with a non-English article or preposition, the preliminary term is generally alphabetized; the phrase is presented in uninverted form.

De Baca County (NM)
De Kalb (IL)
Del Mar (CA)
El Cajon (CA)
La Crosse (WI)
Le Mans (France)
Los Angeles (CA)

## Identifiers for Geographic Names

It is often desirable to provide a clear identifier for a geographic name. This is especially true when the same name appears in several distinct contexts:

Los Angeles (CA)
Los Angeles (Chile)
Los Angeles County (CA)

If a common set of identifiers will be used in the index, such as abbreviations for states in the United States, the indexer must use the abbreviations in a consistent manner. It is not proper to abbreviate California as "CA" in one place and as "Calif." in another place.

## References

Indexers who handle material that contains references to geographic names would do well to have a geographical dictionary at hand, such as *Merriam-Webster's Geographical Dictionary (1997)*. If a more detailed reference is required, in the United States information about the standard forms of geographic names can be obtained from the United States Board on Geographic Names (U.S. Geological Survey, Reston, VA 22092 or http://geonames. usgs.gov/bgn.html). The following quotation is from the BGN Web site:

> The U.S. Board on Geographic Names (BGN) is a Federal body created in 1890 and established in its present form by Public Law in 1947. Comprised of representatives of Federal agencies, appointed for 2-year terms, the Board is authorized to establish and maintain uniform geographic name usage throughout the Federal Government. Sharing

its responsibilities with the Secretary of the Interior, the Board has developed principles, policies, and procedures governing the use of both domestic and foreign geographic names as well as underseas and Antarctic feature names. Although established to serve the Federal Government as a central authority to which all name problems, name inquiries, and new name proposals can be directed, the Board also plays a similar role for the general public.

The USGS Geographic Names Information Systems (http://geonames .usgs.gov) provides the standard format for U.S. place names and links to gazetteers for many other countries. Even the International Astronomical Union's *Gazetteer of Planetary Nomenclature* is listed.

On Britain, K. G. B. Bakewell (1988, 28) states that "the standard gazetteer of Britain is *Bartholomew Gazetteer of Britain* compiled by O. Mason (Edinburgh: Bartholomew, 1977), which has about 40,000 entries compared with the 90,000 entries in the same publisher's earlier *Gazetteer of the British Isles* (Edinburgh: Bartholomew, 1970). The English Place-Name Society publishes separate volumes on the place names of each English county."

Oliver Mason (1986) has also complied the *Bartholomew Gazetteer of Places in Britain*. The English Place-Name Society maintains a Web site at http://www.nottingham.ac.uk/english/research/EPNS/.

## Organization Names

The names of organizations, like other types of names, are not without their problems. It must be decided where to post an organization's name and whether to provide a cross-reference. In some cases the decision is an easy one. For example, the utility company Pacific Gas and Electric would be entered in its full form in the *P*'s. But since most customers of this utility company refer to it as "PG&E," a *See* cross-reference should be provided from the abbreviation to the full name.

More troublesome are names that begin with what appears to be a forename, such as the John Deere Company. While inverting a name like this might seem natural, it is a sounder practice to enter the name in uninverted form in the index. "The most conspicuous difference between the indexing of personal and corporate names is that the latter are always entered in the order of all words, that is, *without any inversion*" (Wellisch 1995, 103).

The formal name of a winery often begins with a forename. The general practice is to include the name without inversion in the index.

A list of index entries for Sonoma County (California) wineries would look like this:

> Alexander Valley Vineyards
> Barefoot Cellars
> B. R. Cohn
> Davis Bynum Winery
> Dry Creek Vineyard
> Eric Ross Winery
> F. Teldeschi Winery
> Kenwood Vineyards
> Kunde Estate Winery
> Mark West Winery
> Matanzas Creek Winery

Nonprofit foundations often feature personal names. These names are also entered in the index without inversion. If it is likely that readers may not remember the first name or initial, then a cross-reference can be used. For example,

> Bill & Melinda Gates Foundation
> Getty Trust. *See* J. Paul Getty Trust
> Grant a Wish Foundation
> Hewlett Foundation
> J. Paul Getty Trust
> Richard and Rhoda Goldman Fund

Many business owners do not think of the alphabetizing consequences of the names they choose. Take a book that discusses both Tony Roma and Tony Roma's, the latter being a restaurant. Tony himself would be indexed as *Roma, Tony*. However, Tony's restaurant name would correctly appear in the *T*'s. In the *R*'s we might find the following:

> Roma, Tony, 35–39
> Roma's, Tony (restaurant). *See* Tony Roma's

Another type of business name is one that is pronounced differently from its spelling. In my town there is a local restaurant named Hs. Lordships. When the townspeople refer to this restaurant, they say "His Lordships." A cross-reference such as the following would be appropriate for a name like this:

> His Lordships. *See* Hs. Lordships

The general rule is that organizational names should appear in uninverted form; cross-references should be provided when necessary. But the topic of how to handle organizational names cannot be wrapped up without discussing some exceptions to the rule.

In some situations it would make more sense to double-post a name in both direct and inverted format rather than provide a cross-reference:

> American Society of Indexers
> American Translators Association
> Japanese Translators Society
> Society of Indexers

could be double-posted as

> Indexers, American Society of
> Indexers, Society of
> Translators Association, American
> Translators Society, Japanese

This advice applies when there are only a few reference locators at each of these entries. Thus, the double-posting of information saves space in the index.

When confronted with a text that cites many organizations that begin with the same title, such as "Association of . . . ," the indexer may invert the names to pull the important portion of the name forward. Such a decision will help readers who are not certain of the formal name of an organization. They need not worry whether the name is Association of American Indexers or American Indexers Association or Society of American Indexers or American Society of Indexers.

If a decision is made to handle the index in an unusual way, the headnote to the index must explain the convention used. An example of a subject index that handled the names of organizations in an unconventional but useful way can be found in the 1989–1990 edition of the *Washington Information Directory*, published by Congressional Quarterly Inc. *WID*, as the directory is fondly called, is a lengthy (more than a thousand pages) compendium of who's who in the greater Washington, D.C., area. It includes names and addresses of people from the executive branch, Congress, trade associations, and nonprofit groups. Agencies, subagencies, divisions, subdivisions, committees, and subcommittees are all included. There are thousands of organizational names. The following headnote precedes the subject index (1989–1990, 960):

> If the title of an agency or organization begins with one or more of the words listed below, it is not listed under those initial words. Rather, it is indexed under the next word in the title. For example, the National Gallery of Art is listed alphabetically not under "National" but under "Gallery of Art, National." In addition, agencies and groups are indexed under KEY words. The National Gallery of Art will also have an entry under "Art, National Gallery of."
>
> Academy
> Advisory

Agency
American
Association
Bureau
Center
Coalition
Commission
Committee
Council
Department
Federal
Foundation
Fund
Institute
International
National
Office
Society
U.S.
United States

This introductory note makes quite clear the scheme that has been used in this index. Although a generally accepted indexing rule has been broken, the usability of the index has been greatly enhanced by this decision. The designer of this index clearly put the readers' needs first.

Even more than other types of names, corporate names seem to be in a state of flux. Some businesses have more than one formal, legal name. Others have one formal name but may also have other names that are protected by trademark or service mark. Indexers working with a variety of names for a corporation will need to settle on one name and cross-reference from the others. Generally, the form of the name most frequently used in the text will be the name at which to post the information:

**International Business Machines Co.** *See* **IBM**

Some companies do file the necessary papers and formally change their names. If it is decided that information will be posted at the current name, then a cross-reference from the old name to the current name is appropriate. For instance, in a discussion about the changing world of computer retail sales, the author may point out that the Soft Warehouse changed its name to CompUSA because the company's inventory began to include a great deal of hardware in addition to software. The new company name, it is felt, better reflects the goods now being sold. The names may appear in the index as

**CompUSA** (*formerly* **Soft Warehouse**)
**Soft Warehouse.** *See* **CompUSA**

If the author makes no mention of the old name, such a cross-reference is not needed. Again, the text should be the indexer's guide. The indexer need not research the posting of every company name and provide cross-references from former names to current names when the older names are not mentioned in the text.

Mergers and acquisitions of companies provide yet another indexing challenge. For example, in 1884 the National Cash Register Company was founded. The name of this company was changed to NCR Corporation in 1974. In 1991 NCR Corporation was acquired by AT&T, but continued to operate under its own name. However in 1994, the NCR name was changed to AT&T Global Information Solutions (GIS). Then in 1995 AT&T announced the spin-off to shareholders of AT&T GIS, which would become an independent, publicly traded company. In 1996 AT&T GIS changed its name back to NCR Corporation. The index to a book that charted the history of this company would surely include index entries for all of these names. The entries for *NCR Corporation* might include qualifiers for various time periods

> **NCR Corporation (1974–1991)**
> **NCR Corporation (1991–1994)**
>   *See also* **AT&T Global Information Solutions**
> **NCR Corporation (1996–2005)**

The main difficulty with organization names is determining how to post the name. While it may be comfortable to establish the rule that all such names will be posted at their formal spelled-out versions, this may not meet the needs of the readers. Readers may tend to look up *AT&T*, not the *American Telephone and Telegraph Company*. Ideally there will be entries for both *AT&T* and *American Telephone and Telegraph Company*. But one of these entries will be a *See* cross-reference to the entry where information has been gathered. If readers of the book will tend to look up the shortened form of the name first, then that is where the information should be posted.

### Alphabetizing of Names

Names are alphabetized in the same way that the rest of the index is alphabetized. Be aware that word-by-word and letter-by-letter sorting schemes will often place entries in very different positions in the index. Because of the space following the *U*, *U S WEST* will fall at the beginning of the *U*'s, far removed from other entries such as *US Sprint* if word-by-word alphabetizing is followed. Most readers looking up this term will think of it as *us west* and look for it in the *us* portion of the index. A letter-by-letter sort would interfile this entry with the other *US* entries in the index.

This problem brings us back to the discussion of how to choose an alphabetizing method. If an index will contain many terms with spaces within entries, the indexer may wish to consider the use of a strict letter-by-letter sort. Fine examples of word-by-word alphabetizing that sorts the punctuation within an entry can be found in the white pages name listings in phone books. Go to the beginning of any letter group and examine the names. In the *G* section of one phone book we find the following alphabetized list:

> **G-Style Body & Sound**
> **G A Photography**
> **G & A Systems**
> **GAB BUSINESS SERVICES**
> **GE COMPANY**
> **GHL International**
> **GTE Cellular Communications**
> **G W Paving & Construction**
> **Gaal, Ronald P**
> **Gaar, Tony**
> **Gabato, Ronald**

Admittedly, the list above is a hybrid. Upon close examination we find that it really does not follow any conventional sorting arrangement. Most of us who have had to use lists like this in the phone book are grateful that we can get directory assistance by dialing 411. The listing above illustrates what happens when unconventional decisions are made regarding the sorting of terms. Indexers faced with many entries that contain spaces, punctuation, and other symbols must seriously consider the alphabetizing order that will help readers locate the entries. Improvising one's own arrangement scheme should be avoided simply because it will very likely confuse the readers (and readers cannot dial 411 for index assistance!). See chapter 6 for a discussion of nonalphabetic characters in index entries.

## Names of Works

### Books, Musical Compositions, Motion Pictures, and Artworks

*The Chicago Manual of Style* recommends (2003, 18.51) that English-language titles beginning with *The, A,* or *An* place the article at the end of the title in main headings. In subheadings the placement of the article depends upon the format of the index. In an indented index the article is placed at the end; in a run-in index the article retains its natural position but is not alphabetized.

*Alamo, The*, 234
*Book on the Bookshelf, The* (Petroski), 34–39

Petroski, Henry
  *Book on the Bookshelf, The*, 34–39
  *Invention by Design*, 112–15
  *Pencil, The*, 184–89

Petroski, Henry, *The Book on the Bookshelf*, 34–39;
  *Invention by Design*, 112–15; *The Pencil*, 184–89

Chicago recommends that articles in foreign-language titles be retained in the index and handled in the same manner as English titles (2003, 18.52):

  *Bohème, La* (Puccini), 89
  *trovatore, Il* (Verdi), 23

Chicago cautions the indexer to make certain that the article is not a number: "French *un* and *une*, for example, and German *ein* and *eine* can mean *one* as well as *a*. In the absence of verification, the indexer will do better to alphabetize all foreign titles just as they appear in text, without inversion. Inversion is customary but not mandatory, whereas faulty inversion will confuse or irritate the user and embarrass the publisher" (2003, 18.52).

Titles beginning with function words other than articles are not inverted.

### Newspapers and Periodicals

The names of newspapers and periodicals are handled in this manner (*The Chicago Manual of Style* 2003, 18.48–49): if the name begins with an article, the article is omitted for English-language publications; it is retained and inverted at the end of the entry for foreign-language publications. *The New York Times*, *Le Monde*, and *Der Spiegel* would appear in the index as:

  *Monde, Le*
  *New York Times*
  *Spiegel, Der*

In conclusion, the handling of names in an index can be troublesome. The arrangement of name indexes must be carefully evaluated. More often than not, word-by-word alphabetizing will gather similar names together. There are situations in which we must seriously reconsider the arrangement of names and usability. Edward Tufte (1990, 42–44) presents an interesting discussion of the arrangement of names on the Vietnam

Veterans Memorial in Washington, D.C. "The memorial's designer, Maya Ying Lin, proposed that the names be listed by date of death rather than alphabetically." The memorial originally included 58,000 names, and there were over 600 Smiths. A directory of names was created. Visitors look up a name in the directory, where the stone panel and line number for the memorial indicate the location of the name. "Thus the names on stone triple-function: to memorialize each person who died, to make a mark adding up the total, and to indicate sequence and approximate date of death. A directory-book alphabetically lists all the names and serves as finder, pointing viewers to the location of a single engraved name" (Tufte 1990, 44).

# Chapter Eight

## FORMAT AND LAYOUT OF THE INDEX

The indexing style guide that is provided to the indexer will explain how the publisher wants the index formatted. The format of an index includes items such as

overall style: indented or run-in
format and placement of cross-references
special typography used within the index

Additionally, the style guide will outline the final submission format of the index. Most indexes are submitted via e-mail as file attachments. However, there are still times when an editor will request manuscript copy of the index. Both manuscript and electronic formats are discussed later in this chapter.

There is an important relationship between the layout and design of the index and its usability. Ideally, all decisions regarding index format take into consideration the needs of its users. Unfortunately, we do not live in an ideal world. All too often indexes are squeezed into a limited number of pages and their usability is greatly compromised. But with a little advance planning and an understanding of index design issues, an index can be presented so as to enhance its usefulness.

In chapter 1 Gérard Genette's notion of paratext was introduced. The index was discussed as a paratext of the book text. In this chapter we can think of the index as a text with its own associated paratext. In other words, decisions about the format and layout of an index directly affect the presentation of the index to the reader.

If we agree that an index should provide quick and easy access to information, we cannot ignore the crucial role played by the format and layout of the index in this regard. Indexes are rarely read in a linear style, that is, from beginning to end. Readers jump into the index at various points. The overall design of the index should provide for easy scanning of entries by the readers. Readers should be able to ascertain very quickly, at any place, where they are in the index. The index text pages should be clean, inviting, and easy to scan rather than dense and cluttered. In reference books, where the index is very likely the most heavily used portion of the book, its format and layout are especially important.

This chapter will discuss general format considerations and more specific index submission formats, matters that directly involve the indexer. Once the index is submitted to the publisher, the production department must lay out the index; we will discuss layout issues later in the chapter.

## Overall Index Style

Indexes are printed in the same typeface as the text of the body of the book but often two points smaller. If the body text of the book is printed in 10-point Times Roman with 12-point leading, the index text will be printed in 8-point Times Roman with 10-point leading. In this context *leading* refers to the amount of space between lines of text.

Indexes are often printed in multiple columns. In many books, the index is printed in two columns per page. Books with oversize pages can accommodate three or four columns of index text per page.

The body text for many books is set in a right-justified column. This means that the right side is straight and even. The alignment of the right-hand margin of the index, however, is almost always *ragged right*, allowing the lines to break where they may—the effect is an uneven right margin. When the columns are narrow, such a format is easier to proofread, typeset, and read.

The two general formats for indexes are *indented* and *run-in*. The distinguishing feature of these two styles is the way subheadings are formatted. In both formats, main headings are flush left—they are not indented—and runover lines are indented. This arrangement is what is known as *flush-and-hang style*. This simply means that subheadings and runover lines are indented in some fashion under the main heading. Following are examples of index entries formatted in indented and run-in styles:

| Indented Style | Run-in Style |
|---|---|
| dogs | dogs: breed clubs, 242–48; |
|   breed clubs, 242–48 |   breeding of, 180–95; herding |
|   breeding of, 180–95 |   group, 135–42; hound group, 67– |
|   herding group, 135–42 |   72; nonsporting group, 23–29; |
|   hound group, 67–72 |   obedience training for, 275–84; |
|   nonsporting group, 23–29 |   registration of, 210–15; showing |
|   obedience training for, 275–84 |   of, 250–62; socialization of |
|   registration of, 210–15 |   puppies, 198–206; sporting |
|   showing of, 250–62 |   group, 56–60; terrier group, |
|   socialization of puppies, 198–206 |   125–30; toy group, 86–94; |

Indented Style *(continued)*
    sporting group, 56–60
    terrier group, 125–30
    toy group, 86–94
    working group, 34–39
    *See also* American Kennel Club

Run-in Style *(continued)*
    working group, 34–39. *See also*
    American Kennel Club

## Indented Style

In an indented-style index, each subheading begins on a new line with a specific measure of indentation, or indention. This type of layout is also referred to as *setout, hierarchical, outline,* or *line-by-line* style. The amount of indention for lines appearing under a main heading is a function of the level of the line in the hierarchy. Subheadings could be indented 1 em, with sub-subheadings indented 2 ems. (An *em* is a linear measurement used in printing that is equal to the point size of the type. As an example, if the index is in 8-point type, then 1 em is 8 points wide, 2 ems is 16 points wide, and so forth.)

The indented format allows for clear display of sub-subheadings:

    *Arctostaphylos*
      *andersonii,* 550
      *bakeri,* 550
        ssp. *bakeri,* 550
        ssp. *sublaevis,* 550
      *densiflora,* 551
      *glauca,* 552
      *montaraensis,* 554
      *pallida,* 555
      *stanfordiana,* 556–558
        ssp. *decumbens,* 556
        ssp. *raichei,* 556
        ssp. *stanfordiana,* 558
      *uva ursi,* 558
      *viscida,* 558–559
      *wellsii,* 559

As the example above illustrates, the various levels in an indented-style index are easy to follow. When there are multiple levels in an index—that is, subheadings, sub-subheadings, sub-sub-subheadings, and so on—this is the correct format to use. However, do note that there are variations. See the discussion below about other styles.

When an indented index is set within narrow columns, there will be lines that do not fit within the column width. Lines that must be continued on the next line are called *turnover, wraparound,* or *runover lines.* The indention of a turnover line must be different from the indention for subheadings or sub-subheadings. Turnover line indention will be discussed in more detail later in this chapter.

## Run-in Style

There is one, and only one, reason to use a run-in format for an index: that reason is to save space. The two format styles shown at the beginning of this chapter illustrate the space-saving attribute of run-in style. But subheadings formatted in run-in style are not as easy to scan or locate as in an indented format.

Run-in subheadings follow one another with no line breaks in between. Subheadings are separated from each other by a semicolon. Sometimes the subheadings begin indented under the main heading and its locators. But since the purpose of this type of format is to save space, more often than not the subheadings are run off from the main heading; they begin on the same line as the main heading.

The run-in format does not lend itself easily to the display of sub-subheadings. The run-in format should be used only when the index is composed of main headings and one level of subheadings. This format should not be used when the index contains more levels. Unfortunately, this advice is not always followed; some publishers have concocted ingenious punctuation schemes for further cluttering a run-in index with sub-subheadings. The problem of sub-subheadings and run-in format will be discussed shortly.

The only situation in which the run-in format saves a useful amount of space is where there are many main entries that have subheadings. If an index is composed of mostly main entries, the space ultimately saved by the run-in style is negligible.

A run-in format should be considered only when there is not enough room for an indented index. Sadly, many publishers routinely format indexes in run-in style regardless of space considerations. Choosing a run-in format should be a conscious decision that takes into consideration that to some extent the usability of the index will be compromised. The user of the index may find it particularly annoying to struggle through a run-in index of densely packed subheadings only to discover several blank pages following the index that could have accommodated an indented style. Given the powerful formatting capabilities of dedicated indexing software, it is a very simple matter to format an index in both indented and run-in styles and see how much space is needed for the two formats.

Like the indented format, the run-in format also indents the runover lines under the main heading. The indention is generally 1 em. Since there are no sub-subheadings, no further indention will be required.

More details regarding both types of formats will be presented in the layout section of this chapter. Subtle variations can be used with both formats to enhance the usability of an index.

## Other Styles

Any decision to set an index in a style other than the traditional flush-and-hang format should be made with caution. One common deviation from the standard indented format can be found in some legal books. In these books the indexes are printed two columns per page, main headings set in capital letters in bold type centered across the column width, with subheadings set underneath, the first subheading level set flush left and the second, indented:

| **AFFIRMATIVE ACTION** | **CIVIL ACTIONS** |
|---|---|
| Generally, 5:1 | Age Discrimination in Employment Act |
| Bakke revisited, 2:29 | EEOC civil actions, 5:17 |
| EEOC guidelines, 2:34 | Federal employee civil actions, 5:18 |
| Rehabilitation Act | private civil actions, 5:16 |
|   Federal employment, 6:11 | Equal Pay Act |
|   Federal grants, 6:7 | EEOC civil actions, 4:16 |
|   government contracts, 6:3 | private civil actions, 4:15 |

Such a format is useful only in indexes in which every main heading has at least one subheading. A main heading would look quite odd standing alone centered within a column on a page. Setting the first subheading level flush with the left margin saves space by reducing the number of turnover lines.

Another variation is the use of both indented and run-in styles in indexes with three levels. The University of Chicago Press recommends that "if an index requires a second level of subentries (sub-subentries), a mixture of run-in and indented styles can be used" (2003, 18.26). Indeed, this format was used to good advantage in the index for the fifteenth edition of *The Chicago Manual of Style*. Here is what it looks like (some subentries are shortened or omitted):

> alphabetizing
>   abbreviations, 18.39–39, 18.62, 18.91
>   basic rule of, 18.55
>   cross-references, 18.16
>   letter-by-letter, 18.56–57, 18.59, 18.125, 18.148–49
>   names: compound 18.70; foreign, 18.74–85; with initials vs.
>     spelled-out, 18.61; with *Mac* or *Mc*, 18.71; with *O'*, 18.72; with
>     particles, 18.69, 18.82; *Saint, St.,* and such, 18.42, 18.73, 18.91
>   numerals, 18.63–64
>   subentries, 18.66–68

Years ago it was not unusual to see indexes with their locators set flush right, preceded by leader dots. This format produced a right-justified index. In general, this format is frowned upon today. It is difficult to proofread. Also, the user must carefully follow a trail of leader dots to the locator. I have recommended the use of this format only once—when both the entries and the locators were cryptic. The index was easier to use with the locator physically separated from the entry. For example:

```
BDCHa ................................. 3C:libpt:BDCHa
BDClear ............................. 3C:libpt:BDClear
BDCompare ................. 3C:libpt:BDCompare
BDConv .............................. 3C:libpt:BDConv
label
    create ........................ 3H:libpxio:LabCreat
    length ................................... 4D:getInfo
    print ........................... 3H:libpxio:LabPrnt
    read .............................. 3H:libpxio:LabRd
ldxep .............................. 5H:stdio-libh:Xep
LFBuff ................................ 2C:libtool:Lbuff
```

In general, though, right-justified indexes are more difficult for readers to use and should be avoided. For an interesting discussion of typography and the layout of indexes see Nan Ridehalgh's (1985) article, "The Design of Indexes." The article provides examples of many typographic and design elements in printed indexes and delves into the history of some of these considerations.

## Cross-reference Format and Placement

An indexing style guide will indicate the format and placement of cross-references within index entries. Many, many variations exist. Some of the more common examples will be presented here. See also table 3.1 in chapter 3 for a synopsis of various publishers' styles for cross-reference format and placement. Designers should strive to enhance the readability of the typeset index in their specifications.

The format of main heading cross-references must be different from that of subheading cross-references. Also, readers should easily be able to ascertain whether a cross-reference leads to more information about a main entry or about a subheading.

### *See* Cross-references

Generally *See* cross-references for main headings are run off from the main heading in both indented and run-in-style indexes. The *See* itself may or may not be capitalized. It is almost always set in italics. Sometimes the *See* reference is preceded by a period and space; other times the *See* and the term referred to are placed within parentheses:

**AKC.** *See* **American Kennel Club**
**AKC,** *see* **American Kennel Club**
**AKC** (*see* **American Kennel Club**)

One problem with placing the cross-reference inside parentheses arises when the entry referred to also contains a parenthesis. Earlier we discussed the debate about the completeness of cross-references. Many editors would like to see the full main entry, *American Kennel Club* (*AKC*), cited in the cross-reference. When the entire cross-referenced text is placed inside parentheses, the result can be visually distracting:

**AKC** (*see* **American Kennel Club [AKC]**)

Such awkward arrangements are to be avoided when possible.

The cross-reference is occasionally placed as a subheading under the main heading. The problem with this format is that two lines are used instead of one. Many consider this a waste of space:

**AKC**
    *See* **American Kennel Club**

The first example above—"AKC. *See* American Kennel Club"—is a more flexible format when there is also a need to provide *See* references for subheadings, which can then be styled within parentheses immediately following the subheading, which helps distinguish it as relating to a subheading. Regardless of the format used for a subheading *See* cross-reference, such a reference is far easier to format and read in an indented index than in a run-in index. An indented index with a *See* reference for a subheading can be formatted in the following way. Notice the subheading *obedience training*.

**dogs**
    **breed clubs,** 242–48
    **breeding of,** 180–95
    **herding group,** 135–42
    **hound group,** 67–72
    **nonsporting group,** 23–29
    **obedience training** (*see* **training**)
    **registration of,** 210–15
    **showing of,** 250–62
    **socialization of puppies,** 198–206
    **sporting group,** 56–60
    **terrier group,** 125–30
    **toy group,** 86–94
    **working group,** 34–39
    *See also* **American Kennel Club**

The identical entry formatted in run-in style can use the same format for the subheading cross-reference:

> dogs: breed clubs, 242–48; breeding of, 180–95; herding group, 135–42; hound group, 67–72; nonsporting group, 23–29; obedience training (*see* training); registration of, 210–15; showing of, 250–62; socialization of puppies, 198–206; sporting group, 56–60; terrier group, 125–30; toy group, 86–94; working group, 34–39. *See also* American Kennel Club

In a run-in index, the situation that must be anticipated is the presence of a subheading cross-reference at the last subheading, which is then followed by a cross-reference for the main heading. Readers must be able to distinguish the two cross-references easily. If we take the entry above and create a cross-reference for the last subheading, *working group,* the entry would look like the following:

> dogs: breed clubs, 242–48; breeding of, 180–95; herding group, 135–42; hound group, 67–72; nonsporting group, 23–29; obedience training (*see* training); registration of, 210–15; showing of, 250–62; socialization of puppies, 198–206; sporting group, 56–60; terrier group, 125–30; toy group, 86–94; working group (*see* Akitas; Great Danes; Rottweilers). *See also* American Kennel Club

This format may not be pretty, but it does work. It distinguishes clearly between a subheading cross-reference and a main heading cross-reference.

In general, *See* cross-references from subheadings should be avoided in an index. As pointed out earlier, the primary function of a *See* cross-reference is vocabulary control. Vocabulary control is done at the main heading level and not repeated at the subheading level. But there are situations where a subheading *See* cross-reference cannot be avoided. Careful formatting of these references will make the index easier to read and use.

### *See also* Cross-references

More elements are at work in the placement and format of *See also* references for main headings than there are in the format and placement of *See* references. Placement will be discussed first.

In both indented and run-in indexes, a *See also* reference that refers from the main heading can be placed either at the top of the entry or at the bottom of the entry as the last subheading. In an indented index the two placements may look like this:

| dogs | dogs. *See also* American Kennel Club |
|---|---|
| breed clubs, 242–48 | breed clubs, 242–48 |
| herding group, 135–42 | herding group, 135–42 |
| hound group, 67–72 | hound group, 67–72 |
| nonsporting group, 23–29 | nonsporting group, 23–29 |
| registration of, 210–15 | registration of, 210–15 |
| sporting group, 56–60 | sporting group, 56–60 |
| terrier group, 125–30 | terrier group, 125–30 |
| toy group, 86–94 | toy group, 86–94 |
| working group, 34–39 | working group, 34–39 |
| *See also* American | |
| Kennel Club | |

In the entry on the right, the placement of the *See also* reference at the top of the entry—run off from the main heading—eliminated two lines, thus saving space. But keep in mind that, unlike here, main headings are often followed by page numbers. Placing the *See also* reference after the main heading page numbers may result in a turnover line and no saving in space:

dogs, 1–6, 39–42. *See also* American
Kennel Club (AKC)

Placement of *See also* references has proponents on both sides. Those who favor placement at the bottom present the following arguments.

1. Readers are not distracted by references suggesting that they look elsewhere in the index for information.

2. The overall appearance of the entry is neater because *See also* references placed at the top, running off from the main heading, often result in turnover lines that add unnecessary visual complexity to the printed page.

3. Since the index entry is a hierarchy, less important information within the entry should come last.

Those in favor of placing the reference at the top of the entry counter as follows.

1. Readers should be immediately informed of related information that may be germane to their search.

2. When an index contains lengthy lists of subheadings, readers might not see the cross-reference placed at the end of the list.

Regardless of which placement is chosen, the decision must be applied uniformly throughout the index. *See also* references must appear in the same place within all entries. When the *See also* reference is placed at the bottom as the last subheading in an indented-style index, it is important to maintain correct subheading indention regardless of the level of the entry preceding the cross-reference:

dogs
  breed clubs, 242–48
  herding group, 135–42
  hound group, 67–72
  nonsporting group, 23–29
  registration
    breeds registrable, 10–14
    forms, 210–15
    litter registration, 35–38
    refusal of registration, grounds for, 125–30
  *See also* American Kennel Club

Like *See* references, *See also* references may appear in a variety of formats. The *See* may be capitalized or lowercase; the entire reference may stand alone or be placed within parentheses.

  *See also* American Kennel Club
  *see also* American Kennel Club
  (*see also* American Kennel Club)

Following are examples of formats and placements of *See also* references for main headings in run-in-style indexes:

  dogs (*see also* American Kennel Club): breed clubs, 242–48;
    breeding of, 180–95; herding group, 135–42; hound group,
    67–72; nonsporting group, 23–29; obedience training, 275–
    84; registration of, 210–15; showing of, 250–62; socialization
    of puppies, 198–206; sporting group, 56–60; terrier group,
    125–30; toy group, 86–94; working group, 34–39

  dogs: breed clubs, 242–48; breeding of, 180–95; herding
    group, 135–42; hound group, 67–72; nonsporting group,
    23–29; obedience training, 275–84; registration of, 210–
    15; showing of, 250–62; socialization of puppies, 198–206;
    sporting group, 56–60; terrier group, 125–30; toy group, 86–
    94; working group, 34–39. *See also* American Kennel Club

  dogs, 10–20 (*see also* American Kennel Club); breed clubs,
    242–48; breeding of, 180–95; herding group, 135–42;
    hound group, 67–72; nonsporting group, 23–29; obedience
    training, 275–84; registration of, 210–15; showing of, 250–62;
    socialization of puppies, 198–206; sporting group, 56–60;
    terrier group, 125–30; toy group, 86–94; working group, 34–39

  dogs, 10–20. *See also* American Kennel Club; breed clubs,
    242–48; breeding of, 180–95; herding group, 135–42;
    hound group, 67–72; nonsporting group, 23–29; obedience
    training, 275–84; registration of, 210–15; showing of, 250–62;
    socialization of puppies, 198–206; sporting group, 56–60;
    terrier group, 125–30; toy group, 86–94; working group, 34–39

## General Cross-references

A *general cross-reference* refers to a class of entries rather than a specific entry. Although its placement follows the same format as that of other cross-references, general cross-referenced entries are usually set in italics to distinguish them from actual entries that are referenced:

> **Southeast Asia.** *See specific country names*

The use of italics for "specific country names" indicates to readers that this is a general instruction; there is no entry in the S's for *specific country names*. Instead, the reader is instructed to look up countries by name throughout the index. Additionally, *The Chicago Manual of Style* requires that the general cross-reference be placed after any other cross-references even if it is out of alphabetic order (2003, 18.22).

### Cross-references to Entries in Italic

Some publishers prefer that a *See* or *See also* be set in plain roman (non-italic) type when it is followed by a reference in italics (*The Chicago Manual of Style* 2003, 18.21):

> **dogs. See also** *Travels with Charley*
> **Twain, Mark. See** *Life on the Mississippi*

## Special Typography

By their very nature, indexes tend to be dense. A good rule of thumb is that the more simple and plain the typography, the better. Most of the text in an index will be set in regular type. Italic will be used for *See* and *See also* references and titles of books. But in some situations the use of simple typographic devices can enhance the usability of the index and provide information at the same time.

Reference locators can be set in a different typeface when they refer to a particular type of entry. For example, a reference locator that refers to an illustration might be set in italic type:

> **Beef Wellington,** 45, *54*

The entry above indicates that a recipe can be found on page 45 and a picture of the dish can be found on page 54. This simple typographic device saves space in the index. Of course, an introductory note explaining the use of italic page numbers must appear at the beginning of the index.

Often bold type is used with reference locators that indicate where the reader can find definitions or substantial discussion of a term:

> **random access memory (RAM),** 35, **41–43,** 78–79

Readers looking at the entry above know immediately that pages 41–43 contain the definition and description of the term. Once more, space has been saved. The subheading "defined" is not needed to indicate the relevance of the material on these pages. Again, an introductory note must explain this particular use of bold type.

In some indexes the typeface used within the text for particular kinds of terms is retained in the index. For example, some software manuals use a monospaced Courier font to indicate commands that users type themselves. When the commands are index entries, the same monospaced font is used in the index:

> FORMAT command, 56–58, 65–67
> **formatting disks**
> **floppy disks**, 57, 78
> **hard disks**, 65–68, 79

It is easy to overdo the use of typographic variations. Too many changes in typefaces can make the index pages overly dense and busy. Some indexes use large and small caps for the names of authors to distinguish them from the names of other individuals in the index. Rarely is the use of such typography truly helpful.

On the other hand, setting the main headings in bold type may greatly enhance the usability of indexes with a preponderance of subheadings. This method is frequently used in legal indexes. The bold type helps readers locate information on dense index pages; it helps to focus the eye. But in an index with many main headings and few subheadings, the bold type in main headings can add annoying density to the index page.

When special typography is used in an index, the indexer usually needs to know what devices to use before the indexing begins. If pages that contain illustrations are to be set in italic, the indexer must code these entries for italic when the entry is written. It would be extremely tedious and time-consuming to insert the coding after the index has been completed.

All too often the actual design of the index pages is given little forethought. Ideally, the design is set before the indexer receives final pages. The addition of typographic codes for particular types of entries will increase the time needed for indexing. First, the indexer must know what additional keyboarding is to be done. Second, any special typography that is called for in the design will have to be proofread carefully by the indexer and the book editor.

Indexers who suspect that special typography may be useful in an index should bring the matter up with the editor as early in the indexing process as possible. Experienced indexers, without even seeing pages of the book, can often anticipate when the use of special typography will be helpful. But if the matter is not discussed early on, the editor is unlikely to allow extra time for indexing so that the indexer can go back into the index and, for example, add italic codes to specific page numbers.

## Final Submission Formats

Although beginning indexers may think their task will never end, there does come a time when the index is finished and must be turned over to the editor. Writing brilliant and robust indexes is certainly part of the indexer's job; submitting the index in the format desired by the editor is also an important part of the job. When the index is submitted, there is not a lot of time remaining in the publishing schedule. It is extremely important that the indexer understand at the beginning of the project exactly how the editor wants the index submitted. Two submission formats will be described: manuscript format and electronic format.

### Manuscript Format

While an indexer will rarely be asked to submit an index as manuscript only without an electronic file, submission of an index in manuscript form along with an electronic file is sometimes requested. Most editors do not edit from the indexer's printout; it is used only for reference or if there are problems with the electronic file. When the indexer's manuscript will not be used for editing, the indexer can submit a single-spaced printout. Other editors expect the index to be submitted as a typed, double-spaced manuscript so that the editor or proofreader can insert corrections. The discussion that follows will assume that the manuscript will be used for editing purposes.

Many publishers' style guides include a section devoted to manuscript submission format. Some common submission guidelines follow:

1. Paper size is 8 ½ inches by 11 inches.
2. Margins are at least 1 inch on the top, bottom, and right and left sides.
3. No hyphens are added in order to break lines.
4. Double-spaced lines are used throughout the index, with one column of entries per page.
5. Each manuscript page is numbered.

Variations on these guidelines of course exist. Some publishers will want larger margins; others will specify an index line length. Some will require a monospaced type. Regardless of minor variations, indexers should understand the importance of following the submission guidelines.

The index manuscript should be very neat. The type should be dark and easy to read. Handwritten corrections made by the indexer should be minimal. Submitting a manuscript littered with corrections is unprofessional.

It is wise for the indexer to keep a copy of the index manuscript and the page proof in case the originals are lost in transit. The indexer may also need the copies for reference, in case the editor has questions.

### Electronic Format

Authors preparing their own indexes in a word-processing program need only identify entry levels, special characters, and special typographic treatment in their indexes. It is important to follow your editor's instructions, and do not wait until the last minute to ask questions. An editor might send a note like this to an author:

> About the index: I've enclosed an extra copy of the proofs and our indexing brochure for that purpose. (It's a good idea for you to mark corrections on both copies.) Although it's all spelled out in the brochure, I would stress that when you type the index, you shouldn't try to put it into columns or format it to look like an index. Please use hard returns only to move to a new entry, never within an entry or subentry. Please do not use tabs, unless you use the indented style for subentries, and then use them only to begin a new subentry, never within an entry or subentry.

The rest of this discussion about electronic format is intended for professional indexers working for a variety of publishers. These indexers use specialized indexing software that helps them create files that meet the needs of their clients. Indexes are usually submitted to clients through e-mail as file attachments. It is essential that the indexer discuss before work begins which file formats the publisher will accept. The most common format produced by dedicated indexing programs is Microsoft's Rich Text Format (RTF) which allows for easy and reliable exchange of files no matter what word processor or operating system the publisher uses.

An RTF file is a plain text or ASCII file. The file itself is unformatted; it contains no proprietary codes. However, the file will include plain-text coding for various elements in the index, such as typeface changes. Here is the RTF coding for *See also* in italic:

```
\i See also\i0
```

Notice that there is a code to begin italics, (\i), and a code to end italics, (\i0). Typeface changes are indicated with beginning and end codes.

Dedicated indexing programs will provide style sheets for RTF formatting of the index. There is usually no need for the indexer to set up this coding format. It is helpful to understand the elements of an index that need coding in order for the publisher's computer system (hereafter the *target system*) to interpret them accurately. We will look at common elements:

1. Beginnings and ends of lines
2. Indentions
3. Typeface changes
4. Special characters

The code examples will be RTF coding. Over the years RTF has evolved into a complex markup language. The codes provided here are very simple. We will not consider the "header" information at the beginning of an RTF file. This information is required and fully discussed in Microsoft's *Rich Text Format (RTF) Specification Version 1.7* (Microsoft 2001).

**▮ Beginnings and ends of lines.** Until the index file has been formatted with particular font and leading instructions, it is not possible to know exactly where each line will break. The indexer's responsibility is to indicate clearly where an entry ends and the next entry begins in a way that the target system can recognize.

**▮ Indentions.** In the case of an indented-style index, the target system must have a means of recognizing various heading levels. For example, the target system must treat subheading lines differently from main heading lines or sub-subheading lines. Subheading indention levels are often indicated by generic coding, that is, the insertion of a unique code, such as [S1] for subheadings and [S2] for sub-subheadings. Some target systems use the tab character as an indention indicator. Subheadings can be indented with one tab, sub-subheadings with two tabs, and so on. The advantage of using a tab character is that the actual width of the tab space can be set on the target system. The RTF code for the tab character is \tab (a space follows the code). Following is an example of indented format with RTF codes for a main heading and four subheadings:

```
migratory pollinators\par
\tab bats, 73, 122-29\par
\tab bees, 249\par
\tab international protection, 259\par
\tab monarch butterflies, 119-22\par
```

A run-in-style index will not have the multiple indention levels of an indented index, although it will undoubtedly have many lines that turn over. Since line breaks are unpredictable in advance of typesetting, many target systems require that run-in subheadings be strung off from the main heading and continue one after another until the end of the entry. The target system will identify the text between the beginning of the line and the end of the line as a complete entry and will format it in run-in style appropriately.

■ *Typeface changes.* Any text in the index that changes from the regular typeface to another typeface must be indicated in some manner. For example, if the *See* and *See also* text in an index is to be set in italics, the target system must have a way of knowing when the typeface change begins and when it ends. Any typeface change, whether it be to italics, to bold, to small caps, or to monospaced font, or to other more exotic fonts, must be indicated in a unique manner within the text file. The target system must be instructed to change from the regular typeface to the new typeface and then back again to the regular typeface. This may be done with generic coding by creating typed beginning and end codes and providing a list along with the index. For instance, small caps in the phrase "treatment of AM and PM" might be indicated as follows.

```
treatment of <sc>am</sc> and <sc>pm</sc>
```

RTF codes may also be used to indicate a change of typeface. As always, it is good to know your publisher's preferences beforehand.

■ *Special characters.* What is a special character? In regard to letters, a special character is a letter not included in the Roman alphabet *A* to *Z*, upper and lower case. The following words all contain special characters:

> Académie française
> Mädchen
> Juan Alberto Peña Montalvo

It is important for indexers to understand that special characters usually require special treatment. Even if indexers can see the special characters on their computer screens, it does not necessarily follow that their clients will enjoy the same view. In fact, it is very likely that the special characters will not appear in the same way on the target system's computer screen. If RTF coding is used for the above examples, they would look like this:

```
Acad\'e9mie fran\'e7aise
M\'e4dchen
Juan Alberto Pe\'f1a Montalvo
```

In addition to letters, there are symbols that may need special treatment. The following symbols are considered standard and do not need to be coded:

! " # $ % & ' ( ) * + - . / : ; < = > ? @ [ \ ] ^ _ ` { | } ~

Any symbol not included in the list above will require special coding. One of the most common symbols used in indexes that needs coding is the en dash. Many publishers, including the University of Chicago Press (2003, 18.99) use an en dash rather than a hyphen in inclusive locator ranges. Generic coding for en dashes might render the entry *cats, 45–50,* like this:

```
cats, 45<en>50
```

The RTF coding for, "cats, 45–50," would look like this:

```
cats, 45\endash 50
```

■ *Generic coding.* As we have seen in the paragraphs above, generic, or ad hoc, coding may be devised by the indexer or the publisher. It simply refers to a code markup scheme that is unique. For example, heading levels may be coded in this way:

[M1] = main heading level
[S1] = subheading level
[S2] = sub-subheading level

Ad hoc markup is often used for indexes that include many non-Roman characters. The *Chicago Manual of Style* tells us that "consistency is essential. The copyeditor may need to invent codes for unusual elements. Whether a manuscript is typeset in house or by an outside supplier, the editor must furnish a list of codes used, with their definitions" (2003, 2.89). Of course, the list of codes for special characters must be supplied to the indexer. Such a list might look like this:

[lig ae] = æ
[lig AE] = Æ
[lower thorn] = þ
[upper thorn] = Þ

The index file would include only the generic codes. For example, *Ælfric* would appear in the index file as:

```
[lig AE]lfric
```

It is not hard to imagine how difficult it would be to proofread a heavily coded electronic manuscript. Luckily, such files are imported directly into the target system's software and printed so that it can be quickly seen whether or not the coding is correct. Indexers who use dedicated indexing software can have the software automatically insert RTF or generic codes into the index text file. Coding a text file manually would be very time-consuming and errors easily introduced. Some indexing software vendors provide the ability to build user-defined code tables that can be used for ad hoc generic codes.

## Layout of the Index

Rather than an exhaustive discussion of typography and layout considerations regarding indexes, this section is a discussion of general page design principles for attractive index presentation. Since many publishers work with page design software in-house to produce camera-ready copy, formatting suggestions for desktop publishing software will be presented. Lastly, design suggestions for the presentation of electronic indexes will be offered.

Most of the discussion that follows will focus on the layout of an indented-style index. As was pointed out earlier, an indented index is the most usable format. A run-in index format should be used only as a last resort when the number of pages available for the index is at a premium.

### Index Title and Introductory Note

The index should be titled. If there is only one index, then the simple title *Index* appears at the top of the first index page. If there are multiple indexes, each should be clearly titled—for example, *Subject Index, Name Index, Author-Title Index, Index to Cases*. An introductory note is needed to explain any special conventions used in the index. The note appears at the beginning of the index, between the index title and the beginning of the index entries.

### Type Size and Columns

Indexes are usually set in two or more columns per page in a type size that is smaller than the type used in the body of the book. The type size for the index is often two points smaller, with the leading reduced proportionately.

At first it may seem that printing the index in the same type size as the book at one column per page would help the reader—the larger type size would be easier to read. But if the body text of the book is 10-point type with 12 points of leading, an index formatted in this size can be quite lengthy. If the index were printed at one column per page, readers would have many more pages to thumb through in order to locate index entries. The index would be quite cumbersome.

The index page design goal is to fit as many entries on a page as possible while ensuring that the entries are easy to scan. The page designer should remember that indexes are not read like the body text of a book. Instead, index users jump into the index at some point and scan the pages for the alphabetic section that contains the index entry sought. Ideally, readers will be able to ascertain easily where they are in the index at any point on a page.

### Text Alignment and Hyphenation

As noted earlier in this chapter, the alignment of the right margin of the index text is usually ragged right, or unjustified. When words in index entries are hyphenated, more characters will fit on an index column line. Many desktop publishing programs offer automatic hyphenation. If this feature is activated, the production editor will need to review the hyphenation carefully so as to avoid unsightly and confusing breaks within index lines. See the discussion about bad breaks below for more information. Because indexers rarely provide indexes in final format for printing, indexers never add hyphens to indicate end-of-line breaks.

### Indention and Turnover Lines

In an indented index a style must be established that clearly indicates the different levels within entries. Indention within an index visually establishes the hierarchy of the entries. When the hierarchy is clearly presented, the usability of the index is greatly enhanced. The indention levels, although related to index usability, also impart information. For example, a reader scanning an index entry that contains indented sub-subheadings knows that the specificity of entries changes as the indention level increases.

Publishers often use a combination of em spaces to indicate indention levels. Generally, the main heading is set flush left with no indention, subheadings are indented 1 em, sub-subheadings are indented 2 ems, and so on.

Many desktop publishing programs allow for the use of points as a linear measurement. Such programs also offer other linear measures such as inches or centimeters. Regardless of which unit is used, a consistent indention measurement must be set up for each level present in the index. Each indention level is indicated by an even, incremental increase in indent length. If inches are used as the linear measure, main headings are set flush left, subheadings could have an indent of 0.2 inches, sub-subheadings could have an indent of 0.4 inches, and so on, with each subsequent level 0.2 inches greater than the preceding level.

Index text files that will be imported into desktop publishing software are often formatted by the indexer with main headings flush left, sub-headings indented one tab, sub-subheadings indented two tabs, and so on. The actual linear measure of the indent is set up within the desktop publishing program by defining a particular length for the tab character. In the example described above, the tab would be set equal to 0.2 inches. Or if points are used as the measure and the index is set in 8-point type, the tab will be set equal to 8 points.

Closely connected to the formatting of indention levels is the formatting of turnover lines. If each line in an index always fit within the column width, turnover lines would not be a problem, since there would not be any. It is rare, though, to find an index with no turnover lines. A turnover line must be indented in a way that will easily distinguish it from a subheading or sub-subheading indentation. The example below illustrates the problem that arises when a turnover line is indented with the same measurement as a subheading indent.

> **journals**
> abbreviations of titles, 34–38, 54, 90, 115
> copyediting of, 23
> printing cost reduction using offshore printing
> facilities, 120–25
> storage of back issues
> in sealed containers, 67
> warehouse facilities for, 234
> worldwide distribution of, 335

The third subheading above (printing cost reduction . . .) is a long line that will not fit across the column width; it turns over and continues on the next line. Since the turnover line indent is not set correctly, the last portion of the entry, *facilities*, appears to be another subheading that is not in alphabetic order. As the example shows, it is necessary to set up a specific way of handling turnover line indention.

Many publishers handle turnover line indention by indenting both main-heading and subheading turnover lines by the same amount of space; often this amount is slightly more than the indent for a subheading. This method works quite well for two-level indexes—that is, indexes that do not have sub-subheading levels.

Another method of handling turnover line indention is to add a discrete measure to the indention of the particular level of the index that is affected. Many typesetters use an en space as the turnover line indention increment. An en space is equal to half of an em space. If the em space is equal to 8 points, then the en space will be equal to 4 points. The turnover line indent is arrived at by adding 1 en to the em-space indention for each level. In this case the turnover line indent for a main heading will be 4 points (1 en space), the turnover indent for a subheading will be 12 points (1 em plus 1 en), and a sub-subheading turnover line will be indented 20 points (2 ems plus 1 en).

We can use the same method when working with inches as a linear measure. If the indention levels are in increments of 0.2 inches, then the turnover line indentions will be an additional 0.1 inches (half of 0.2 inches) that is added to the amount of the indention level. The entry below, using inches as a measure, illustrates the various indentions for levels within the entry and turnover lines within levels.

> 0″ for main heading
>  0.1″ for main heading turnover line
>   0.2″ for subheading indent
>    0.3″ for subheading turnover line
>     0.4″ for sub-subheading indent
>      0.5″ for sub-subheading turnover line

What's important in the example above is that the turnover line indents are different from the indents that indicate subheading levels. The turnover line indention length is a static number that is added to the indention of the level of the line that turns over.

If the *journals* entry example were formatted with a correct turnover line indent, it would look like this:

> journals
>     abbreviations of titles, 34–38, 54, 90, 115
>     copyediting of, 23
>     printing cost reduction using offshore printing
>         facilities, 120–25
>     storage of back issues
>         in sealed containers, 67
>         warehouse facilities for, 234
>     worldwide distribution of, 335

Notice that the runover word *facilities* is indented differently from both the subheading indent and the sub-subheading indent.

Indention and turnover lines can also be easily handled in a RTF file in which every line begins with a style. For example, in an index with two levels, main heading and subheading, there would be two styles, "Main" and "Sub." Each style would be set up as a paragraph with a hanging indent. The Main style would be flush left with no indention. The Sub style would be indented. Once the RTF index file were imported into the publisher's program these styles could be easily redefined.

## Bad Breaks

Bad breaks are unsightly and confusing line breaks from column to column and from page to page in the index which compromise the usability of the index. Bad breaks do not become apparent until the type and layout of the pages are set. Indexers rarely deliver indexes in camera-ready format. Once the index is submitted, the indexer has no control over or responsibility for the appearance of bad breaks in the typeset index. Reformatting the index in order to remove bad breaks is usually the responsibility of the production editor. Dealing with bad breaks should not begin until it is certain that the text of the index is stable. Adjusting for a bad break on one page often has a domino effect on the pages that follow. In other words, adding a line to the second column on the fourth page of the index can move all the remaining lines back another line, thus creating new bad breaks later in the index.

One of the most common types of bad breaks is the splitting of an entry's subheadings from one column or page to another. The result is a new column that begins with a subheading:

| | |
|---|---|
| journals | storage of back issues |
|    abbreviations of titles, |    in sealed containers, 67 |
|     34–38, 54, 90, 115 |    warehouse facilities |
|    copyediting of, 23 |     for, 234 |
|    printing cost reduction using |    worldwide distribution |
|     offshore printing facilities, |     of, 335 |
|     120–25 | |

Users looking at the entry on the right have no way of knowing that the entry *storage of back issues* is a subheading of the main heading *journals*. A simple way of dealing with this problem is to repeat, at the top of the continuation page or column, the main heading with the word *continued*, in parentheses, inserted as demonstrated below. (In order to save space and avoid turnover lines, many production editors abbreviate the word as *cont'd.*)

| | |
|---|---|
| journals | journals (*continued*) |
|    abbreviations of titles, |    storage of back issues |
|     34–38, 54, 90, 115 |     in sealed containers, 67 |
|    copyediting of, 23 |     warehouse facilities |
|    printing cost reduction |      for, 234 |
|     using offshore printing |    worldwide distribution of, 335 |
|     facilities, 120–25 | |

Notice that the correct indention of the various levels is maintained in the example above. The word *continued,* often in italic type, follows the level at which the break occurred. If the break occurred within the sub-subheadings for *storage of back issues,* the carried-over part of the entry would look like this:

| | |
|---|---|
| **journals** | **journals** |
|   **abbreviations of titles,** |   **storage of back issues** |
|     **34–38, 54, 90, 115** |     *(continued)* |
|   **copyediting of, 23** |     **warehouse facilities for, 234** |
|   **printing cost reduction** |     **worldwide distribution of, 335** |
|     **using offshore printing** | |
|     **facilities, 120–25** | |
|   **storage of back issues** | |
|     **in sealed containers, 67** | |

Again, notice how the correct indention levels are maintained so that readers can easily see the entry's hierarchy.

To save space, many publishers choose to use *continued* lines only when an entry breaks at the end of the last column on a right-hand page and carries over to the left column on a left-hand page. Ideally, however, any break within an index entry will be so noted, including breaks that occur between columns on the same page. The use of *continued* lines is particularly helpful to readers of indexes of large-format books with three or more columns of index text per page. When *continued* lines are provided in such indexes, readers can look at the top of each index column and easily know where they are in the index. Some editors suggest that intercolumn breaks on the same page of an index do not need to be adjusted with the use of *continued* lines because readers can easily scan the bottom of the previous column to locate the entry that is modified. But editors almost unanimously agree that a break that occurs between a right-hand page and a left-hand page must be compensated for by the insertion of a *continued* line. Examples of such attention to detail by production editors can be found in the indexes that have received the ASI–H. W. Wilson Award for Excellence in Indexing (see appendix B). The award-winning books are examples of not only excellence in indexing but also excellence in index page design and layout.

Other types of bad breaks include the top of an index column beginning with reference locators that are carried over from another entry:

    **67, 82–89, 135**
    **dogs, 55**
    **donkeys, 89**

In addition to being unsightly, this arrangement leaves the reader fumbling for direction and, hence, is unacceptable.

Two other types of blemishes to avoid are a single line at the beginning of an alphabetic section *orphaned* (standing alone) at the bottom of a column, or a single line at the end of an alphabetic section *widowed* at the top of a column. Readers could easily miss these entries.

Bad breaks such as the three described above can often be eliminated by reducing the leading within a column so that one or two more index lines can fit within the column. If the leading is increased, one or two more index lines can be forced to the next column. Another remedy for these types of bad breaks is to move a line of the index from one column to the next. This method works quite well when the index columns are not vertically justified on the page. Sometimes an entry can be shortened by judiciously tightening up the language. But such editing must be done in such a way as not to change the meaning of the entry.

**Page Design Tips**

When working with a lengthy, dense index that is set in small type (anything less than 9 points), page designers might consider using a dictionary-style guide word across the top of each page. As in dictionaries, the running head on the even-numbered pages would contain the main heading that begins the page; the running head on the odd-numbered pages would contain the main heading that ends the page.

Indexes that make heavy use of special notation within the entries will contain a headnote that explains the notation. If several items require explanation—for example, abbreviated, compound reference locators that refer to different volumes in the collection—the designer may consider adding a running foot to each index page that translates the abbreviations. This would save readers time; they would not need to turn over and over again to the headnote at the beginning of the index.

*Header letters* are sometimes used to distinguish the individual alphabetic sections within a lengthy index. In an index that is set in 8-point type, a large (14-point) capital *A* could appear before the A section, a capital *B* before the B section, and so on. Such visual guides can greatly help readers navigate through the index pages. If there is not enough space for header letters, an attempt can be made to provide at least a blank line or two between the alphabetic sections.

## Electronic Display of Indexes

Indexes are frequently displayed in various electronic formats: on Web pages, in e-books, online help, and PDF files. In a printed book, index pages are naturally dense. They contain a great amount of information and when correctly formatted offer readers quick access to the topics they seek. When visually dense printed pages are moved directly to a computer screen display without modification, usability decreases dramatically. Jan C. Wright (2001, 208) points out, "Designing indexes that work equally well in any of the various interfaces a document may be displayed in, whether print, help, PDF, or on the Web, presents a real challenge." In her paper "Single-source Indexing," Wright discusses the many issues involved with the preparation and display of indexes for print, online HTML help, PDF, XML, and plain HTML.

Jakob Nielsen, a Web usability expert, has written extensively over the years about the presentation of information on a computer screen.

> As an online publishing enthusiast, I sometimes get ridiculed for having written a traditional printed book about hypertext and the Internet. I don't feel apologetic about publishing something in print because paper remains the optimal medium for some forms of writing, especially for long works like a book.
>
> It is an unfortunate fact that current computer screens lead to a reading speed that is approximately 25 percent slower than reading from paper. (Nielsen 1996)

In 1997 Nielsen wrote, "How Users Read on the Web" and found that "people rarely read Web pages word by word; instead they scan the page, picking out individual words and sentences. In a recent study John Morkes and I found that 79 percent of our test users always scanned any new page they came across; only 16 percent read word-by-word" (Nielsen 1997).

Of course, printed book indexes are meant to be scanned, and they often include navigational aides, such as guide words and *continued* lines, that are all too often lacking in electronic indexes. The electronic index is inherently much more difficult for readers to scan.

Thomas R. Williams, writing in the Society for Technical Communication's journal *Technical Communication,* offers practical suggestions for ensuring that text on the computer screen is presented in a usable manner:

In our efforts to ensure that text is readable, we can draw on knowledge gained from literally hundreds of years of practice in the art of typography as well as recent research that specifically addresses the special typographical challenges posed by the comparatively low resolution of today's computer screens. . . . As the "perceptual" differences between paper and screen lessen, then, we should be increasingly confident in our ability to apply paper-based typographical principles to the screen. (2000, 388–389)

Barnum et al. found that users had difficulty using a visually dense index in a PDF file (2004, 201). Some complained that the hyperlinked numbers associated with the index entries were difficult to click on (200). These findings coincide with Nielsen's thoughts: "Users get lost inside PDF files, which are typically big, linear text blobs that are optimized for print and unpleasant to read and navigate online" (2003).

Large indexes presented online are even more challenging. Dan Scott and Ronnie Seagren (2002, 190–191) present three HTML format options for the 24,000-entry master index that is the subject of their article. The format was developed internally at IBM Canada and includes an interesting twist: "The solution for this project was to provide an expanding, collapsing master index. . . . To assist in scanning, the HTML master index presents only the primary entries at first, but enables users to drill down to secondary and tertiary entries to find exactly the information they need." They found that "initial usability sessions on the current index presentation format indicate that users understand how to work with expanding and collapsing lists, prefer this format to our previous index format, and find the performance of the index from an intranet or from a local workstation acceptable."

What are we to do? Williams's (2000, 389) first recommendation is to use a san serif typeface for text displayed on a screen. His second recommendation is to use 12- to 14-point type. I would add the following recommendations for the electronic display of indexes:

1. Display the index in indented format.

2. Display the index in one column.

3. Link all cross-references to the target index entries so that readers can click on the referenced entry rather than scroll through the index manually.

4. Provide an "A to Z" navigation bar so that readers can quickly access the various letter groups.

5. For lengthy indexes, provide the ability to search the index for terms, and consider the expanding/collapsing format.

Even as computer screen resolution improves, we must keep in mind that simply converting a printed index to electronic format often compromises its usability. Double-column lists of index entries on a printed page can be extremely easy to scan. The same cannot be said of double columns of dense index text on a computer screen.

As more material is presented in electronic format, it is important that we critically examine what works and what does not work when paper-based page design is moved to a computer screen. To date, one of the most comprehensive discussions about these issues can be found in the second edition of Andrew Dillon's *Designing Usable Electronic Text (2004)*.

# *Chapter Nine*

## EDITING THE INDEX

When the indexer comes to the last page of a great book he
rejoices to have finished his work; but he will find by experience,
when he calculates the arrangement of his materials, that he
has scarcely done more than half of what is before him.
—Henry B. Wheatley, *How to Make an Index*

In 1979 G. Norman Knight found Wheatley's comment a fitting introduction to his chapter on editing indexes. It is just as meaningful now as it was in 1902 when Wheatley's book, *How to Make an Index,* was published.

This chapter will discuss editing by the indexer, review of the index by the book author, and editing by the copyeditor. Unfortunately, many indexes do not receive treatment from all three parties. Quite often professionally prepared indexes are not reviewed by authors. Authors who prepare their own indexes frequently turn over to their copyeditors material that is in need of extensive editing, which would be best done by the authors themselves.

It is extremely important for all parties to budget time for review and editing of the index. Professional indexers should build editing time into their work schedules. If an index is to be reviewed by an author, a minimum of three to four days should be added to the schedule so that the author has time to receive the index, review it, and work with the indexer to integrate any changes. After the author and indexer have completed their collaboration, the index is turned over to the copyeditor at the publishing house. The copyeditor may be expected to deliver the index to the production department within a day or two after its receipt. Of course, the time estimates above are tentative. Long and complex indexes will obviously require more editing time.

Authors must understand how little time is available for index review. Because of time considerations, many publishers do not encourage the author to review the index at all. One editor describes the situation in this way: "We give the author very little time for review. The index is sent by e-mail to her in manuscript—only if she asks for it. She has to phone in her changes, but she is not encouraged to have any. Otherwise, the author receives page proofs to look at via FedEx; any response must be made by phone. This last chance is all we give the author. Of course, by this point it is mostly a pro forma OK we are looking for."

## Editing by the Indexer

Like any piece of writing, an index will require editing by its author. When an indexer reaches the last page of text and enters the last entry, what lies before her is a first draft of the index. The work that follows involves several types of editing skills: substantive editing, copyediting, and proofreading. While the publisher will undoubtedly perform these tasks as well, the indexer should provide an index manuscript that is in need of few, if any, copyediting or proofreading changes.

Because an index is internally complex, substantive editing tasks—that is, the rewriting or reorganization of material—should be left to the indexer alone. Careless reorganization of an index can easily result in a breakdown of its conceptual interrelationships.

Editing is an integral component of the indexing process. As an indexer works with the text, editing decisions are made along with entry selection decisions. Frequently, the structure of the index does not emerge until after a few chapters of a book have been indexed. Early in the indexing process the indexer may return to the first 25 percent of the entries and completely restructure them.

The index is molded and remolded throughout the first sweep through the text. This is one reason that an editor's or author's interim review of an index is often not of great benefit. The draft of the index that is sent off for review on day ten may bear little resemblance to the index on day fifteen. An index contracts and expands as it develops. Term selection that made sense on page 125 may not make as much sense by the time the indexer reaches page 230. She may go back to the entries on page 125 and rephrase them in light of new information.

As the indexer adds new entries, old entries are constantly being manipulated. A biological metaphor for this process would not be far off the mark. New cells grow and old cells divide; synergy is at work that results in a functioning organism in which renegade or mutant aberrations have been identified and eliminated. Index writing integrates substantive editing into the initial creative writing process.

The important role that dedicated indexing software plays in the editing process cannot be ignored. Indexers who are able to work with the emerging index in sorted order at all times are able to get a sense of the overall structure of the index quickly. Global search-and-replace operations greatly aid in the restructuring of entries. Indexers who work with this type of software claim that many editing tasks are completed during the index-writing stage; there is far less editing to do at the final stages. Perhaps this intense integration of editing into the index-writing process occurs because of the short amount of time allowed for indexing. Whatever the cause, experienced indexers know when the proper structure for an index has emerged. They can feel it. Once the structure is in place, the cadence of work changes. Term selection seems to move faster. The indexer knows where to place new entries within the index network.

Experienced indexers also know when the structure is not working. But the sense that an index structure is not working is often a good sign. It is what precedes finding the proper structure. Indexers must pay attention to their inner voices. Indexers have even been known to discover the key while dreaming at night. In the morning she returns to the index, reworks it, and "feels" the index fall into place.

One of my colleagues, when asked the question, "What is it that really goes on in indexing?" answered, "Magic!" While magic may or may not play a role, the intense synergy between creativity and editing that grips the indexer is an integral part of the indexing process.

By the time the indexer has reached the last page of text, a definite index structure will be in place. It is now time for the indexer to change modes; the final editing process requires a very different perspective than did the writing process.

### Substantive Editing Tasks

The most difficult and time-consuming aspect of editing for the indexer will be the review of the structure of the index. The indexer, although intimately involved with the index, must be able to develop an "editorial distance" from the work and view it with the eyes of the readers. However, indexers must be careful at this point. Surely there will be index entries to add and entries to eliminate. Assuming that a carefully designed index has emerged, it is important not to interfere with the inherent structure of the index.

▮ *Main headings.* Main headings need to be evaluated one by one, keeping in mind that they are the primary access points in the index. Do they make sense? Are they clear and concise? Are they worded in the way that readers are likely to look them up?

As the indexer proceeds through the index, inevitably inconsistencies and new relationships between concepts will emerge. Inconsistencies should be eliminated; new relationships must be molded into the structure of the index. The need for consistency is paramount. For example,

> baseball, 35–49
> football
>    history of, 80–82
>    professional teams, 92–95
>    rules of, 82–91
>    San Francisco 49ers, 94

The entries above reveal an inconsistent treatment of a similar topic. Assuming that the discussion of baseball covers the same type of topics as the football discussion, either the baseball entry should be divided into subheadings or the football entries should be condensed into one main heading *football, 80–95.* If space allows, the baseball entry could be reworked as

> baseball
>    history of, 35–36
>    professional teams, 42–49
>    rules of, 37–42

The football entry contains one more inconsistency. Why are the San Francisco 49ers the only team mentioned as a subheading? What about the Chicago Bears or the Green Bay Packers? If in fact all the football teams are discussed on pages 92–95, there is no need to list individual teams under the heading *football.* Instead, the subheading *San Francisco 49ers* should be eliminated and changed to a main entry. The indexer should also check the teams described on pages 92–95 to be sure they all appear as main headings within the index.

Similar kinds of topics in an index should be treated in a consistent manner. Readers depend upon this consistency when using the index.

Long strings of undifferentiated reference locators at the main heading level should be broken down into subheadings. Exactly what constitutes a "long" string of page numbers is often defined in a publisher's style guide or, unfortunately, by the space allowed for the index. A common rule of thumb is that more than five reference locators should be differentiated by the addition of subheadings:

> dogs, 23, 29, 35–39, 98–103, 123–127, 158–164, 213–220

The number of locators provided in the entry above places an excessive burden on the reader. The entry is in need of further analysis by the indexer. The indexer will likely return to the text and provide subheadings:

>**dogs,** 23, 29
>>**breeding of,** 35–39
>>**as companions,** 158–164
>>**military use of,** 213–220
>>**obedience training,** 98–103
>>**search-and-rescue operations with,** 123–127

▮ *Subheadings.* Subheadings, like main headings, must be evaluated for their clarity and conciseness. Do they make sense? Are they worded in a way that readers will be likely to look up? Are they necessary? At the subheading level, typical candidates for editing are the single subheading under a main entry and the group of subheadings that all have the same page number. The entry

>**chicken recipes,** 45–49
>>**Chicken Divan,** 53

can be condensed to *chicken recipes, 45–49, 53* without a loss of information.

In the next example the subheadings should be eliminated and then examined as possible main entries:

>**file management,** 35–36
>>**copying files,** 36
>>**deleting files,** 36
>>**moving files,** 36

If these subheadings do not already appear as main entries, the indexer may decide to convert them to main entries:

>**copying files,** 36
>**deleting files,** 36
>**file management,** 35–36
>**moving files,** 36

This type of rearrangement leaves intact the information provided by the original main heading, *file management,* and at the same time provides multiple access points for specific information about the topic. Subheadings that all have the same page number should be eliminated.

▮ *Cross-references and double-postings.* Each cross-reference in an index must be verified. The indexer must be sure that the referenced term does in fact exist in the index. If a cross-reference reads "judiciary, federal. *See* federal courts," the indexer must be sure that there is a complete entry for *federal courts.* Remember that a complete entry will contain at least reference locators and often subheadings as well. All circular cross-references must be eliminated:

judiciary, federal. *See* federal courts
federal courts. *See* judiciary, federal

Cross-references must also be direct. We do not want to send the readers on a convoluted path to the proper term. If the indexer has decided to post information at *federal courts,* then all cross-references from synonyms should directly lead to *federal courts.* The following cross-references are in need of editing:

courts. *See* judiciary, federal
federal courts, 35–42
   appointment of judges, 67
   jurisdiction of, 78
   political influence in, 83
judiciary, federal. *See* federal courts

The entry "courts. *See* judiciary, federal" should be changed to "courts. *See* federal courts."

Cross-references that send the readers elsewhere in the index only to pick up one or two references can often be changed to double-postings:

autos. *See* cars
cars, 67–72

Rather than force readers to spend time going to another portion of the index, the indexer could add the page numbers at the *autos* entry and eliminate the cross-reference. Such double-posting is often best done during the final editing stage. Indexers should be cautious of double-posting information while writing the index. The danger is that the two double-posted entries may not contain the same information in the long run.

A crucial part of the final editing process is checking to see that all double-posted entries are mirror images of each other:

autos, 67–72
   compacts, 74
   sedans, 128
cars, 67–72
   compacts, 74
   sedans, 128
   station wagons, 88–89

In the example above, the double-posted information under *autos* is incomplete. Readers turning to the *autos* entry will not find the information about station wagons. Readers should be able to go to an entry and feel confident that all related information about the topic has been gathered together at the entry. Readers should not have to second-guess the indexer and try to think of synonymous terms.

While it is often beneficial to provide multiple access points for information, the danger in excessive double-posting is that information will be scattered in the index. Scattered information forces readers to look in many places in order to gather all information about a topic. It is the indexer's job to pull related information together. The following series of entries is an example of scattered information:

> oak trees, 82–88
> pine trees, 89–93
> trees, 78–80

Ideally, the indexer will add subheadings to the *trees* entry:

> oak trees, 82–88
> pine trees, 89–93
> trees, 78–93
>> oak trees, 82–88
>> pine trees, 89–93

Lastly, the indexer will review the treatment of synonyms in the index. As noted above, posting information at two or more synonymous terms may lead to scattered information. Such problems must be resolved during the final editing stage. But often during final editing the indexer will add cross-references for synonymous terms. The addition of such cross-references will add to the usability of the index and provide for a more coherent structure.

After the indexer is satisfied that the structure of the index is robust, still more editing tasks remain. The indexer must now wear the hats of a copyeditor and proofreader.

### Copyediting and Proofreading Tasks

Many of the tasks that follow are performed by the indexer throughout the indexing process. However, all index manuscripts will benefit from a final review of the following items.

■ *Alphabetizing.* All main headings and subheadings must be sorted in the alphabetic order desired by the publisher. Even if the indexer uses dedicated indexing software, a review of alphabetic order is still needed. Check the publisher's style guide at this stage to make sure that desired alphabetic order has been followed.

■ *Spelling.* All words in the index should be spelled correctly. Any proper terms, such as personal names, must be proofread against the text. Indexers who use computerized spelling checkers must still manually review the spelling of terms in the index because, as we all know, computerized spelling checkers do not catch all spelling errors. The other problem with computerized spelling checkers is that many of the specialized, as well as proper, terms in an index will not appear in the online dictionary; the spelling checker will tag these terms as misspellings.

■ *Accuracy of reference locators.* All reference locators must be correct. Undoubtedly during the editing process, the indexer looked up many entries in the text. But there certainly will not be time at this point to check the accuracy of each and every entry. The indexer can at least make sure that reference locators are sensible. A locator such as "7883" may be in need of a hyphen or an en dash: "78–83." More troublesome is the incomplete locator, say, "125–." In this case the indexer must return to the text and supply the missing portion. Finally, all reference locators should appear in ascending numeric order, generally with roman numerals preceding all arabic numbers.

■ *Parallel construction.* Main headings and subheadings will follow a consistent grammatical format, whenever possible and whenever parallel construction does not distort the meaning of the entries or make them unwieldy. In the example below, the subheading *move* can be changed to *moving of* so that parallel construction is maintained within the entry:

> **files**
> copying of
> deleting of
> move

■ *Punctuation.* All entries must be checked for the correct use of punctuation in accordance with the publisher's style guide. A comma followed by a space separates multiple reference locators. Multiple cross-referenced terms are separated by a semicolon followed by a space.

Main headings that are followed immediately by a comma and one subheading may benefit from rewording:

> **books, teenagers and, 90**

In the example above, *teenagers and* turns out to be the only subheading for the main heading *books*. The entry would read better as *books and teenagers, 90.*

■ *Capitalization.* The index must be reviewed for correct capitalization. If a publisher asks that every main heading be capitalized, this must be checked. If only proper names and nouns are to be capitalized, this too must be checked.

■ *Format of the index.* If an index is presented in an indented format, indention levels must be coded correctly.

■ *Cross-reference format and placement.* The indexer must check that correct style and placement of cross-references have been followed throughout the index. For example, if *See also* cross-references are to appear as the last subheading, then there should be no *See also* cross-references running off from main headings that are followed by subheadings.

■ *Special typography.* The indexer must be sure that the correct typography has been used throughout the index. Titles of works are usually printed in italics. Any other special elements used in the index must be thoroughly reviewed. If italic page numbers indicate pages containing illustrations, the indexer must check the page numbers for italic. At this point it would help to check the index citations against a list of illustrations from the publisher.

■ *Query resolution.* Any unanswered questions that have emerged during the indexing process must be resolved. For instance, if the indexer has noted inconsistent spellings of an individual's name, the editor or author must be queried unless the indexer is certain of the correct spelling. If the indexer is certain that a name or term has been misspelled, it is kind to provide the editor with this information so that the misspelling can be corrected in the text.

There are types of queries that should not be left until the end of indexing. If the indexer notices any error that may affect the placement of text on pages of the book—such as a misplaced illustration—the editor should be contacted immediately.

■ *Introductory note.* If the index includes any use of special symbols, abbreviations, unconventional sorting methods, or typography, the indexer will write a note that explains the use of such devices. Additionally, if portions of the text are deliberately not indexed, this information is included in the note. The introductory note is placed at the beginning of the index, preceding all entries. It should be worded as succinctly as possible. If it looks too lengthy, users of the index will resist reading it.

■ *Submission format.* An index is usually submitted through e-mail as a file attachment. At a minimum, the indexer will check the file for proper coding. For example, one could locate a term that should be coded for small caps and make sure that the beginning and end codes are correct. Codes that indicate levels in the index should be checked. The indexer should be sure to scroll through the index to make sure that the entire document, from *A* to *Z*, is included in the file.

### Indexer's Editing Checklist

Main headings: clear, concise, sensible

Subheadings: clear, concise, sensible

Cross-references: verified

Cross-references: correct format and placement

Double-postings: complete mirror images of one another

Alphabetizing

Spelling

Reference locators: accuracy of

Reference locators: no long strings of undifferentiated locators

Parallel construction

Punctuation

Capitalization

Format of the index

Special typography

Query resolution

Introductory note

Submission format

### Copyfitting the Index

When the indexer has been informed that the index must fit into *x* number of pages, it is important to deliver an index that fits. Following is a description of a quick and easy way to estimate the length of your index. If you know that the index will have to be shorter than is ideal, it is a good idea to copyfit the index periodically as you work.

In order to estimate actual index length the editor needs to provide the indexer with three bits of information: the number of pages available for the index, approximate number of characters per line of the index, and the number of columns of index text per page. Here is an example of how to apply this information.

> There are 20 pages available for the index. Each page will have 2 columns of index text. Each column will have 48 lines. If we multiply 48 lines by 2 columns we see that there are 96 lines of index text per page. Then multiply 96 lines by 20 pages. There will be room for 1,920 lines of index text. Lastly, there is room for approximately 35 characters per line. The next step is to format the index for a narrow line width, in this case 35 characters, and see how many lines are in the file.

Formatting an index in progress to a narrow line width is very easy to do with dedicated indexing software. For example, if you are halfway through indexing the book and you already have over 1,000 lines in the formatted index and there is room for only 1,920 lines, then you will want to consider reducing the density of indexing.

## Review by the Author

Authors who prepare their own indexes should also perform the editing tasks described in the previous section. Authors who review an index prepared by someone else will do best to focus on the conceptual content of the index. Of course, if the author notices any misspellings or typographical errors, these errors should be pointed out to the indexer.

Authors need not concern themselves with stylistic matters. Rather, they should review the index for completeness and access to information. Before actually looking at the index, some authors find it helpful to reflect on the content of their books and to compose a list of their major topics. With this list in hand, authors can check their indexes by looking up the terms.

Some authors prefer to sit down with the index and read it. They will look up in the text any entries whose meaning is unclear. Authors can also randomly flip through their set of page proofs and attempt to locate index entries for selected pages.

The author may find it helpful to ask the indexer to provide a listing of index entries in page number order as well as a copy of the formatted index. The page number-order listing can be used when the author cannot locate index entries for a particular item on a particular page. The page-number-order listing will provide a list of entries for the page in question; the author will doubtless locate the entry in this listing. It is possible that the indexer has phrased the topic differently than the author would have. At this point the author may suggest a cross-reference that will guide most readers to the entry. Or the author may wish to have the entry changed.

Authors must try to avoid substantial restructuring of the index. If entries are not phrased in the same manner that the author might phrase them, then cross-references can be inserted in the index. Undoubtedly the author will be reminded by both the copyeditor and the indexer that there is very little time available for review of the index. Authors are often expected to return comments about the index within a day or two of its receipt.

It is best if the indexer makes the author aware of any restrictions that the publisher has placed on the index. Many problems that arise during the author review stage are due to the author's lack of understanding of the constraints under which the indexer worked. The most common restriction is space—forcing the index into a limited number of pages. If the indexer has followed particular space-saving procedures, the author needs to know what they are. If written works are posted only as titles and not by authors' names, for example, this convention should be explained to the author.

The author who has abdicated involvement with the index up to this point is not in a good position to insist on major changes that would affect the length of the index or the production schedule for the book. On finding the index unsatisfactory, the author should contact the editor immediately and be prepared to indicate its structural problems clearly and calmly.

A properly prepared index will very likely impress the author. It is easy for the author to be swept away by the depth and intricacy of the index and fail to review it in a detailed manner. Many authors look at a well-prepared index and say, "I didn't realize that I discussed all of that!" Authors must try to approach the index from the perspective of their intended audience. They should look up concepts and topics in the index as a reader might.

If particular topics seem to be missing, authors should contact the indexer. Chances are good that the material is covered somewhere in the index. The indexer and the author can then discuss a better way of providing access to the information.

Ideally, the author will have an opportunity to review the index before it is sent to the publisher and the indexer will be allowed to integrate the author's suggestions into the index before it is submitted to the publisher. But the publishing world rarely operates within an ideal time frame. It is more likely that the author will receive the index from the publisher after the indexer has submitted it. All too often the indexer is out of the loop at this point; the index is in the hands of the editor. However, any substantial changes in the index should be discussed with the indexer, who is in the best position to revise the index. Frequently, the indexer is not consulted about such changes and the integrity of the index is compromised.

It may come as a surprise to many authors that no one outside the publishing house will review the page proofs of the index. Although many indexers offer to review them, rarely are they given the opportunity. All indexers have stories to tell about gross formatting errors in at least one of their indexes. This type of error could have been easily avoided had the indexer been able to review the page proofs. Authors who want to see the final pages of the index must make this desire known to their editors early in the production cycle so that time can be allocated for this final review. Authors may also wish to include the right of final review of the index in their book contracts.

## Editing by the Editor

Ideally, by the time the editor receives the index, little editing will be required. If the indexer and the author have worked together on the index, the editor need only proofread and review it for conformance to desired specifications. After that, the editor need only copyfit the index and send it to the production department for typesetting and final layout.

But most editors will not receive indexes that have been both professionally prepared and thoroughly reviewed by the book author. All too often at this critical point in the production cycle, an editor receives an index that is in need of heavy editing.

The advice found in the thirteenth edition of *The Chicago Manual of Style* is worth repeating. "Copyediting a well-prepared index can be a minor pleasure, an ill-prepared one, a major nightmare. You cannot, as editor, remake a really bad index yourself. . . . You cannot turn a sow's ear of an index into a silk purse" (1982, 18.126).

### Copyediting Issues

The copyeditor's first task is to assess the overall quality of the index. Ill-prepared indexes fall into one of two categories: salvageable and unsalvageable. Since time is of the essence at this point, editors must be able to judge indexes quickly. Following are a few tips that may help the editor assess overall quality.

▪ *Length.* A very short index is immediately suspect. If an index is excessively short, it is most likely unsalvageable. The ideal solution would be to have the material reindexed. An index that is excessively long poses different problems. Such an index is probably in need of thorough and time-consuming restructuring. Information in the index is probably scattered, with little or no pulling together of related information. While this type of index may be salvageable, salvaging it will require the attention of someone very familiar with the text and with indexing. The time required to edit an index of this type must be balanced against the time required to reindex the material from scratch.

▪ *Undifferentiated reference locators.* Another telltale sign of an ill-prepared index is the appearance of entries followed by long strings of refer-

ence locators. While an editor may be able to live with eight or ten locators following an entry, having twenty or more locators is unacceptable.
At first glance it may appear that breaking down these strings of locators
into subheadings will fix the problem. But the fact that long strings of
undifferentiated locators exist at all is symptomatic of a lack of analysis
that will very likely affect other aspects of the index.

■ *Cross-references.* An index that lacks cross-references is suspect.
However, if the index passes muster in other respects, the editor can add
appropriate cross-references without unduly compromising the production schedule.

■ *Subheadings.* Look over lists of subheadings carefully. If you find that
there are subheadings all with the same page numbers, they should be
eliminated and the page numbers moved up to the main heading level
if not already present.

■ *Term selection.* The editor must review the conceptual content of the
index, just as we recommended that authors do. When the editor is
familiar with the text, checking for coverage of major topics will not be
difficult. If major topics are missing, the quality of the index is suspect.
If, upon looking up several entries in the index, the editor still does
not understand the meaning of the entries, the quality of the index is
in serious doubt. When the scope and depth of an index do not reflect
the scope and depth of the text, the material most likely needs to be
reindexed.

A word of caution is called for here. Frequently the editor who receives
the index is not the book editor and is, instead, a production editor or project manager familiar only with the table of contents, the style sheets, and
the type specs for the book. Review of term selection in an index should
not be attempted by editors who are not intimately knowledgeable about
the content of the book. If the book editing has been contracted to a freelance editor, the index should be sent to the freelance editor for review.

■ *Accuracy.* A copyeditor's rule of thumb for checking accuracy in an
index is to randomly look up 10 percent of the entries in the referenced
pages. If only one or two inaccurate entries are discovered, then the
editor should check another 10 percent of the entries. If no inaccuracies
are found in the second group, one can hope that the inaccuracies of
the first group are anomalous. But if more inaccuracies are discovered,
the entire index must be checked. This can be a tedious and error-prone
task. The main problem is how to resolve the inaccuracies. If an entry
cites page 78 as its reference when in fact the page should be 178, it

could be very difficult for the editor to locate the correct reference. The editor who attempts to resolve such inaccuracies will have time only to check for inverted digits (such as 87 instead of 78) and dropped digits (such as 178 instead of 78), but not to leaf through the text, hunting for other kinds of errors. If the reference cannot be corrected quickly, it should be deleted. If an index is full of inaccurate reference locators, it is not usable.

### Ill-prepared Indexes: Available Options

*The Chicago Manual of Style* advises, "If an index cannot be repaired, you have two choices: omit it or have a new one made by a professional indexer—thereby delaying publication" (2003, 18.135). A third option is to publish the index as is.

Unfortunately, in this age of bottom-line publishing, we see the third option frequently exercised. Assuming that the index fits in the space reserved, publishing it as is in the short term is the most cost-effective approach. It is easy to sympathize with editors who are tired of dealing with troublesome authors and have little energy left to demand that the index be rewritten. It is also understandable that delaying the production schedule in order to rework an index can be costly. By the time the index is in the hands of the publisher very likely not much remains in the book's budget to accommodate preparation of a new index.

However, the publication of ill-prepared indexes can have long-term, undesirable effects. First and foremost, such an index reflects badly on the author and the publisher; it indicates a lack of quality and professionalism. In some books the index has a direct effect on sales. For example, instructors reviewing books for classroom use rely heavily on the index. When an instructor is faced with six possible textbook choices, the index is often the initial filter in the review process. If the instructor cannot find pertinent topics in the index, very likely the book will be put aside and the next index scanned. Acquisition librarians have strong feelings about good indexes in books. When it is necessary to decide between various books for purchase, the acquisition librarian will be more likely to purchase the book with the better index.

The first option available to the editor, not publishing an index at all, is the least desirable of the options. Access to information is severely compromised if an index is lacking. But if a given index would be an embarrassment to print, it might be better to be criticized for not providing an index rather than ridiculed by reviewers for publishing a bad one. Another problem with bad indexes is that they can be very misleading. Potential buyers of a book may look at an index, not find a topic, and assume that the topic is not covered in the text, concluding that the book is of little or no value to them. It may not occur to the potential buyer that the index is bad; indeed, many people will assume that the index accurately reflects the content of the book.

The second option, delaying production and having the index redone, may be the most desirable option, but it is probably the least feasible. It is the rare production schedule that has an extra two or three weeks available for last-minute reindexing. And locating an indexer at the eleventh hour can be very difficult.

What is especially frustrating about the submission of bad indexes is that the situation is avoidable. Many publishers are acutely aware of the need to employ or contract with skilled editors, skilled proofreaders, skilled production personnel, and skilled printers and binders. It would be unthinkable for a publisher to turn over a book-length manuscript to an individual for copyediting when that individual has demonstrated no experience in copyediting. And yet, often little thought is given to the professional qualifications of the writer of an index.

As soon as an author has submitted a manuscript, the editor should begin thinking about who will index the book. If the editor knows that the index will be written by an inexperienced indexer, every effort must be made to include time in the production cycle for extensive revision or rewriting. Just as someone who has never before copyedited would not be expected to provide satisfactory services the first time around, so too would it be rare for someone who has never before indexed to provide a satisfactory index.

### Good Indexes: What to Do with Them

The editor who receives a good index that has benefited from thorough review by the indexer/author must still examine the index. An index, like any other piece of writing, will benefit from another stage of copyediting and proofreading. If the index has been submitted electronically, it should be printed as soon as possible to ensure that no computer problems are lurking in the background.

The following checklist is for editors who find the structure of the index in good order and must perform only basic copyediting and proofreading tasks.

**Copyeditor's Checklist**

Check alphabetizing of main entries and subheadings.

Check order of subheadings if the order is not alphabetic.

Check spelling of all words in the index.

Check punctuation.

Verify cross-references.

Check accuracy of reference locators.

Check typography.

Check that formatting is correct, especially of cross-references.

Some of the editing tasks listed above can be done at the manuscript stage. Other tasks, though, are best left until the index page proofs are in hand. In particular, matters relating to typography will need to be checked on the final typeset pages. Editors who must mark up an index manuscript for typesetting should follow the same general procedures used for the markup of any manuscript copy. Additional information about copyediting indexes can be found in *The Chicago Manual of Style* (2003, 18.135–18.137) and Amy Einsohn's *The Copyeditor's Handbook* (2000, 302–306).

## Reducing the Length of an Index: Tips for Editors

For the purpose of the discussion that follows, we will assume that all layout and formatting options that squeeze more index entries onto a page have been fully exploited, and still an index needs to be reduced in size. Eliminating entries from a well-prepared index is a thankless task. Eliminating entries from such an index reduces to some extent the access to information; it should be attempted only by someone intimately familiar with both the index and the text. Ideally, the indexer will be asked to reduce the size of the index. The indexer knows the index thoroughly and will be in a better position to shorten it without severely compromising its internal structure.

The number of index lines that need to be deleted should be ascertained. If only a 1 percent reduction in size is needed, removing the necessary amount of entries will not be difficult. However, a 10 percent reduction in size can prove to be quite complicated.

In an indented-style index, the first candidate for elimination would be sub-subheadings. All sub-subheadings can be eliminated and their reference locators pulled up to the subheading they modify.

If the index is a two-level index (main headings and subheadings), the editor can scan the index for subheadings that are followed by only one page number. These subheadings can be eliminated and their reference locators pulled up to the main heading that they modify.

Another method that can be used to save space is to examine all the index lines that turn over in an indented index. It may be possible to rephrase the entry so that it fits on one line. In a run-in index, the same method can be used: shorten as many entries as possible without distorting their meanings. Always make sure that rephrased entries are alphabetized correctly.

If the index needs to be shortened additionally, the next items to consider deleting are the *See also* cross-references to obviously related topics. It is strongly recommended, however, that an attempt be made to retain all cross-references, since they are integral navigation aids.

If it is house style to distinguish between continuous and noncontinuous discussion of a topic on consecutive pages, editors are cautioned to resist the temptation to consolidate page numbers like "Faulkner, William, 65, 66, 67" by changing them to "65–67". Remember that the comma indicates separate discussion about a topic on the referenced pages whereas the en dash indicates a continuous discussion.

After the index has been reduced in size, it must be copyedited again. First, any entries that have been rephrased need to be checked for correct alphabetization. Second, entries referred to in cross-references in the original index may have been eliminated; the editor must make sure that such terms still exist.

## Revising an Index for a Revised Edition

When a revised edition of a book is published, the editor must decide whether to revise the original index or to write a new one. Three factors that will determine which is the better option are (1) the quality of the index to the original edition, (2) the extent of changes in the text, and (3) whether the original index exists in electronic format. The discussion that follows assumes that the person revising the index either is its original author or has obtained revision rights through copyright assignment or some other contractual agreement.

If the original index is not of good quality, there is no point in revising it. The revision process is not likely to improve the quality of a bad index.

Changes in the text can be editorial additions or deletions and pagination changes. If editorial changes are isolated and not extensive, chances are good that the original index can be revised. But if editorial changes are sporadic and occur throughout the book, probably revising the index will not save time. One critical factor is the effect of editorial changes on the original pagination of the book. If new material is added in chapter 3 and the pagination after the addition is increased in full-page increments, the index entries that are attached to the remaining pages can also be increased by adding the difference to the original reference locators. But if the editorial changes result in the movement of text by paragraphs rather than full pages, repagination of existing index entries can be very time-consuming. Even when an indexer is able to work with the original index in page number order (see below), tracking new pagination on a paragraph-by-paragraph basis is tedious. If the "creeping paragraphs" are restricted to a discrete portion of text, say, twenty pages in chapter 4, it may be cost-effective to revise the index entries for the affected pages and then repaginate the remaining entries automatically.

In order to make a reasonable decision about the revision or rewriting of indexes, the editor must keep track of the changes in the text. Ideally, an editor who decides to revise an index will provide the indexer with the changed pages and a copy of the old pages. For example, the indexer may receive 50 revised pages from chapter 5 of a 300-page book, which result in adding 13 pages to the chapter. The indexer's assignment is to revise the entries for those 50 pages. The entries from chapter 6 onward will be repaginated by adding an increment of 13 to each page number.

An unsatisfactory and expensive arrangement would be to give the indexer old pages and new pages and ask the indexer to figure out where the changes have occurred. It is much better if during the revision process the editor has tracked every textual change that might affect index entries and every pagination change that will affect index entries. Armed with this information, the editor will be in a good position to ascertain whether revising an index is feasible.

If the editorial changes to a book are substantial, the index should be completely rewritten. Changes affecting more than 30 percent of the text are considered substantial. Because the index is an intricate network of interrelationships, substantial changes in the text will greatly impact the structure of the index. A structure that worked well for the original text may need extensive revision if it is to fit the new text. A properly prepared index is not a structure that lends itself well to insertion or deletion of its parts.

If the original index does not exist in electronic format, any thought of revision is best approached with great hesitation. Revision of an index should not be attempted unless it is possible to work with the index entries in page number order. The absence of a page-number-order listing greatly increases the opportunity for error. Anyone revising an index must be certain that all entries on the changed pages have been found on the text pages. The only way to ensure 100 percent accuracy is to work with a page-number-order listing.

Since the mid-1980s, professional indexers have had access to dedicated indexing software that allows them to retain archive copies of index files that can be used at a later date for revision purposes. Many publishers receive indexes in electronic format. However, the electronically submitted indexes are generally formatted versions. Many publishers fail to ask for (or require) simultaneous submission of the archive index files that could be used in the future.

If an index archive file, or data file, is not available, some formatted index files can still be successfully converted to a data file format. There are conversion services and programs that can prepare a formatted index file for import into a dedicated indexing program.

But it is often the case that no electronic version of the index exists. Sometimes publishers find it cost-effective to have the original index pages optically scanned. The files created by the OCR (optical character recognition) process are then edited, converted into index data file format, and imported into dedicated indexing programs for revision. The cost-effectiveness of this procedure must be weighed against the cost of reindexing from scratch.

It would appear that the use of embedded indexing software would greatly alleviate the problems associated with the revision of indexes. Indeed, the ability to quickly generate revised indexes from original text files is the primary raison d'être for such software. However, the use of embedded indexing software is not without its problems. In the next chapter its advantages and disadvantages will be discussed.

Many publishers know from the beginning that a book will go through revisions in the future. Planning for later editions can help make the indexing revision process manageable. The primary index component to consider is the format of the reference locator.

Using section or paragraph numbers as reference locators in the index, as in legal indexing, may be helpful. The primary benefit of using a section or paragraph number as the reference locator is that it is not tied to the actual pagination of the book. Paragraphs can be inserted, deleted, and edited; they can shift from page to page without affecting the index entries that follow.

Publishers of computer documentation revise their material frequently. Quite often computer documentation is paginated using a chapter/page number sequence that begins each chapter anew with page 1. With this method, an unlimited number of editorial changes can be made to one chapter without affecting the index entry pagination for other chapters.

In some material, changes to the text are so frequent that a unique reference locator format must be designed. But all too often, little or no thought is given to the issue during the book design process. Updating and maintaining a thorough and accurate index under such circumstances can be a maddening and difficult task. Early consultation with an indexer can be very beneficial. For example, I was asked by a book design consultant to work out a pagination format for a set of policy and procedures manuals for a large bank. There were approximately fifteen hundred pages of text. The publications manager for the bank said that various portions of the text were revised biweekly. The publications department needed to be able to insert new pages at virtually any point within the set of manuals. The department also wanted to be able to produce a monthly cumulative index for all the manuals. A reference locator format was eventually designed that could accommodate the almost continuous revision of material. With the use of dedicated indexing software, the revisions were handled quickly and new cumulative indexes generated as desired.

Finally, electronic versions of indexes should be retained for future use. Both the formatted version of the index and an archive data file version of the index should be stored by the publisher. In the future, when a revised index is needed, the data files can be put into a dedicated indexing program that generates entry listings in page number order and later can be used to repaginate entries in even increments. Remember that the index data files will not contain any editing changes made to the index after it was submitted to the publisher. So it is also a good idea to retain a copy of the edited index manuscript. Should the index data files be used in the future, the original editing changes can be incorporated into the new index.

# Chapter Ten

## TOOLS FOR INDEXING

The preceding chapters have presented different aspects of index structure and design. This chapter will discuss various methods used to produce indexes. Regardless of which tool the indexer uses, the index must meet the specifications of the publisher that assigned the work. The adage "the right tool for the job" is as appropriate here as it is in carpentry. Just as the carpenter can choose between a hand drill and a power drill, so, too, the indexer can choose between manual and electronic tools. The first portion of this chapter will present manual methods for index production. The automatic indexing tools will be discussed next, followed by a discussion of computer-aided software tools. Lastly, ideas about the future of indexing and indexing tools will be presented.

Each indexer has her or his own way of working. There is great truth in what Delight Ansley said about methods of producing indexes: "The best way to make an index is the way that the indexer finds most convenient. If the result is a good index, nobody will care whether it was made with a notebook, a computer, or knots in a piece of string" (quoted in Knight 1979, 39).

## Manual Methods

In this age of the computer, many scoff at the notion of using manual methods to produce an index. While professional indexers may find the idea of writing index entries by hand on 3″ × 5″ cards ludicrous, the manual method of indexing still has its place. It is not hard for me to imagine an author, tethered for months and months to a computer writing the book, wishing to take page proofs and a stack of index cards to a remote cabin by a lake and prepare the index using 3″ × 5″ cards.

While it is cost-effective for professional indexers to invest $500 or so in dedicated indexing software, authors who index occasionally will likely not want to purchase such software. Aside from the capital investment required to take advantage of computer-aided indexing tools, there is also a significant investment in learning time to consider. In the long run, occasional indexers may be able to produce indexes more quickly using manual methods.

Long before the appearance of the computer, indexes were produced manually, and various methods have emerged over the years. Here, only two methods—the use of index cards and the typing of entries into a text file on a computer—will be presented. G. Norman Knight describes several other manual methods in his chapter "The Mechanics" (1979, 33–39).

### The 3" × 5" Index Card Method

We have all used index cards for one thing or another. These cards can also be used to produce an index. The procedure involves writing entries on the cards, alphabetizing the cards, editing the cards, and typing an index manuscript from the cards.

Each card usually has only one index entry. In this context, an *index entry* refers to a main heading, subheading, and reference locator; or a main heading and cross-reference. If sub-subheadings are used, then the card will contain the main heading, subheading, sub-subheading, and reference locator. The following formatted index entry would be broken down into three index card records:

> **dogs**
>   **feeding of, 56**
>   **walking of, 89**
>   *See also* **American Kennel Club**

The alphabetized cards would look as they do in figure 10.1 (read up from the bottom).

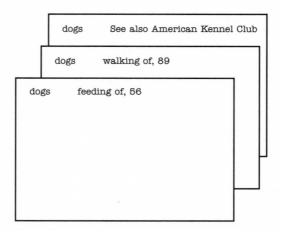

Figure 10.1. Alphabetized index cards

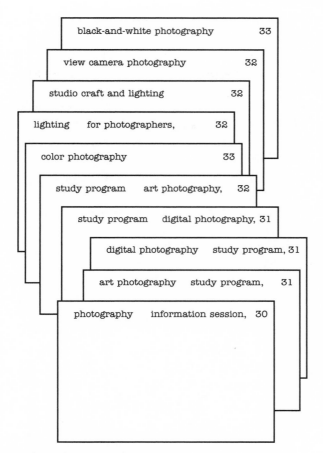

Figure 10.2. Index cards in entry order

When the cards are first written, they are not immediately alphabetized. Instead, the cards are placed face down in a stack so that before the entries become scattered throughout the alphabetic sections of the index, the reference locator can be verified for each card. Prior to alphabetizing, the cards will be in page number (or other locator) order. This is a good time to think about adding cross-references to the cards. Such a stack of cards in entry order might look as they do in figure 10.2.

When a small stack of cards accumulates, the page numbers are checked for accuracy and then the cards are alphabetized and placed in a container with alphabetic dividers. There are special filing boxes built to hold 3" × 5" index cards; these boxes can be several feet long. Shoe boxes can also be used to hold the cards. In any case, a box of some size will be needed for a book-length index, which may require several thousand index cards.

Once a batch of perhaps several hundred cards has been alphabetized and filed, the indexer will perform minor editing tasks when filing new cards. Entries on previously filed cards will be looked up to ensure consistency in terminology.

After the first sweep through the page proofs has been completed and cards have been written and filed for all entries, the next step is to review and edit the cards. At this point, a large work space is helpful. The index cards can be spread out on a large table so that various entries can be compared. Many of the editing tasks described in chapter 9 are performed at this time, as are reorganization and rearrangement of the entries. Corrections to entries are written on the cards. If necessary, the edited card is realphabetized. The goal at this stage is to prepare the cards for typing.

The last stage of the process is typing the index manuscript. At this point all term selection decisions and editing tasks have been completed. The index entries are typed in a word-processor file in the correct format. The file is then sent to the publisher.

## The Text File Method

Using a computer as a manual indexing method may seem a contradiction. But when the indexer must perform such mundane tasks as alphabetizing, we are still in the realm of manual methods of indexing. Please see later sections of this chapter for a discussion of more sophisticated computer-aided indexing methods.

The *text file method* of index production is quite simple. The entries are typed into a text file. Subheadings are placed under main headings and indented, usually with a tab character. As the indexer adds entries to the file, the entries are placed in alphabetic order. For example, the subheading *painting, 149* would be inserted as the third line of the following:

> **art classes**
> **monoprinting, 56**
> **watercolor, 89**

One drawback to this method is that the indexer must think of not only term selection but also alphabetizing at one and the same time. The indexer working with index cards can focus on term selection and perform alphabetizing tasks at another time. Another drawback to the text file method is that as the file grows in length, moving from the end of the file to the beginning of the file to insert a new entry in the various sections of the alphabet can be quite tedious. One way to speed up this process is to insert alphabetic header letters in a unique way that allows for quick searching. For example, on the line above the *C* entries, the indexer can place the sequence "C$." When it is necessary to go to the *C*'s to insert an entry, the indexer can search for C$ and quickly be taken to the *C* portion of the index.

Benefits of the text file method include the ready availability of common word-processing tools. For instance, the text file can be quickly searched if the indexer wishes to look up another entry. Also there are features that check spelling. The index can be printed at any time, providing a useful reference for the indexer working with long indexes. The primary benefit of this method is that there is no separate step required for typing the index manuscript. Assuming that the indexer is able to alphabetize quickly, the text file method may take less time than the index card method.

Those who use the text file method will naturally be tempted to let the computer alphabetize the index entries. As we shall see in the discussion that follows about embedded indexing software, allowing the computer to sort the entries is not an option. Even if the sorting modules available in word-processing software could sort properly, there is the added problem of subheadings beginning with a tab character or spaces that indicate an indention level. The character or characters used to indicate indention levels will be sorted along with the text characters that follow if a line-by-line sorting method is used. Such a sorting method will completely jumble the structure of the index. Some suggest using a spreadsheet program to enter index entries. However, this is not an efficient solution. If I had to choose between the manual methods, I would opt for writing entries on index cards—with a pencil, of course.

## Automatic Indexing

> automatic: *adj.* 1 a : involuntary either wholly or to a major extent so that any activity of the will is largely negligible : of a reflex nature : without volition <the *automatic* blinking of the eyelids> b : like or suggestive of an automaton : MECHANICAL <the *automatic* smile of a tired store clerk> c : performed without conscious awareness <an unthinking *automatic* response> (Merriam-Webster, Inc. 2004)

Automatic indexing conjures up images of indexing at the push of a button, the computer taking care of all the drudgery and the thinking involved in creating an index. With respect to the way that indexing has been discussed in this book, the phrase *automatic indexing* is an oxymoron. There is nothing automatic about the index-writing process. There is no automatic indexing tool available that could produce the index in the back of this book. Many of the automatic indexing tools available are not intended to be used with book-length narrative text. Instead, they were designed to process massive amounts of textual data in open systems. So automatic indexing is not *indexing* as the word is used in this book.

Automatic indexing has been a research focus in information science for decades. An online search for "automatic indexing" returned over 65,000 hits in early 2005. Readers wanting more information about this topic will find it in James Anderson and José Pérez-Carballo's excellent book *Information Retrival Design* (2005). Additionally, Donald O. Case (2002) in his book, *Looking for Information: A Survey of Research on Information Seeking, Needs, and Behavior*, thoroughly presents historical and contemporary concerns in information retrieval.

In chapter 1 the distinction between closed-system indexing and open-system indexing was introduced. In this book the focus has been on closed-system indexing, within a single document. Automatic indexing tools are used for open systems. Search engines like Google use automatic indexing tools to locate specified search terms on the ever-changing Web. The Web is an open system, constantly in flux as material is added and deleted worldwide, twenty-four hours a day. Search engines must use automated tools; there is no other choice.

A book, be it on paper or on a screen, is a closed system. Automatic indexing of books has failed miserably, as will be discussed below. A properly prepared book index is the product of a human mind. The human mind has a significant advantage over automatic tools: it can think.

### Intellectual versus Algorithmic Analysis of Text

Automatic tools for indexing are distinguished from computer-assisted indexing tools primarily by their lack of intellectual analysis of text. When computer-assisted tools are used, a human selects the text to include in the index; the computer manipulates the text and produces a listing in the format of an index. When automatic tools are used, the software selects text for the index on the basis of the algorithms that are part of the software's instruction set.

The distinction between the intellectual and algorithmic analysis of text has particular importance in regard to the writing and preparation of indexes as stand-alone documents. While there is interesting and challenging work going on in natural language research, computers are not

| Analyse | Helpful | Relationships |
|---|---|---|
| Arrange | Identify | Relevant |
| Arrangement | Index | Scattered |
| Based | Indexed | Seeking |
| Being | Indicate | Series |
| Chosen | Information | Significant |
| Concepts | Locate | Subheadings |
| Cross-references | Material | Subject |
| Direct | Means | Subjects |
| Discriminate | Mention | Synthesize |
| Document | Nothing | Systematic |
| Entries | Offers | Terminology |
| Exclude | Order | Terms |
| Function | Passing | Treated |
| Group | Potential | User |
| Headings | Produce | |

Figure 10.3. Concordance listing for the "Function of an Index" (BS 3700: 1998)

able to analyze and synthesize text as efficiently as the human mind can. No automated indexing program currently available can compete with the experienced human indexer. No such program can produce an index that conforms to the ASI–H. W. Wilson Award criteria for the content of an index. None can fulfill the *British Standard*'s criteria for the function of an index. Most significant, no automated indexing program available can be used to produce a proper book index.

The previous statement might appear to be incorrect since a common feature of most PC-based word-processing programs is automatic indexing. And although many of those programs also offer computer-assisted embedded indexing functions, it is the automatic indexing feature that we see advertised. What we have here is a terminology problem. The common feature found in word-processing software is not *automatic indexing*; rather, it is *automatic concordance generation*. A *concordance* is a list of words that appear in a document followed by a reference locator. Unlike an index, no analysis of the text is required to produce such a list. There will be no subheadings in such a list, no cross-references, no gathering together of related information. A concordance listing for the "Function of an Index" (BS 3700: 1988) discussed in chapter 1 would look like figure 10.3.

One of the most egregious attempts at automatic book indexing made its way to market in 1994—the program Indexicon. Here are some quotes from the Indexicon package:

- Indexicon pays for itself after 50 pages of referencing* (*Based on professional indexing pricing of $3 per page)
- The Standard for Indexing is Here!

- With just a click of the mouse, you create back-of-the-book indexes
- Produce professional quality indexes at a rate of up to 50 pages per minute

A review of Indexicon published in the American Society of Indexers newsletter concluded, "Automatic indexing was never intended to produce back-of-the-book indexes. As Indexicon demonstrates so well, back-of-the-book indexes cannot be automatically generated" (Mulvany and Milstead 1994). After this review appeared, Steven Waldron, president of the company that published Indexicon, apologized to the indexing community:

> With regard to professional or human-quality claims made about the product, these will be clarified in all advertising and p.r. in general, as well as on all future packaging. Obviously, there are ads, articles and packages already in circulation that are impossible to correct. I deeply regret these errors in communication and pledge that all future ads, p.r. and packaging will describe only those product capabilities which are readily demonstrable. (Waldron 1994)

Within a few years Indexicon was pulled from the market.

Back in 1992 Hans Wellisch (1992, 75) summed up the situation in this way:

> Yet the human faculty of understanding, the grasping of meaning and context, is a process that depends on "knowledge of the world" (a vast microcosm of experiences, memories, relations and intuitions) and whose workings are essentially still an enigma. It can therefore neither be successfully performed nor even approximated by machines, fraudulent claims to the contrary by artificial intelligence enthusiasts notwithstanding.

Wellisch's words still ring true today, especially in regard to closed-system indexing. A computer is capable of quickly processing massive amounts of data while humans can process only limited amounts of material at one time. But when access to information is the goal, the intellectual and analytical skills of human beings are far superior to the algorithmic skills of the computer. It is unfortunate that the sheer mass of material published in both the print and the electronic media precludes the writing of indexes for each and every document.

## Computer-aided Indexing

Tools for computer-aided indexing manipulate index entries by alphabetizing and merging the entries, and by formatting the entries into a structured index. Entry selection is performed by the indexer. The indexer decides exactly how to phrase all entries. Ideally, computer-aided indexing tools free indexers from mundane tasks such as alphabetizing and allow them to focus attention on term selection and the structure of the index.

Computer-aided indexing software can be divided into two categories: embedded and dedicated. Embedded indexing software is generally a feature found in word-processing or page design software such as Microsoft Word or Adobe Framemaker. It allows the indexer to insert index entries (or tags for entries) directly into the document's text files. Dedicated indexing software is stand-alone software that requires the indexer to type index entries and reference locators into the program. The sole purpose of such software is the production of indexes. Programs such as MACREX (http://www.macrex.com), SKY Index (http://www.sky-software.com), and CINDEX (http://www.indexres.com) are examples of dedicated indexing software. Both types of computer-aided indexing tools will be discussed in this section.

### Embedded Indexing Software

Embedded indexing software allows the indexer to insert index entries (or tags for the entries) into a document's text file or files. The indexer inserts entries in one of two ways: (1) the entries are typed using special codes or commands that distinguish the entries from the actual text, or (2) terms in the text are marked in a unique way that identifies them as index entries. After entries are embedded, the software will generate an index by scanning the text, extracting the embedded entries, attaching page numbers, and then sorting and merging the entries to construct an index.

Many document-processing programs have contained embedded indexing modules since the mid-1980s. While we have witnessed dramatic improvements in the capabilities of document-processing software, the indexing modules have remained surprisingly unsophisticated (Mauer 2000; Mulvany 1990, 1999; Wittmann, 1991; Wright 1998).

Although the way that index entries are embedded in text files varies from program to program, some generalizations can be made about this method of producing an index. In some programs, embedded index entries are treated as "hidden" text. This means that after an entry has been inserted, it is not visible on the computer screen unless a special command is issued. Figure 10.4 shows a few paragraphs that were indexed with Word.

---

Noeline Bridge{ XE "Bridge, Noeline" } (2002) identifies six patterns of name problems:

1. order in which to enter names
2. length or brevity of names
3. one-word names
4. distinguishing between names that are similar
5. names that change
6. spelling of transliterated names

These are indeed issues that every indexer will face at some time or another. While it is not necessary or practical for the working indexer to know every rule for every situation, it is important to know where to turn for authoritative guidance.
{ XE "reference resources:personal names" }
The American Library Association's *Anglo-American Cataloging Rules* { XE "*Anglo-American Cataloging Rules*" }{ XE "AACR2" \t "See *Anglo-American Cataloging Rules*" }(2d ed., 2002 Revision) has been used as a primary reference source for personal names. Particular references to this tome will be cited as follows: (AACR2 section number). When appropriate, more specialized reference sources will be mentioned. One of the most comprehensive sources of reference information is K. G. B. Bakewell's{ XE "Bakewell, K.G.B." } *Information Sources and Reference Tools,* { XE "*Information Sources and Reference Tools*" } particularly chapter 3, "Reference Tools for the Indexer." Various online reference sources are included. Some were obtained from Noeline Bridge's article, "Verifying Personal Names on the Web," that appeared in April 2003 issue of *The Indexer.*

---

Figure 10.4. Embedded index entries

The program generated the following index entries from the embedded index tags.

> AACR2. See *Anglo-American Cataloging Rules*
> *Anglo-American Cataloging Rules*, 1
> Bakewell, K. G. B., 1
> Bridge, Noeline, 1
> *Information Sources and Reference Tools*, 1
> reference resources
>    personal names, 1

Other programs require the indexer to type the index entry on a separate line preceded by special codes that indicate that the text is an index entry. When index entries are embedded in this way, they are usually visible on the screen at all times. Embedded entries can be edited like other text in the file.

Regardless of how they are embedded, when the document is printed the index entries do not appear with the rest of the text. Embedded entries will appear only after the indexer has asked the software to generate an index.

Most embedded indexing software provides two ways to designate entries. One method involves marking text in the document file and issuing a command to include the marked text as an entry for the index. The second method is used when the indexer needs to include an entry that does not appear verbatim in the text. The indexer issues a command to indicate that an entry should be embedded at a specific point in the text. The indexer then types the exact text for the entry.

Indexers who embed entries in the text files need not worry about assigning reference locators; the software adds the locators to the entries when the index is generated. That index entries can be written independently of the assignment of reference locators provides two primary arguments in favor of this indexing method:

1. Indexing can begin before page proofs are ready.

2. Future revisions of the text will not require reindexing of the entire text since index entries will be retained in the text that remains unchanged. Because the entries are not tied to locators, additions or deletions of text will not affect the entry locators; the software will assign new locators if the text is repaginated.

The second argument in favor of embedded indexing has taken on even more weight as the technical writing industry has moved to single-sourcing. This refers to the creation of one set of documents that can be output in a wide variety of formats, such as print, online, Web files, and online help files. Regarding the indexing component of single-sourcing, Jan Wright provides this description (Mulvany 2003a, 2):

Single-source indexing is an environment of tools and techniques, developed to help the client write one set of documents and then output them in a variety of ways, carrying along the content, formatting, and indexing into each version. An example would be a set of manuals for a software product that comes in two versions, a "light" version and a "professional" version that has more features. As the writers work, they craft two versions of the text in one document. Some text will appear in both books, some text will only appear in the light version, and some text will only appear in the professional version. The index must cover all the versions and compile correctly for each one. Software packages like Frame allow the writers to create "conditional" text—that is, text that appears in a version when certain rules are met. For this scenario, text would be tagged either as "all," "light," or "pro," and the rules pull out the "all" text and the "light" text to create the light version, and similarly the "all" text and the "pro" text for the pro version.

It gets even more fun. If this same group wanted to create online help from the same set of files, they could tag some paragraphs as "online only" or "print only." You now have four versions of output (online light, online pro, print light, print pro). The indexer has to identify the least flexible interface (e.g., online vs. print) for all of these outputs, and design the entire index around those constraints. Usually it is the online interface that is the most demanding and inflexible—it must be coded correctly or it breaks. The print index usually suffers somewhat from being forced to look like an online index in print. But with just one set of index entries for all four outputs you have to choose to sacrifice some niceties.

On the face of it, these arguments in favor of embedded indexing are quite convincing. However, very serious problems with embedded indexing tools lurk beneath the surface. In the discussion that follows every effort has been made to distinguish between technical problems with embedded indexing software and practical problems with this method of index writing. Technical problems can be solved by reprogramming. Practical problems require reevaluation of the entire approach. The practical problems will be discussed first.

▮ *Practical problems.* Time is of the essence when an indexer is creating an index from page proofs of a book, as has been pointed out many times. Once proofs have been produced, the book is almost ready to go to the printer for manufacturing. Any method that would give the indexer more time to write the index is alluring. Using embedded indexing tools, index writing can begin before the page proofs are generated. However, we must ask ourselves, at what point is it practical to begin indexing?

It is sometimes suggested that index entries be embedded by authors as they write their texts. But as noted earlier, writing narrative text and writing index text are two very different forms of writing. How many authors are capable of switching from one writing mode to another in midstream? How many would *want* to? If index entries are embedded in concert with the writing, how many index entries will remain through the editing and rewriting stages? How many first drafts of a book go unchanged? How much of the original indexing work will have to be eliminated as the text is edited?

Many authors who do embed index entries do not do so as they are in the process of writing the text. Instead, they return to the text files and embed index entries as a procedure separate and distinct from the writing process. Some wait until the text has gone through several stages of review and editing. Often the indexing does not begin until the document is undergoing a final review. While the author waits for comments, he or she embeds index entries in text that is assumed to be fairly stable. Authors who wait until the final review stage to begin indexing have a much clearer picture of the structure of the book. Far less time will be spent reorganizing and rethinking the index if the general structure of the book is known before indexing begins.

In some technical writing environments a professional indexer rather than the writer creates the index. File management is a major concern. Let's use the example of a five-hundred-page software manual. The manual will be broken into many separate files, often by chapter. The indexer will embed entries chapter by chapter. However, the complete index is compiled from entries embedded in all of the files. Frequently the indexer will embed entries in one file and then return the file to the project manager and begin work on the next file. Jan Wright (2004) describes the work flow in this way:

> The biggest problem with embedding is that the indexer needs the files. The indexer can have them one by one during the embedding process, but he or she needs all of the files to compile the index. That's often a problem at this stage of book production—right when the illustrators need to make changes and copyeditors want to fix the ragging in the files, that's when the indexer needs sole access. The way the software designers designed the indexing modules guarantees a bottleneck. So the indexer is stuck with seeing one file at a time, not getting the big picture until the very end, and taking the chance that someone else is opening a copy of the same file she is working in. If someone works on a copy of the file and makes copy changes, the two files—one with indexing that the indexer has been working on, and the one with copy changes—must be merged somehow later. It means copying over tedious edits, because someone forgot the file was checked out to the indexer. You must practice version control and file management.

Most book authors use word-processing software to produce their texts. But most writers whose books are published by traditional publishers are not using the software that will be used to typeset and paginate their books. For example, authors may use Microsoft Word and deliver Word files to their publishers. What often happens at this point is that the Word files are converted by the publisher or typesetter to another format for typesetting.

The page breaks in the Word files are not the same as the page breaks in the typeset copy of the file. In order for the correct page numbers to be assigned to embedded index entries in the Word files, authors will need to repaginate the files, usually by forcing new page breaks, to duplicate the pagination of the typeset book copy. This will mean waiting until the page proofs of the book are in hand. At best, this is a tedious, time-consuming, error-prone task to perform on a megabyte or two of text files—a common size for a book-length manuscript. Surprisingly, some publishers continue to recommend this method to their authors (see the excerpt from the Columbia University Press *Guide for Authors* in chapter 2).

Another problem with current embedded indexing software is that it is cumbersome for the indexer to move between various parts of the text. Many indexers refer forward and backward through the pages of a book while indexing to check other discussions of similar material. Most book-length documents are not stored in one file; instead, the text is often divided into separate files, perhaps one chapter per file. To examine text in another chapter, then, one must open separate files. The indexer will often avoid this step and instead leave loose ends that will have to be cleared up later during the editing stage. Wright (2004) cautions that "you must increase your editing time for embedded projects by nearly 40 percent of the total project due to this problem."

Some technical writers who index their own work using embedded indexing tools work from a printed copy of their documents before embedding entries in the text files. These writers claim that they save a great deal of time by marking entries on the printed pages, primarily because the printed pages are much easier to read than the computer screen. They also keep a printed copy of the entire manuscript close by solely for the purpose of referring to other portions of the text while indexing. Another advantage of working with printed text pages is that the writers can indicate exactly where to embed entries on the printed page. Then, when they work with the text file, they know where to insert the entries. Later, when the entries need to be edited, they can refer to their marked copy of the pages and easily locate the embedded entry.

By far the most important reasons cited above for embedding index entries in text files are to avoid reindexing the text when it is revised in the future and to accommodate single-sourcing and the translation and internationalization requirements. Even in the face of technical problems that increase the time needed for indexing two- to threefold when compared with the use of dedicated indexing software tools, many publishers find that embedded indexing is still cost-effective.

In chapter 9 some of the problems inherent in the revision of indexes were presented. Even if we put aside the technical problems found in current versions of embedded indexing software (discussed below), we are still faced with the practical problems of revising indexes. While it is true that embedded entries will be carried along when text is moved from one part of a document to another, it is also true that embedded entries will be deleted when the text is deleted. When a document is extensively revised, we must ask ourselves, how much of the original indexing work will remain? Do the remaining entries still make sense, or has the basic organization of the index been undermined? If a significant number of the index entries are eliminated, those entries that remain must be reexamined in light of the changed material, whether that material has been added or removed.

Another problem with revising embedded index entries is that their coding can easily be corrupted when writers return to a document and do not turn on the display of the embedded index entries. (Figure 10.4 illustrates why many authors do not want the hidden entries to be displayed.) For example, a block of text within a paragraph is moved to a sidebar on another page. Because the display of index entries is not turned on, the index entry is overlooked in the move. It remains with the rest of the paragraph, referring to material that has been moved. Wright (2004) points out, "If a book is heavily revised, it's best to remove the embedded entries and start over. Troubleshooting bad codes can take more time than it is worth. On the other hand, if the technical writing style is highly modularized, as it is in many technical documents, the indexing often remains good for several releases unchanged."

An index is an interconnected network of access points to information in the text. Tampering with the network links through deletions and additions of entries can significantly affect the integrity of the entire index structure. When a document undergoes extensive revision, the new index that is generated from the embedded entries must be thoroughly reviewed and edited. This type of review, in and of itself, can be time-consuming. Every cross-reference must be verified. The new index must be compared to the old index to make sure that important entries have not been left out by mistake. When we add up the time it took to embed the entries in the first version and the additional time it took to embed new entries in the second version and then add the editing time needed to ensure that the integrity of the index structure has not been compromised, we see that it would often take far less time to reindex the material from scratch.

Regarding single-source documents that will be output in various formats, many of the problems of maintaining index integrity can be resolved by producing extremely simple, and often unhelpful, indexes. While inadequate indexes are unfortunately common in computer documentation, this trend of producing simple indexes is appearing in mainstream publishing as well.

Some publishers require the indexer to assign unique numeric codes as reference locators to the index entries. Then the indexer indicates on printed or electronic copy of the document where these codes should be embedded. Although the indexer is not physically embedding the index entries, the idea is the same. Index entries are associated with discrete pieces of content. Once the index entries have been embedded, a piece of content can be extracted along with the index entries attached to that content and reused. For example, chapter 15 from an economics textbook can be pulled out into a separate XML file. All the formatting and index entries would come along and the content could be placed on a Web site or in another book. If the content of chapter 15 is placed in another book, it would not require indexing, because the index has already been embedded. No thought is given to the fact that the original index entries were designed for a closed system, the original twenty-chapter economics textbook. How these index entries will work in another context is not usually considered.

Fortunately, there are situations in which the reuse of index entries can work effectively. A primary requirement is the realization that a great deal of prior planning is needed. Without this planning, there is no guarantee that moving index entries from one context to another will work well. The planning involves applying open-system indexing principles. Jan Wright (2004) describes one successful project:

> I have designed systems where you can pull a topic with its index entries out of context, and merge it into another document successfully. This worked only because I established a 20,000-line controlled vocabulary throughout the entire company's documentation indexing, and because the topics were very modular. The entries from over 80 files and 6 books all meshed, and it worked when you pulled an assortment of topics out and put them into another file during revisions or for a

separate product. But few companies spend the time to develop that front-end vocabulary control. I was in on the first release of the software, and was able to maintain vocabulary control through 6 releases. It made the indexing easy to revise, but updates still meant checking each topic for changes. I would check a topic's existing indexing, and make any changes or corrections under the constraints of the master index vocabulary. I could also predict what new indexing would look like, where it would fit into the open system. This level of planning is out of the ordinary, but it works nicely, as long as you have an indexing tsarina.

**▮ Technical problems.** Technical problems with embedded indexing software are related to software design or hardware limitations. Unlike some of the practical problems discussed above, technical problems can be resolved through reprogramming and the use of more capable hardware. A detailed discussion of the technical limitations of popular embedded indexing programs can be found elsewhere (Mauer 2000; Mulvany 1990, 1999; Wittmann 1991; Wright 1998). The discussion here will focus on general problems common to most embedded indexing programs. Technical problems can be divided into two categories: (1) problems related to actual index entry manipulation, and (2) problems related to user interface design.

*Index entry manipulation.* Index entry manipulation includes the sorting of entries, the formatting and placement of cross-references, the handling of reference locators, and the formatting of the index as a whole. As has been pointed out in previous chapters, there are different ways to sort entries in an index. The indexer needs the flexibility to sort index entries in a manner that will provide the best access to information for readers. In addition to choosing between a word-by-word or letter-by-letter alphabetizing sequence, the indexer must be able to control the sorting of numeric entries and special types of entries, such as names beginning with "St." or "Mc." Many embedded indexing programs do not even offer a choice between word-by-word and letter-by-letter alphabetizing.

The least sophisticated programs alphabetize the index entries in strict ASCII order. It is easy to spot this type of sorting because capitalized entries will precede all entries beginning with lowercase letters. One notch above the programs that rely on a strict ASCII sort are those that use a slightly modified ASCII sort. This type of program will typically sort letters without regard to whether they are upper- or lowercase. However, the extent of the modifications to a strict ASCII sort is usually limited to letters of the alphabet and letters that appear in the international character set. Often punctuation marks and other symbols are not assigned a new sort order; they retain their ASCII sort values. For example, *"Who Is Duffy?"* will sort before *apples* because the ASCII value of the double quotation mark (034) is lower than the ASCII value of a lowercase *a* (097).

Some embedded indexing software is programmed to ignore such characters as double quotation marks and parentheses. But as a rule, these programs do sort on the space character, which means that letter-by-letter alphabetizing is not possible. Even if word-by-word alphabetizing is desirable, embedded indexing programs usually do not sort numbers in ascending numeric order.

The documentation for most of these programs rarely provides a thorough discussion of the sorting sequence used, but the indexer needs to know how entries will be sorted. Following is a short list of terms that can be used to test the sorting order of an embedded indexing program. These terms are sorted in three ways: (1) in strict ASCII order, (2) in word-by-word order, and (3) in letter-by-letter order. In both the word-by-word and letter-by-letter lists, numbers have been sorted in ascending numeric order.

| Strict ASCII Sort | Word-by-Word Sort | Letter-by-Letter Sort |
| --- | --- | --- |
| "Who Is Duffy?" | data structure | database |
| FORMAT statement | database | data structure |
| Intel 80386 | format command | format command |
| Intel 8088 | FORMAT statement | FORMAT statement |
| data structure | Intel 8088 | Intel 8088 |
| database | Intel 80386 | Intel 80386 |
| format command | "Who Is Duffy?" | "Who Is Duffy?" |

Embedded indexing programs that do not allow the indexer any control over the sort order of the entries force the indexer to carefully review and alphabetize the index entries manually. In a book-length index, resorting index entries can take a great deal of time.

Most publishers require that leading prepositions, articles, and conjunctions in subheadings not be sorted. Additionally, some publishers ask that names beginning with "St." or "Mc" be sorted in a special manner. Lastly, many publishers require that numbers be sorted as if they were spelled out. Some embedded indexing programs allow the indexer to force a particular sort order through the use of a "Sort as" field. The program often provides the indexer with a dialog box where the index entries are input along with any "Sort as" instructions. For example, if the indexer wanted the subheading *of host mode* to sort as *host mode*, the index entry dialog box might look like figure 10.5. The "Sort as" field instructs the

```
┌─────────────────────────────────────┐
│           Mark Index Entry           │
│                                      │
│  Main Heading:    RAM requirements   │
│  Sort as:                            │
│                                      │
│  Subheading:      of host mode       │
│  Sort as:         host mode          │
│                                      │
└─────────────────────────────────────┘
```

Figure 10.5. Dialog box 1

```
┌─────────────────────────────────────┐
│           Mark Index Entry           │
│                                      │
│  Main Heading:    5th Avenue         │
│  Sort as:         fifth avenue       │
│                                      │
│  Subheading:                         │
│  Sort as:                            │
│                                      │
└─────────────────────────────────────┘
```

Figure 10.6. Dialog box 2

```
┌─────────────────────────────────────┐
│           Mark Index Entry           │
│                                      │
│  Main Heading:    data structure     │
│  Sort as:         datastructure      │
│                                      │
│  Subheading:                         │
│  Sort as:                            │
│                                      │
└─────────────────────────────────────┘
```

Figure 10.7. Dialog box 3

computer to ignore the *of* when this subheading is sorted. Likewise, the indexer could instruct the computer to sort a numeric entry as though it were spelled out, as in figure 10.6.

In theory, the indexer could force a letter-by-letter sort through the use of a "Sort as" field. Using the entry list above, the *data structure* entry could be entered in the dialog box as shown in figure 10.7. In practice, however, indexers are unlikely to have the time to force a letter-by-letter sort in this way, because of the additional typing of entries that is required.

Most embedded indexing programs allow the indexer to insert *See* and *See also* cross-references. The indexer, however, is usually limited to one predefined format and a predefined placement for them. Some programs will automatically place a *See also* cross-reference as a subheading at the end of a subheading list. If the indexer or the publisher/client wants the cross-reference placed at the top of the entry, run off from the main heading, it will have to be moved manually after the index has been generated. Some programs will not merge multiple cross-references into a single entry, so the indexer must either add them all at one time or merge them manually after the index has been generated. For example, some programs produce

> *See also* **formatting commands**
> *See also* **graphics**

instead of

> *See also* **formatting commands; graphics**

Unlike some dedicated indexing programs, embedded indexing software does not always provide for cross-reference verification. The indexer will have to make a manual check that each referenced term exists elsewhere in the index.

Embedded indexing programs will assign page numbers to entries. Some programs will automatically concatenate consecutive page numbers to form a page range. For example, "dogs, 3, 4, 5, 6" will appear as "dogs, 3–6" in some indexes. However, the indexer usually does not have the option of making distinctions between a consecutive discussion of a topic on pages 3–6 and a sporadic discussion on pages 3, 4, 5, and 6. The page-number concatenation feature is applied to all entries with consecutive page numbers; it cannot be turned off for a single entry.

A handful of embedded programs provide for page-range compression or elision of numbers. Most of the few programs that do perform compression of page numbers follow the abbreviation sequence used in *The Chicago Manual of Style* (2003, 9.64); other compression methods—which may be required by clients—are not allowed.

Programs that can handle multipart page numbers allow the indexer to specify the character(s) used as the page-number concatenator. In a book that renumbers pages with each chapter, the following format for a page range is possible:

> **roses, fertilizer for, 4-5 to 4-10**

Many embedded indexing programs will assign only page numbers as reference locators, however. It is not possible to use a section number or paragraph number as a reference locator.

While many of the programs allow the indexer to specify that a page number be printed in italic or bold type, annotated page numbers are usually not allowed. For example, the indexer could not use the following types of notations:

> **Beef Wellington, 34–36, 42(illus.)**
> **minimalist writing techniques, 124n**

The majority of indexes produced by embedded indexing programs are printed in indented style, although a handful of programs can format a run-in-style index. If the software tools are selected carefully, moreover, some embedded programs can create hyperlinks for reference locators when the index is converted from print to an electronic version. But in general, when compared to the formatting capabilities of dedicated indexing software, embedded indexing software formatting options seem extremely limited.

*User interface design. User interface design* refers to the way a user works with software and includes what the user sees on the computer screen. In document-processing software, user interface design varies greatly. While it is difficult to address the specific design aspects of individual programs, some general comments can be made.

Many embedded indexing programs are designed to tag index entries in text files. This means that the indexer can mark a word in the text file and the software will automatically include that word in the index. The design of these programs is based upon the spurious notion that index entries always appear verbatim in the text files. Unfortunately, this is not the case. It is extremely unlikely that a main heading and its subheading will appear in natural form in the text file. So, ultimately, the marking of existing terms is of little use to the indexer. Instead, it is often necessary for the indexer to type the entry in a form appropriate to the index.

On the whole, embedded indexing programs require the indexer to perform more typing tasks than do dedicated indexing programs. For instance, most embedded indexing programs lack an automatic inversion function. If an indexer wants to include both *California, counties* and *counties, California* as entries, the indexer must type the two entries individually. On the other hand, many dedicated indexing programs will automatically invert the first entry (thereby creating the second entry) at the touch of a key. Far too many embedded indexing programs require the opening and closing of dialog boxes in order to create an entry. This lack of functionality demonstrates a lack of understanding about index creation. Ideally, the indexer would work with a database grid for records and fields that was always open rather individual dialog boxes for each entry.

The weakest aspect of the user interface design of embedded indexing programs becomes apparent during the index editing process. Although some programs and plug-ins display index entries previously created, the displayed entries are usually in a separate window with extremely limited functionality. For example, it is not possible to group entries based on a search criterion and edit them. Search-and-replace operations that affect only the index entries are not available in these displays. These "preview index displays" do not allow the indexer to toggle between alphabetic and page number order for entries. Most are truly previews, not a dynamic working environment.

The work area context is not right; rather, it is backward. The indexer is striving to create an index, a separate document, and yet the context of most embedded indexing programs is the document being indexed, not the index itself. Index writers are extremely handicapped when they cannot work dynamically with the structure they are trying to mold.

In chapter 9, "Editing the Index," it became clear that even under the best of circumstances editing an index can be a very time-consuming task. Editing an index produced by embedded indexing software is extremely tedious and will take longer than editing index cards or an index produced by dedicated indexing software.

Most embedded indexing programs generate the index as a separate document or block of text; users of these programs are understandably tempted to edit the generated index, without returning to the original document files to correct the embedded entries. If the embedded entries are not corrected, however, the entire purpose of embedding entries in the first place is defeated.

We might find the following entries in the first draft of an unedited index:

> **book market,** 34, 56, 191
> **book markets,** 20–26, 139

If the indexer wanted to post all the references at the entry *book markets,* the entries for *book market* would all have to be changed to the plural form. The text for a book-length document is commonly divided into many separate files. In the example above, the indexer might need to go into three separate files to locate and change the *book market* entries.

Since so much typing is required to get embedded entries into the proper form for the index, there will undoubtedly be spelling errors. Most embedded indexing programs do not allow a spelling checker to run against index entries alone. Correction of spelling errors in index entries can be another tedious task.

The practice of editing only the generated index is quite common. Many technical writers tell me that one of the first things they do when they revise a manual written by another writer is to generate an index from the files. Frequently, the index generated from the embedded entries turns out to be quite different from the index printed in the manual. Apparently, the original writer made changes in the generated index without returning to the document files to correct the embedded entries. Just as writers can fine-tune documents in their final, formatted state, so, too, indexers should be able to work with a formatted index and have the embedded entries automatically updated.

**▌ *Summary.*** For the most part, the sorting routines employed in embedded indexing software do not conform to standard alphabetizing requirements of American publishers or international index standards. The formatting capabilities of such software are extremely limited. The time required to type and then edit embedded entries is much greater than the time required to perform the same tasks using other index-writing tools. It is interesting to note that the conclusions from two journal articles, one published in 1990, the other in 1999, are still applicable.

> The current capabilities of the indexing modules of text processing software are inadequate. Even the most simple needs of the professional indexer are left woefully unfulfilled. At a point in the publishing process when users should be able to focus on the content and structure of their indexes, they are required to spend far too much time "cleaning up" the index that is generated by these programs. Users of such programs clearly should not be forced to devote so much time to mundane and repetitive tasks that could and should be handled by the software. (Mulvany 1990, 113)

> Although embedded indexing programs have improved since 1989, when compared with dedicated indexing software they are still crude tools. It is difficult to understand why so many basic problems still exist. In regard to alphabetizing and index format, *The Chicago Manual of Style* is readily available; it is not an obscure text. During the past ten years no fewer than three books about indexing have appeared; two of them have gone into second editions (Fetters 1994, 1999; Mulvany 1994; Wellisch 1991, 1996). All of these books discuss index structure. Given the availability of information about indexes and indexing it would be difficult for designers of embedded indexing software to claim ignorance. It appears that they are simply inept. (Mulvany 1999, 163)

### Dedicated Indexing Software

Dedicated indexing programs are devoted solely to the preparation of indexes. The top three programs used by book indexers are MACREX (http://www.macrex.com), SKY Index (http://www.sky-software.com), and CINDEX (http://www.indexres.com). They are stand-alone programs in that they do not work with the text files of the document being indexed. Instead, they are designed to enable indexers to type in index entries and reference locators while working from page proofs of the document. Such programs free the indexer from clerical tasks such as the sorting and formatting of index entries; the indexer is able to focus on term selection and the overall structure of the index.

At first it may seem that typing in each index entry is a time-consuming task. But dedicated indexing programs offer various features that reduce the amount of typing—for example, autoinversion of entries, and the ability to copy reference locators and part or all of previous entries.

These programs have also been fine-tuned to sort index entries according to different schemes. The indexer can choose letter-by-letter or word-by-word alphabetizing. Leading prepositions, articles, and conjunctions can be ignored for sorting purposes, if desired. Terms such as "St." and "Mc" can be automatically sorted as though spelled "Saint" and "Mac." Entries that contain numbers will be sorted in ascending numerical order. These programs will also sort roman numerals in correct ascending numerical order.

Cross-references can be verified. Various index formats—such as indented or run-in—can be automatically produced. Generic codes can be automatically inserted.

Because dedicated indexing programs are devoted solely to the task of index preparation, a great deal of time is saved when working with these programs. Professional indexers find that the use of such software is the most cost-effective way to work. Perhaps one of the strongest features of this software is that the indexer can work with the index in sorted order at all times, immediately seeing the placement of a new entry within the index. The structure of the index is constantly emerging and visible. The work area context is the index itself.

Because the indexer can focus on the structure of the index, there are far fewer editing tasks at the end of the process. Simple mistakes such as entering a term in singular form instead of plural form can be corrected immediately. Structural changes such as double-posting entries or deleting entries can be accomplished with a few keystrokes. Do Mi Stauber (2004, 300) sums up the situation this way:

> In general, my most important tool is my indexing software, and my most important strategy is to index directly into the computer. With the page proofs on a rack under my monitor and Macrex open on the screen, I work with the index growing as I make entries. The "track added entry" feature shows me the latest entry in alphabetical context, and the quality of my work benefits. I swim in the index as I read the text, basing new entries on old ones, making global wording changes, breaking down growing locator strings before they get too big. The text structure and my index structure grow together, intertwined. My decisions are based on all of my knowledge about the content of the index. I do not have to index blind.

Some indexing programs allow for the use of a controlled vocabulary and ensure that all entries conform to the vocabulary. The ability to import topic lists or specified fields from bibliography entries for a book can significantly reduce time spent typing. Even professional indexers who embed index entries in a document's text files often write the index first using dedicated indexing software. After the index is written and edited, the indexer can produce a listing of index entries in page number order. The page-number-order file is used to embed the entries in the document's text files.

It is important to remember that the software needs of professional indexers may vary greatly from the needs of authors who prepare an occasional index. While the professional indexer may need to produce a run-in, word-by-word alphabetized index one week and an indented index, sorted letter by letter, the next week, a book author may need to produce an index in a single style only once every few years. Nevertheless, authors would do well to investigate dedicated indexing software. Even the less expensive programs might enable authors to produce an index more quickly than could many of the other types of index preparation tools.

Dedicated indexing software is specialized, with a relatively small user base. Few resources provide information about it. Reviews of this software are not likely to be found in the mainstream computer press. The most comprehensive source of information is the American Society of Indexers (ASI). The ASI Web site (http://www.asindexing.org) maintains a list of software products in the "Resources" section. Vendors of major programs have demo versions available for users to try out.

## The Future

In chapter 1 the distinction between open-system and closed-system indexing was presented. The book, be it in print or online, was described as a closed system. Regarding the indexing of books, however, the line between open and closed systems is becoming blurred. More and more publishers are reusing content in a variety of media. While the lack of functionality in embedded indexing software was an annoyance during the 1980s and 1990s, today it is a costly detriment to information access. The need for improved embedded indexing tools is critical. As our requirements for access to information in a variety of formats increase, we can no longer accept the incompatible, proprietary file formats that cannot carry along metadata of the index from one media to another. Jan Wright (2004) correctly explains:

We need a free form indexing module for embedding indexing codes, most likely XML-based, that allows the indexing to be tied directly into the files, but manipulated easily from outside the files. Unique IDs assigned by the production person to each paragraph when the files are tagged for XML will allow us to index in a tool outside of the content files, finalize the indexing, and then tie the indexing codes into place in the content. This would allow us to change indexing as the content is changed.

Take this a step further: if you use only unique IDs for the target content, you could link it to unique IDs of indexing concepts (or a set of synonym rings) to make the connection between indexing and content chunk truly flexible to maintain. You link the number to the number, and you are free to change the content of the ID on either side of the equation. For example, Susan Chambers no longer equals the mayor. So we update ring no. 345 with synonyms for the new mayor.

People need the indexing codes to tag their data with meaning. It should be easier to do so, and easier to manipulate those codes into whatever we want. We should be able to strip them out of the content, work with them free of the files, add new entries, change existing entries, perform batch operations and grouping, and strip the codes back in with one simple process. We should be able to replace true indexing with synonym rings if needed for an online search environment, or vice versa. We should be able to repurpose the metadata for the environment it is being displayed in and searched in automatically without pain. We should be able to designate which controlled vocabulary we want to use, and which set of preferred terms is displayed, basing the display on a choice of several typical user profiles.

Tools for indexing are varied. Indexers will choose the tools best suited to the job at hand. But whatever tool is used, it is only an adjunct to the intellectual task of indexing. Ideally, our indexing tools will free us from the mundane aspects of index preparation. While we strive to increase the efficiency of our tools, we must remember not to lose sight of the art of indexing.

A tool is just a tool—an implement for facilitating or performing mechanical operations. Instead of shuffling and alphabetizing index cards by hand, we have software that performs this task. However, there is no tool that thinks for us. There is no tool that will decide which terms work as main headings and which terms should be subheadings. There is no tool that will automatically control the vocabulary in an index. The indexer must critically read and identify ideas and relationships between ideas.

The indexer's ability to recognize patterns and relationships is a unique human skill cannot be automated, at least not in the near future. Computers can build concordances that list every word in a text; they can perform frequency analysis and weighted string pattern matching. But computers cannot identify ideas. Computers cannot construct the intricate network of interrelationships that we call an index. A good index folds the ideas and terminology of a text into patterns that make sense to others. There are many paths that lead to information within the index. This type of access to information has been described as "pre-wiring the thinking so that a person doesn't have to think. You build the links, and if you're good, people aren't even conscious of it. People can find whatever they want without any effort—it's so well organized" (Larson 1989).

Book indexes have been the subject of quantitative studies. But counting the numbers of entries per page or the number of words in subheadings or the frequency of cross-reference use does not get to the heart of the matter. Until we know more about the human ability to identify ideas and provide public access to those ideas, there will be an aspect of indexing that seems like magic.

Neil Larson (1989) said that "indexing is adding value that never existed in the original material." That is the magic of an index. The index goes beyond the words in a text. It provides a gateway to ideas and information that is accessible to others. An index, whether it appears in the back of a book or on a Web site, is a knowledge structure. Access to information is the added value the indexer brings to the material.

Without a doubt, indexing software tools will improve and the demand for indexing will increase. Given the profusion of published material, another certainty is that there will not be enough people skilled in knowledge structure design to meet the information access needs of the marketplace. The book or online text that includes a thoughtfully written and structured index will stand out from the crowd.

The back-of-the-book index is not a relic of seventeenth-century technology; rather, it is an excellent prototype of an efficient information access device. Master the art of book indexing, and you will experience the magic of sharing knowledge.

# *Appendix A*

Title _____

Editor (name) _____

(phone #) _____

(e-mail) _____

Author (name) _____

(phone #) _____

(e-mail) _____

Indexer will receive proofs

❏ via courier

❏ as a PDF via e-mail

❏ as one complete set; Date of delivery

❏ in batches:

Date of delivery of initial portion _____

Date of delivery of last portion _____

Date of delivery for the index _____

Table of contents provided?

❏ Yes    ❏ No

Bibliography provided?

❏ Yes    ❏ No

References/Endnotes provided?

❏ Yes    ❏ No

## NUMBER OF INDEXES

❏ Single index

❏ Multiple indexes

❏ Author-title

❏ Authors cited

❏ Other_____

## STYLE GUIDE
- ❏ *Chicago Manual of Style*
- ❏ House Style
- ❏ Other_____

## FORMAT
- ❏ Indented (number of levels allowed___)
- ❏ Run-in (only 2 levels)

## ARRANGEMENT OF ENTRIES
Main heading alphabetizing
- ❏ Word-by-word
- ❏ Letter-by-letter

Subheading arrangement
- ❏ Alphabetic
- ❏ Chronologic
- ❏ Page number order

## ARRANGEMENT OF NUMBERS IN ENTRIES
- ❏ Numeric order
- ❏ As spelled out
- ❏ By size

## ARRANGEMENT OF SYMBOLS IN ENTRIES
- ❏ ASCII/Unicode order
- ❏ As spelled out
- ❏ Another order_____

## CROSS-REFERENCE FORMAT AND PLACEMENT
Main heading cross-references

- ❏ term. *See* xyz
- ❏ term, *see* xyz
- ❏ term (*see* xyz)
- ❏ *See also* xyz
- ❏ *see also* xyz
- ❏ (*see also* xyz)

*See also* placement
- ❏ At the top of the entry run off from the main heading
- ❏ At the bottom of the entry as the last subheading
- ❏ Indented as the first subheading

Punctuation before *See also* in run-in format_____

Subheading cross-references

- ❏ term. *See* xyz
- ❏ term, *see* xyz
- ❏ term (*see* xyz)
- ❏ *See also* xyz
- ❏ *see also* xyz
- ❏ (*see also* xyz)

*See also* placement
- ❏ Run off from the subheading
- ❏ Other_____

**PUNCTUATION**

Indented index
- ❑ None
- ❑ Colon after main heading/subheading
  without locators

Run-in index

Punctuation after main headings without locators _____

Punctuation after main headings with locators _____

Punctuation between multiple subheadings _____

Between entry and locators
- ❑ Comma followed by a space
- ❑ Two spaces

Between multiple locators
- ❑ Comma follwed by a space
- ❑ Semicolon followed by a space for a change
  in volume number

Between cross-references
- ❑ Semicolon followed by a space
- ❑ Other _____

**MAIN HEADING CAPITALIZATION**

- ❑ Proper names & nouns only
- ❑ First letter only
- ❑ Entire heading

**REFERENCE LOCATORS**

Citation Unit
- ❑ Page numbers, consecutive
- ❑ Page numbers, modular
- ❑ Paragraph/section numbers
- ❑ Other unit _____

Format for continuous discussion of a topic
Consecutive numbers
- ❑ Numbers in full with en dash (125–129)
- ❑ Numbers compressed; what style? _____

Modular number concatenator
- ❑ 10-5 to 10-9
- ❑ Other _____

Format for noncontinuous discussion on consecutive pages
- ❑ Follow style above for continuous discussion (12–14)
- ❑ Separate page numbers with commas (12, 13, 14)
- ❑ Use *passim* (12–14 passim)
- ❑ Other format required _____

## LENGTH

Is there a length limit?

        ❏ No     ❏ Yes

        If yes, number of index lines allowed _____

                 number of characters per line_____

## DELIVERY FORMAT

File format

        ❏ ASCII text file with generic codes

        ❏ RTF file

        ❏ Other_____

Delivery method

        ❏ E-mail attachment

        ❏ On disk with printout

Provide a list of entries in page number order?

        ❏ No     ❏ Yes

## MISCELLANEOUS

Endnotes/Footnotes:

        Indexable?     ❏ No     ❏ Yes

        Locator format_____

Display material:

        Indexable?     ❏ No     ❏ Yes

        Locator format_____

Acronyms/Abbreviations:

        Special posting rules?

        ❏ At acronym     ❏ At spellout     ❏ Other

Articles at beginning of titles:

        ❏ Invert     ❏ Drop     ❏ No inversion

Initial function word in subheadings:

        ❏ Alphabetize     ❏ Ignore, do not alphabetize

# *Appendix B*

## RESOURCES FOR INDEXERS

# Professional Associations

### American Society of Indexers (ASI)
10200 West 44th Ave., Ste. 304
Wheat Ridge, CO 80033
United States
Phone: (303) 463-2887
Fax: (303) 422-8894
Web: http://www.asindexing.org

### Association of Southern African Indexers and Bibliographers (ASAIB)
c/o Dept. of Information Science
P.O. Box 392
Unisa 0003
South Africa
Web: http://www.asaib.org.za

### Australian and New Zealand Society of Indexers (ANZSI)
P.O. Box 2069
Canberra, ACT 2601
Australia
Web: http://www.aussi.org

### China Society of Indexers (CSI)
Mr. Ge
3663 Zhongshan Road (North)
Shanghai
China
Phone: +86 (21) 6356 9074
Fax: +86 (21) 6257 9196

### Deutsches Netzwerk der Indexer (DNI)
Jochen Fassbender
Phone: +49 (0) 421 243 9136
E-mail: info@d-indexer.org
Web: http://www.d-indexer.org

### Indexing and Abstracting Society of Canada/Société canadienne pour l'analyse de documents (IASC/SCAD)
P.O. Box 664, Station P
Toronto, ON M5S 2Y4
Canada
Web: http://www.indexingsociety.ca

### Society of Indexers (SI)
Blades Enterprise Centre
John Street
Sheffield S2 4SU
United Kingdom
Phone: +44 (0)114 292 2350
Fax: +44 (0)114 292 2351
Web: http://www.indexers.org.uk

## Standards Organizations

**American National Standards Institute (ANSI)**
1819 L Street, NW, 6th Fl.
Washington, DC 20036
United States
Phone: (202) 293-8020
Fax:(202) 293-9287
Web: http://www.ansi.org

**International Organization for Standardization (ISO)**
1, rue de Varembé
Case postale 56
CH-1211 Geneva 20
Switzerland
Phone: + 41 22 749 01 11
Fax: + 41 22 733 34 30
Web: http://www.iso.org

**National Information Standards Organization (NISO)**
4733 Bethesda Avenue, Ste. 300
Bethesda, MD 20814
United States
Phone: (301) 654-2512
Fax: (301) 654-1721
Web: http://www.niso.org

**World Wide Web Consortium (W3C)**
Massachusetts Institute of Technology
Computer Science and Artificial Intelligence Laboratory
32 Vassar Street
Room 32-G515
Cambridge, MA 02139
United States
Telephone: (617) 253-2613
Fax: (617) 258-5999
Web: http://www.w3.org

## Internet Discussion Group: INDEX-L

To subscribe to INDEX-L you may send an e-mail message to LYRIS@LISTSERV .UNC.EDU. Leave the Subject Line blank. The only text in your message should be SUBSCRIBE INDEX-L Your Name (e.g., SUBSCRIBE INDEX-L Harry Hound). Or, you may subscribe by going to http://lists.unc.edu/read/?forum=index-l

# Training in Indexing

Some colleges and universities offer book-indexing courses through their adult education programs. Book-indexing courses are often part of a publishing certificate program or are offered through a school of library and information science. The following organizations offer in-depth book-indexing courses:

**Book Indexing Postal Tutorials (BIPT)**
The Lodge
Sidmount Avenue
Moffat, Dumfriesshire
Scotland DG10 9BS
Phone/Fax: 01683-220440
Web: http://www.lodge-moffat.co.uk

**Graduate School, USDA**
600 Maryland Ave., SW
Suite 120
Washington, DC 20024-2520
United States
Phone: (888) 744-4723
Web: http://www.grad.usda.gov/

**New York University**
SCPS Registration Office
P. O. Box 1206
Stuyvesant Station
New York NY 10009-9988
United States
Phone: (212) 995-3060 or (212) 998-7150
Fax: (212) 998-7171
Web: http://www.scps.nyu.edu/

**Society of Indexers (Training Course)**
Blades Enterprise Centre
John Street
Sheffield S2 4SU
United Kingdom
Tel: +44 (0)114 292 2350
Fax: +44 (0)114 292 2351
Web: http://www.indexers.org.uk

**University of California Berkeley Extension**
1995 University Ave.
Berkeley, CA 94720-7000
United States
Phone: (510) 642-4111
Web: http://www.unex.berkeley.edu

University of California Berkeley Extension Online
Phone: (510) 642-4124
Web: http://learn.berkeley.edu/

# Publishers of Dedicated Indexing Software

CINDEX (for Windows and Macintosh)
Indexing Research
180 Varick Street, Ste. 1014
New York, NY 10014
United States
Phone: (212) 633-0994
Fax: (212) 633-9049
Web: http://www.indexres.com

MACREX (for Windows and DOS)
MACREX Indexing Services
Beech House
Blaydon Burn
Tyne & Wear NE21 6JR
United Kingdom
Phone: +44 (0) 191 414 2595
Fax: +44 (0) 191 414 1893
Web: http://www.macrex.com

MACREX Support Office: Australia, New Zealand, South East Asia–MASTER INDEXING
5 Kingston Street
East Malvern, VIC 3145
Australia
Phone/Fax: (03) 9500 8715

MACREX Support Office: North America–Wise Bytes
P.O. Box 3051
Daly City, CA 95015-0051
United States
Phone: (877) 463-3901 or (650) 756-0821
Fax: (650) 292-2302

SKY Index Professional (for Windows)
SKY Software
350 Montgomery Circle
Stephens City, VA 22655
United States
Phone: (800) 776-0137 or (540) 869-6581
Fax: (540) 869-6581
Web: http://www.sky-software.com

**wINDEX** (for DOS)
Watch City Software
24 Harris Street
Waltham, MA 02452
United States
Phone: (781) 893-0514 or (877) 408-7299
Web: http://www.abbington.com/holbert/windex.html

## Winners of the ASI–H. W. Wilson Award for Excellence in Indexing

2005 Award not given

2004 Janet Russell, indexer
*Anglo-American Cataloging Rules,* 2nd ed., 2002 rev., 2003 update
(American Library Association, Canadian Library Association, and
Chartered Institute of Library and Information Professionals [London])

2003 Award not given

2002 Margie Towery, indexer
*The Letters of Matthew Arnold* (University Press of Virginia)

2001 Ronald M. Gephart and Paul H. Smith, indexers
*Letters of Delegates to Congress, 1774–1789* (Library of Congress)

2000 Nedalina Dineva, indexer
*Concepts of Mass in Contemporary Physics and
Philosophy* (Princeton University Press)

1999 Richard Genova, indexer
*Brownfields Law and Practice* (Matthew Bender & Co.)

1998 Laura Moss Gottlieb, indexer
*Dead Wrong: A Death Row Lawyer Speaks Out against
Capital Punishment* (University of Wisconsin Press)

1997 Gillian Northcott and Ruth Levitt, indexers
*Dictionary of Art* (Grove's Dictionaries [US] and Macmillan Publishers [UK])

1996 Award not given

1995 Martin L. White, indexer
*The Promise of Pragmatism* (University of Chicago Press)

1994 Patricia Deminna, indexer
*Carnal Israel: Reading Sex in Talmudic Culture* (University of California Press)

1993 Award not given

1992 Rachel Jo Johnson, indexer
*The American Law of Real Property* (Matthew Bender & Co.)

1991 Nancy L. Daniels, indexer
*Beyond Public Architecture: Strategies for Design
Evaluation* (Van Nostrand Reinhold)

1990   Marcia Carlson, indexer
       *Strategic Nuclear Arms and Arms Control Debates* (Cornell University Press)

1989   Philip James, indexer
       *Medicine for the Practicing Physician,* 2nd ed. (Butterworths)

1988   Jeanne Moody, indexer
       *Raptor Management Techniques* (National Wildlife Institute)

1987   Award not given

1986   Marjorie Hyslop, indexer
       *Metals Handbook* (American Society for Metals)

1985   Sydney W. Cohen, indexer
       *The Experts Speak* (Random House)

1984   Trish Yancey, indexer
       *Index and Directory of U.S. Industry Standards* (Information Handling Services)

1983   Award not given

1982   Catherine Fix, indexer
       *Diagnosis of Bone and Joint Disorders* (Wm. Saunders Company)

1981   Delight Ansley, indexer
       *Cosmos* (Random House)

1980   Linda I. Solow, indexer
       *Beyond Orpheus: Studies in Musical Structures* (MIT Press)

1979   Hans H. Wellisch, indexer
       *The Conversion of Scripts: Its Nature, History, and Utilization* (John Wiley)

Note: The award is given for an index published in the United States during the previous year. Therefore, the 2004 award is for an index published during 2003. Applications for ASI–Wilson Award submissions can be obtained from the American Society of Indexers (http://www.asindexing.org).

## Internet Resources

An updated list of the Internet links in this book can be found at Bayside Indexing Service (http://www.bayside-indexing.com/booklinks.html).

# References

*Academic American Encyclopedia.* 1990. Danbury, CT: Grolier.

Akhtar, Nasreen. 1989. "Indexing Asian Names." *Indexer* 16 (3): 156–158.

*ALA-LC Romanization Tables: Transliteration Schemes for Non-Roman Scripts.* http://www.loc.gov/catdir/cpso/roman.html (accessed 2005).

Alexander, Christopher, and Center for Environmental Structure. 2002. *The Phenomenon of Life: An Essay on the Art of Building and the Nature of the Universe.* Center for Environmental Structure Series, 9 Berkeley, CA: Center for Environmental Structure.

American Society of Indexers. 2004. *Criteria for the H. W. Wilson Award.* http://www.asindexing.org/site/awards.shtml#awcrit (accessed 2005).

Anderson, James D., and National Information Standards Organization (U.S.). 1997. *Guidelines for Indexes and Related Information Retrieval Devices: A Technical Report.* NISO Technical Report 2. Bethesda, MD: NISO Press.

Anderson, James D., and José Pérez-Carballo. 2005. *Information Retrieval Design: Principles and Options for Information Description, Organization, Display, and Access in Information Retrieval Databases, Digital Libraries, Catalogs, and Indexes.* St. Petersburg, FL: Ometeca Institute.

*Anglo-American Cataloguing Rules.* 2002. 2nd ed. Ottawa: Canadian Library Association; London: Facet Publishing for Chartered Institute of Library and Information Professionals; Chicago: American Library Association.

Bakewell, K. G. B. 1988. *Information Sources and Reference Tools.* London: Society of Indexers.

Barnum, Carol, Earvin Henderson, Al Hood, and Rodney Jordan. 2004. "Index versus Full-Text Search: A Usability Study of User Preference and Performance." *Technical Communication* 51 (2): 185–206.

*Bartholomew Gazetteer of Britain.* 1977. Comp. O. Mason. Edinburgh: Bartholomew.

Basbanes, Nicholas A. 2003. *A Splendor of Letters: The Permanence of Books in an Impermanent World.* New York: HarperCollins.

Bell, Hazel K. 1989. "Indexing Biographies: Lives Do Bring Their Problems." *Indexer* 16: 168–172.

————. 2004. *Indexing Biographies and Other Stories of Human Lives.* 3rd ed., Occasional Papers on Indexing, vol. 1. Sheffield, UK: Society of Indexers.

Bertelsen, Cynthia D. 1996. *Issues in Cataloging Non-Western Materials: Special Problems with African Language Materials.* http://filebox.vt.edu/users/bertel/africana.html (accessed 2005).

Bishop, Ann P., Elizabeth D. Liddy, and Barbara Settel. 1991. "Index Quality Study, Part I: Quantitative Description of Back-of-the-Book Indexes." In *Indexing Tradition and Innovation: Proceedings of the 22nd Annual Conference of the American Society of Indexers.* Port Aransas, TX: American Society of Indexers.

Booth, Pat F. 2001. *Indexing: The Manual of Good Practice.* Munich: K. G. Saur.

Booth, Pat F., and Mary Piggott. 1988. *Choice and Form of Entries.* Training in Indexing Unit 2. London: Society of Indexers.

Bridge, Noeline. 2002. "Indexing Personal Names, an Introduction: Some Common Problems." *Key Words* 10 (5): 122–125.

————. 2003. "Verifying Personal Names on the Web." *Indexer* 23 (3): 149–156.

*British Standard Recommendation for Preparing Indexes to Books, Periodicals, and Other Documents* (BS 3700: 1988). 1988. London: British Standards Institute.

Browne, Glenda, and Jonathan Jermey. 2004. *Website Indexing: Enhancing Access to Information within Websites.* Blackwood, South Australia: Auslib Press Pty. Ltd.

*Burke's Genealogical and Heraldic History of the Peerage, Baronetage, and Knightage, Privy Council, and Order of Preference.* Irregular. London: Burke's Peerage Limited.

Bush, Vannevar. 1945. "As We May Think." *Atlantic Monthly* 176 (1): 101–118. http://www.theatlantic.com/unbound/flashbks/computer/bushf.htm (accessed 2005).

Case, Donald O. 2002. *Looking for Information: A Survey of Research on Information Seeking, Needs, and Behavior.* San Diego, CA: Academic Press.

Catholic University of America. 2003. *New Catholic Encyclopedia.* 2nd ed. 15 vols. Detroit and Washington, DC: Thomson/Gale / Catholic University of America.

*The Chicago Manual of Style.* 1969. 12th ed. Chicago: University of Chicago Press.

*The Chicago Manual of Style.* 1982. 13th ed. Chicago: University of Chicago Press.

*The Chicago Manual of Style.* 1993. 14th ed. Chicago: University of Chicago Press.

*The Chicago Manual of Style.* 2003. 15th ed. Chicago: University of Chicago Press.

Coates, Sylvia. 2002. "Teaching Book Indexing: Cognitive Skills and Term Selection." *Indexer* 23 (1): 15–17.

*The Columbia Encyclopedia.* 2000. Ed. Paul Lagassé. 6th ed. New York: Columbia University Press. http://www.bartelby.com/65/.

Columbia University Press. 2002. *Guide for Authors.* Columbia University Press. http://www.columbia.edu/cu/cup/press/AuthorGuide_2002.pdf (accessed 2005).

Debrett's Peerage Limited. Annual. *Debrett's People of Today.* London: Debrett's Peerage Limited.

Dillon, Andrew. 2004. *Designing Usable Electronic Text.* 2nd ed. Boca Raton, FL: CRC Press.

Diodato, Virgil, and Gretchen Gandt. 1991. "Back of Book Indexes and the Characteristics of Author and Nonauthor Indexing: Report of an Exploratory Study." *Journal of the American Society for Information Science* 42 (June): 341–350.

Eco, Umberto. 2003. "Vegetal and Mineral Memory: The Future of Books." *Al-Ahram Weekly On-Line.* http://weekly.ahram.org.eg/2003/665/bo3.htm (accessed 2005).

Einsohn, Amy. 2000. *The Copyeditor's Handbook: A Guide for Book Publishing and Corporate Communications*. Berkeley: University of California Press.

*Encyclopaedia Judaica*. 1972. Jerusalem: Keter Publishing House.

*The Encyclopedia Americana*. 1990. International ed. Danbury, CT: Grolier.

Fetters, Linda K. 2001. *Handbook of Indexing Techniques: A Guide for Beginning Indexers*. 3rd ed. Corpus Christi, TX: Fetters Infomanagement Co.

Genette, Gérard. 1997. *Paratexts: Thresholds of Interpretation*. Trans. Jane E. Lewin. Cambridge: Cambridge University Press.

Gibb, H. A. R. 1960. *The Encyclopaedia of Islam*. New ed. Leiden: Brill.

Gibb, H. A. R., and J. H. Kramers. 2001. *Concise Encyclopedia of Islam*. Boston: Brill Academic Publishers.

Henige, David. 2002. "Indexing: A Users' Perspective." *Journal of Scholarly Publishing* 33 (4): 230–247.

Heywood, Valentine. 1951. *British Titles: The Use and Misuse of the Titles of Peers and Commoners; with Some Historical Notes*. London: Black.

Hornblower, Simon, and Antony Spawforth. 2003. *The Oxford Classical Dictionary*. 3rd ed. Oxford: Oxford University Press.

IFLA UBCIM Programme. 1996. *Names of Persons: National Usages for Entry in Catalogues*. 4th rev. and enl. ed. UBCIM Publications, new ser., 16. Munich: K. G. Saur.

International Organization for Standardization. 1996. *ISO 999: Information and Documentation; Guidelines for the Content, Organization, and Presentation of Indexes*. Geneva: International Organization for Standardization.

Jörgensen, Corinne L., and Elizabeth D. Liddy. 1996. "Information Access or Information Anxiety? An Exploratory Evaluation of Book Index Features." *Indexer* 20 (2): 64–68.

Kasdorf, William E. 2003. *The Columbia Guide to Digital Publishing*. New York: Columbia University Press.

Kimber, W. Eliot, and Joshua Reynolds. 2002. "Internationalized Back-of-the-Book Indexes for XSL Formatting Objects." http://www.mulberrytech.com/Extreme/Proceedings/xslfo-pdf/2002/Kimber01/EML2002Kimber01.pdf (accessed 2005).

Klement, Susan. 2002. "Open-system Versus Closed-system Indexing: A Vital Distinction." *Indexer* 23 (1): 23–31.

Knight, G. Norman. 1979. *Indexing, the Art of: A Guide to the Indexing of Books and Periodicals*. London: George Allen & Unwin.

Lancaster, F. W. 2003. *Indexing and Abstracting in Theory and Practice*. 3rd ed. Champaign: University of Illinois Graduate School of Library and Information Science Publications Office.

Larson, Neil. 1989. "Hypertext: Fact, Fiction, and Opportunity." Paper read at 21st Annual Meeting of the American Society of Indexers, May 19–20, at San Francisco, CA.

Lee, David. 1991. "Coping with a Title: The Indexer and the British Aristocracy." *Indexer* 17 (3): 155–160.

Levin, Bernard. 1987. "Authors and Indexers." *Indexer* 15 (October): 238.

Liddy, Elizabeth D., Ann P. Bishop, and Barbara Settel. 1991. "Index Quality Study, Part II: Publishers' Survey and Qualitative Assessment." In *Indexing Tradition and Innovation: Proceedings of the 22nd Annual Conference of the American Society of Indexers.* Port Aransas, TX: American Society of Indexers.

Liddy, Elizabeth D., and Corinne L. Jörgensen. 1993. "Reality Check! Book Index Characteristics That Facilitate Information Access." In *Indexing, Providing Access to Information: Looking Back, Looking Ahead: Proceedings of the 25th Annual Meeting of the American Society of Indexers.* Ed. Nancy C. Mulvany. Port Aransas, TX: American Society of Indexers.

Lohr, Steve. 2001. *Go To.* New York: Basic Books.

Lommel, Arle. 2003. *The Localization Industry Primer.* 2nd ed. Fechy, Switzerland: Localization Industry Standards Association (www.lisa.org).

Lyman, Peter, and Hal R. Varian. 2003. *How Much Information? 2003.* University of California, Berkeley, School of Information Management and Systems. http: // www.sims.berkeley.edu/how-much-info-2003/ (accessed 2005).

Maddocks, Hugh C. 1991. *Deep-Sky Name Index 2000.0.* Reston, VA: Foxon-Maddocks Associates.

Mason, Oliver, comp. 1986. *Bartholomew Gazetteer of Places in Britain.* Rev. and repr. ed. Edinburgh: J. Bartholomew.

Mauer, Peg. 2000. "Embedded Indexing: Pros and Cons for the Indexer." *Indexer* 22 (1): 27–28.

Merriam-Webster, Inc. 1995. *Merriam-Webster's Biographical Dictionary.* Springfield, MA: Merriam-Webster.

———. 1997. *Merriam-Webster's Geographical Dictionary.* 3rd ed. Springfield, MA: Merriam-Webster.

———. 2004. *Merriam-Webster Unabridged.* http://www.Merriam-WebsterUnabridged. com (accessed 2005).

Microsoft. 2001. *Rich Text Format (RTF) Specification Version 1.7.* Microsoft Corp. http: //www.microsoft.com/downloads/details.aspx?FamilyId=E5B8EBC2-6AD6-49F0-8C90-E4F763E3F04F&displaylang=en (accessed 2005).

Miller, Arthur R., and Michael H. Davis. 1990. *Intellectual Property: Patents, Trademarks, and Copyright.* 2nd ed. St. Paul, MN: West Publishing Co.

Milstead, Jessica. 1984. *Subject Access Systems.* Orlando, FL: Academic Press.

Moys, Elizabeth M., Anne P. Coles, Moira Greenhalgh, and Ben Wynne. 1993. *Indexing Legal Materials.* Occasional Papers on Indexing, vol. 2. London: Society of Indexers.

Mulvany, Nancy C. 1990. "Software Tools for Indexing: What We Need." *Indexer* 17 (October): 108–113.

———. 1991. "Copyright for Indexes, Revisited." *ASI Newsletter* 107 (November/December): 11–13. http: //www.bayside-indexing.com/copyrite.htm (accessed 2005).

———. 1999. "Software Tools for Indexing: Revisited." *Indexer* 21 (4): 160–163. http: //www.bayside-indexing.com/tools.pdf (accessed 2005).

———. 2002. "Teaching Book Indexing: A Curriculum." *Indexer* 23 (1): 11–14.

———. 2003a. "Interview: Jan C. Wright, Part 1." *i-TORQUE* 4: 1–5.

———. 2003b. "Interview: Janet Perlman, Part 1." *i-TORQUE* 8: 1–7.

Mulvany, Nancy C., and Jessica Milstead. 1994. "Indexicon, The Only Fully Automatic Indexer: A Review." *Key Words* 2 (5): 1, 17–23. http://www.bayside-indexing .com/idxcon.htm (accessed 2005).

*New Catholic Encyclopedia.* 2003. Washington, DC: Catholic University of America.

*The New Encyclopaedia Britannica.* 2002. 15th ed. Chicago: Encyclopaedia Britannica. http://www.britannica.com.

Nielsen, Jakob. 1996. "In Defense of Print." Useit.com: Alertbox (February). http://www.useit.com/alertbox/9602.html (accessed 2005).

———. 1997. "How Users Read on the Web." Useit.com: Alertbox (October). http://www.useit.com/alertbox/9710a.html (accessed 2005).

———. 2003. "PDF: Unfit for Human Consumption." Useit.com: Alertbox (July). http://www.useit.com/alertbox/20030714.html (accessed 2005).

*NISO TR02.* See Andersen, James D., and National Information Standards Organization (U.S.). 1997.

*NISO TR03: Guidelines for the Alphabetical Arrangement of Letters and Sorting of Numerals and Other Symbols.* 1999. Ed. Hans H. Wellisch. NISO Technical Report. Bethesda, MD: National Information Standards Organization.

*NISO Z39.19-200X: Guidelines for the Construction, Format, and Management of Monolingual Controlled Vocabularies.* 2005. Bethesda, MD: NISO Press. http://www.niso.org/ (accessed 2005).

Olason, Susan C. 2000. "Let's Get Usable! Usability Studies for Indexes." *Indexer* 22 (2): 91–95.

Oler, Harriet. 1989. Chief, Examining Dept., U.S. Copyright Office. Meeting with author, Washington, DC, July 13.

*Oxford English Dictionary.* 1971. Compact ed. Oxford: Oxford University Press.

Rayward, W. Boyd. 1994. "Visions of Xanadu: Paul Otlet (1868–1944) and Hypertext." *Journal of the American Society for Information Science* (May): 235–250.

Ridehalgh, Nan. 1985. "The Design of Indexes." *Indexer* 14 (April): 165–174.

Ritter, R. M., Horace Hart, and Oxford University Press. 2002. *The Oxford Guide to Style.* Oxford and New York: Oxford University Press.

Rockley, Ann. 2001. "The Impact of Single Sourcing and Technology." *Technical Communication* 48 (2): 189–193.

Salton, Gerard. 1988. *Automatic Text Processing: The Transformation, Analysis, and Retrieval of Information by Computer.* Reading, MA: Addison-Wesley.

Scott, Dan, and Ronnie Seagren. 2002. "Creating a Massive Master Index for HTML and Print." In *The 20th Annual International Conference on Computer Documentation* (SIGDOC '02). New York: ACM Press.

Shere, Thérèse. 2004. "Indexing Cookbooks." Workshop handout.

Simpkins, Jean. 1990. "How the Publishers Want It to Look." *Indexer* 17 (April): 41–42.

Stauber, Do Mi. 2004. *Facing the Text: Content and Structure in Book Indexing.* Eugene, OR: Cedar Row Press.

Sun Technical Publications. 2003. *Read Me First! A Style Guide for the Computer Industry.* 2nd ed. Upper Saddle River, NJ: Prentice Hall.

Thomas, Dorothy. 1989. "Book Indexing Principles and Standards." In *Indexing: The State of Our Knowledge and the State of Our Ignorance, Proceedings of the 20th Annual Meeting of the American Society of Indexers.* Ed. Bella Hass Weinberg. Medford, NJ: Learned Information.

Tufte, Edward R. 1990. *Envisioning Information.* Cheshire, CT: Graphics Press.

*The Unicode Standard, Version 4.0: The Unicode Consortium.* 2003. Ed. Joan Aliprand et al. Boston: Addison-Wesley.

*Union List of Artist Names.* 1994. Ed. James M. Bower and Murtha Baca. 4 vols. New York: G. K. Hall. Available at http://www.getty.edu/research/conducting_research/vocabularies/ulan/ (accessed 2005).

Vickers, John A. 1987. "Index, How Not To." *Indexer* 15 (April): 163–166.

Waldron, Steven C. 1994. Indexicon President's Response [email to INDEX-L]. http://www.bayside-indexing.com/idxcon_response.html (accessed 2005).

*Washington Information Directory.* 1989-1990. [Washington, D.C.]: CQ Press.

Weinberg, Bella Hass. 1988. "Why Indexing Fails the Researcher." *Indexer* 16 (April): 3–6.

———. 1997. "The Earliest Hebrew Citation Indexes." *Journal of the American Society for Information Science* 48 (4): 318–330.

———. 2004. "On Index Matrices and Arrays." *Key Words* 12 (2): 42.

Wellisch, Hans H. 1992. "The Art of Indexing and Some Fallacies of Its Automation." *LOGOS* 3 (2): 69–76.

———. 1995. *Indexing from A to Z.* 2nd ed. New York: H. W. Wilson.

———. 2000. *Glossary of Terminology in Abstracting, Classification, Indexing, and Thesaurus Construction.* 2nd ed. Medford, NJ: Information Today.

Wheatley, Henry B. 1902. *How to Make an Index.* London: E. Stock.

Wheeler, Martha Throne. [1957] 1968. "Indexing: Principles, Rules, and Examples." *University of the State of New York Bulletin* 1445 (January).

Williams, Thomas R. 2000. "Guidelines for Designing and Evaluating the Display of Information on the Web." *Technical Communication* (Third Quarter): 383–396.

Wittmann, Cecelia. 1991. "Limitations of Indexing Modules in Word-Processing Software." *Indexer* 17 (October): 235–238.

Wright, Jan C. 1998. "Indexing after the Millennium 1: Getting the Tools Right." *Indexer* 21 (1): 19.

———. 2001. "Single-source Indexing." In *Proceedings of the 19th Annual International Conference on Computer Documentation.* New York: ACM Press.

———. 2003. "An Interview with Nancy Mulvany." *A to Z: The Newsletter of STC's Indexing SIG* 6 (3): 8–13.

———. 2004. Personal communication with author, March.

# Index

Written by Victoria Baker

Page numbers in *italics* denote illustrations or tables.

The style of this index follows the recommendations of *The Chicago Manual of Style* (2003), 15th ed. It is alphabetized letter by letter, and leading function words in subheadings are not alphabetized. This index was prepared using the MACREX Indexing Program. There are 2,315 entries, averaging 8 entries per page. Following the guidelines in the table on page 72 of this book, this is a 10 percent index.